D0378881

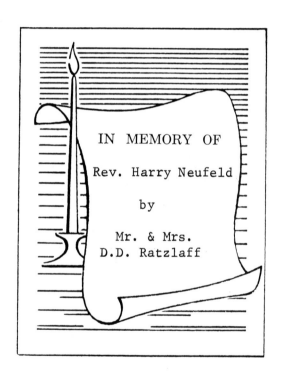

IN MEMORY OF

Rev. Harry Neufeld

by

Mr. & Mrs.
D.D. Ratzlaff

The Exceptional Executive

HF
5500.2
L375

The Exceptional Executive:

A Psychological Conception

by Harry Levinson

Harvard University Press

Cambridge, Massachusetts

WITHDRAWN

HIEBERT LIBRARY
PACIFIC COLLEGE · M. B. SEMINARY
FRESNO, CALIF. 93702

13275

© *Copyright 1968 by the President and Fellows of Harvard College*
All rights reserved

Fifth Printing, 1975

Library of Congress Catalog Card Number 68-25615
ISBN 0-674-27350-8
Printed in the United States of America

*To those dedicated teachers
who made the most difference*

Sarah Haney Zeh

Isabelle M. DeWolfe

Edward W. Geldreich

M. Wesley Roper

George R. R. Pflaum

David Rapaport

John W. Chotlos

Karl A. Menninger

William C. Menninger

Gertrude R. Ticho

Preface

Desire for leadership is like an infectious virus: once it seizes a victim, it rarely relinquishes him. The wish demands attention; the impulse its gratification, even at the sacrifice of pleasures others take for granted. The man who aspires to leadership soars on the fantasies of expectation. He will build, he will mold, he will shape destiny.

Being a leader, however, is as agonizing as it is exhilarating. Leaders do not discuss the anguish because leading is too important to them. Despite the pain, few yield their leadership roles until they are compelled to do so. Each continues to strive, sometimes vainly, for the further gratifications of wielding power.

The anguish of leadership lies largely in achievement devoid of enduring purpose. "Today I am the chairman of the company I helped to create," writes an executive. "I find the prospect of making more money uninteresting. What do I do now?" Thus, the age of success is also the age of failure. Paradoxically, those who succeed most, simultaneously fail the worst. Having achieved extraordinary career success, their lack of enduring satisfaction grates upon them even more harshly. To have so much and yet so little is an exercise in futility.

It is to the executive who seeks a purpose that this book is addressed. He who would gratify his fantasies of social contribution, of making his business a vital and vibrant institution, read on. He who is content with lesser goals need read no further.

In this book I propose to talk about what the organization and what work mean to people. Within a framework of psychoanalytic theory, I shall try to illuminate some aspects of the managerial task which heretofore have been relatively obscure. Then I shall wend my way through an odyssey of contemporary social problems whose resolution, I contend, depends on the effectiveness of business leadership. The reader may become lost, but if he perseveres he will grasp the relevance of the apparent detours.

Re-examining what people require from their work and their leaders will result in questioning some of the more popular psychological truisms about needs and motivation. In doing so, I intend to integrate much of the profusion of contemporary writing on psychological aspects of management, and focus prominent theories into what I think is their proper perspective. That alone should ease the confusion of most executives, already jaded by the parade of clichés and dismayed by the flow of slogans.

This synthesis will also serve as the girders for a new executive role on which I propose to elaborate. Of course, my conception is not really unique. Nothing is. But it does mark a shift from much of the contemporary theorizing about what an executive should do as a leader and defines a new social role for the business organization. I hope that conception is sufficiently different to generate some excitement, offer a vision, and provoke discussion.

The subsequent chapters will not be read quickly. In fact, some, though necessary, are dull. Those who cannot tolerate theory may skip Chapter 2. However, the book will make more sense if the reader is familiar with its theoretical underpinnings.

Of course, I have an underlying motive. I want the reader to do something for me. I want him to make organizations more viable by taking psychological considerations into effective account. Then my social purpose will be served: to strengthen the people who work in them.

Harry Levinson

Topeka, Kansas
February 6, 1968

Acknowledgments

This book began as a lecture on the impact of automation on management. The lecture was part of a week-long session of the Corporate Management Committee of IBM at its Executive Development Center at Sands Point, New York. In the transition from lecture to book, it became apparent that there were more important underlying psychological themes for management than the impact of automation per se. Nevertheless, I am indebted to G. H. Rathe, who invited me to make the presentation, and to the IBM top management group, who stimulated me to turn it into a book.

I am also indebted to the editors of the *Harvard Business Review* for their permission to adapt "Who Is to Blame for Maladaptive Managers?" (43:6 [November–December 1965], 143–158) for Chapter 14; to the editors of the *Administrative Science Quarterly* for permission to adapt "Reciprocation: The Relationship Between Man and Organization" (9:4 [March 1965], 370–390) for Chapter 2; to Harper & Row for permission to use the quotation in Chapter 2 from Aldous Huxley's *The Devils of Loudun*; to the editors of *Think* for permission to reprint "What Work Means to a Man" (30:1 [January–February 1964], 7–11), also for Chapter 2; and to the editors of *The New Yorker* (November 17, 1962), who graciously permitted me to quote at length in Chapter 9 from an article on Eleanor Roosevelt.

Drs. William C. Menninger, Roy W. Menninger, Herbert C. Modlin, and Richard O. Sword and Arthur Mandelbaum made many useful comments on the original paper which was the basis for Chapter 14. Drs. John Turner, Martin Mayman, and Joseph Satten made similar contributions to the original version of "Reciprocation: The Relationship Between Man and Organization." Dr. Lester E. Smith suggested some of the formulations which appear in Chapter 13.

The entire manuscript bears evidence of the editorial skill of Mrs. Janice Molinari. Ronald Molinari and Bruce Littman offered many constructive editorial comments. Mrs. Jean Senecal did the monumental typing job. I am grateful to them all.

During the period this book was written the work of the Division of Industrial Mental Health of The Menninger Foundation was supported in part by grants from the American National Gas Service Company, the International Harvester Foundation, the Detroit Edison Company, the Sears, Roebuck Foundation, the Northwest Paper Foundation, the Marathon Oil Company Foundation, the General Electric Foundation, the General Foods Corporation, the California Portland Cement Company, the Consolidated Natural Gas System Educational Foundation, the Standard Oil Foundation, the Michigan Bell Telephone Company, the Kansas City Power and Light Company, and the Kansas Power and Light Company. During its first three years, the program was given impetus by support from the Rockefeller Brothers Fund. To all of the financial supporters, and to Dr. Roy W. Menninger, president of The Menninger Foundation, for his administrative support and encouragement, I want to express my deep appreciation.

H. L.

Contents

The Exceptional Executive

A great society is a society in which its men of business think greatly of their functions.
Alfred North Whitehead

Management is, all things considered, the most creative of all arts. It is the art of arts. Because it is the organizer of talent.
Jean-Jacques Servan-Schreiber

Part One / The Matrix of Leadership

The world of man is made up of geography and atmosphere, personal psychology and social crosscurrents, changing elements and stable landmarks. His behavior is always a result of his internal drives, his maturing capacities, and both the stimuli and constraints of his environment. Leadership behavior, therefore, is a product of multiple forces. Any effort to understand and modify it must contend with those forces.

To further that understanding, some of the complex interactions of power relationships, personality theory, social change, assumptions about motivation, and technical advances will be examined in this section. The examination will be pointed to subsequent implications for the executive. Behind this examination is the belief that the contemporary executive is a professional, that the executive of the future will be even more professional. A professional is a person who must understand and apply scientific knowledge. Unless he does so, he will be buffeted by forces beyond his control. Given knowledge, the professional can choose courses of action; he remains in charge of himself and his work.

1 / Imbroglio

The problem with being an executive these days is that a man can no longer be an executive in the classical sense. Traditional ways of wielding managerial power have become obsolete.[1]

The historical conception of the executive, whether boss, commander, leader, or bishop, is that he directs and commands. He plans, decides, assigns, and controls. True, he may have assistants with varying responsibilities, but in such a conception, it is he who *does*. If the business year has been a successful one, he has made it so. If the war is won, *he* has won it. He may be magnanimous enough to share his glory with his subordinates or democratic enough to share his decision-making with some of them, but there is no question that when he does so, *he shares*.

Characteristically, the executive has an image of himself as a combination coach, quarterback, linebacker, and end. He designs the plays and calls the signals. He evolves strategy and manages tactics. He tackles the competition head-on, or makes brilliant broken-field marketing runs, or throws surprise product passes over the heads of the competition, or punts the economic ball safely out of danger by merger, cost-cutting, or some other emergency device. And he does it every season.

Such an image is largely fantasy. Realistically, no executive can run an organization that way any more than a football coach can both execute strategy and play on the team. Yet, despite contemporary emphasis on team operation, most executives act as if they can and should. It is in the conflict between this expectation of themselves on one hand and the realities of organizational life on the other that much of the pain of leadership occurs. What are these realities?

Essentially they have to do with the distribution of power. Power exists only in relationship to other people who also have certain kinds of power. These people have expectations of how leadership power should be used. Unless they can be coerced into doing what the leader wishes them to do, they will use their power against him. Therefore, the task of the executive in dealing with these realities is not to pit his power against other sources of power, although sometimes that may be necessary. Rather it is to meet the expectations of the other powerholders in order that they may willingly lend their power to him to be used to further the interests of the organization. There are essentially five sources of power related to organizations. Each has its own expectations.

These facets of power can be illustrated by the experience of a small businessman. A man who goes into business to earn a livelihood may have acquired a skill or invented a product, rented a shop or bought a truck. Sometimes his business grows because he is so capable that it can not help but grow, sometimes because he is innovative, and sometimes because he is lucky. Whatever the case, as soon as his business begins to grow, it is no longer merely a means of earning a livelihood. It becomes a locus of power and he begins to create both expectations of and responsibility for himself.[2]

First, he creates a dual relationship with the public, namely the obligation to serve and the concurrent obligation not to harm. Football fans, the clientele of a government bureau, the customers of a department store, all have one thing in common: each requires services or goods and each demands that certain needs be met. The more they demand of a given vendor or entrepreneur, the more powerful they make him; that is, the larger and more successful he becomes. This success has two consequences. The more powerful he becomes (1) the more he has a vested interest in maintaining and protecting that power; and (2) the greater is his potential power to hurt those who avail themselves of his goods or services.

The leader of such an enterprise loses his power when the fans no longer come to watch the game, the clientele disappears, or the customers turn to other products. He must therefore continuously generate special publics who will turn to him if he is to retain his power.

The executive creates an obligation to serve and, indeed, an organization must exist in order to serve. A company's guarantee means nothing unless the company is in business. Every time it becomes apparent that some people are injured by what he does or sells, the entrepreneur's customer obligations are increased in number and complexity. Government controls were established to counteract the increasing power of the entrepreneur to hurt others, however unintentionally. Every corner drive-in needs half a dozen licenses. Every pharmaceutical manufacturer must conform to the requirements of the Food and Drug Administration before marketing a new drug. If a mail-order book club fails to live up to its promises, the purchaser has the strength of the Post Office Department behind him in his efforts to obtain redress. The entrepreneur as an executive thus incurs both public responsibility and public obligation.

Second, when a man's business grows beyond the corner grocery level, he creates a financial obligation. A fundamental problem of every small business is the fact that the owner rarely has sufficient capital for growth needs. Sooner or later the entrepreneur must "go public" with a stock-offering or obtain long-term credit from banks. In either case he incurs an obligation to those who invest in his business, an obligation backed by law and assorted regulatory bodies. Once he takes this step, others have an interest in the survival of his business beyond his lifetime. If a man were to open a service station today, it might take him as long as forty years to amortize his investment. A generation ago he would have put a gasoline pump in front of his grocery store. Increasingly, businesses require larger amounts of capital for longer periods of time.

This, too, is a power relationship in which he must maintain his own strength while at the same time drawing on the strength of others. The executive must cope with the broad, uncrystallized potential power of mass ownership — whether stockholders, alumni, constituents, or (if he leads a trade association, professional organization, or union) given kinds of publics like grocers, teachers, and bricklayers. From this source of power he must draw and maintain support without harming. He must prevent the inherent power in the mass from being fractionated and destroying the group, as in a proxy fight. If he is to maintain his leadership position, he must also keep that power from being used against himself. He must capitalize on the resources inherent in the mass to further his organization and to return value to the investors exemplified by the use of capital provided by stockholders and alumni.

Third, he then has to contend with the concentrated distillation of the power of the mass in the form of a board of directors or its equivalent. This means that he has to deal with others who are, as he experiences them, intruders into his business. Furthermore, in many organizations, and in some facets of all organizations, the government shares control with the corporation's board (anti-trust, the Federal Trade Commission, the Federal Communications Commission, the Interstate Commerce Commission, the National Labor Relations Board, etc.) to minimize harm to the public.

Fourth, he enters his power into competition with the power of others when he begins competing for customers, students, parishioners, or al-

legiance. Much of the time he competes under tournament rules: codes of ethics, trade association policies, informal norms, industry self-policing, and accrediting bodies. In addition, he often has the protection of governmental practices: tariffs, rate controls, inspections, and quotas. These controlling and protecting devices also become instruments for the survival of the organization beyond the individual. The license to operate a television station, a farmer's wheat allotment quota, a truck freight line's authorized route, all have commercial value and insure the continued function of that production or service unit.

Fifth, he incurs obligations to the people to whom he gives direct leadership — employees, subordinates, colleagues. This is the facet of power with which the modern executive has the most difficulty and the greatest pain. The degree of difficulty is reflected in the repetitive issue in labor relations, "management's right to manage," and in the widespread phenomenon called "management by guilt." [3]

The social importance of the executive's power in his relationship with his employees is evident in the process of hiring and firing. A firm with only a few employees would create little stir if it went out of business or discharged long-term employees. But a larger firm which does the same is resented by the community at large for being irresponsible. Both employees and community regard such action as unfair. The employer's obligation to his employees is reinforced by court decisions holding that a man has a vested interest in his job. His employer cannot move the firm capriciously to deprive him of that interest, nor does he lose it upon merger.[4] Economic obligations to employees are now fixed by tradition and union contract.

There are also psychological obligations to employees. These result in a psychological contract, a set of mutual expectations between organization and employee.[5] If either the economic or psychological expectations of colleagues or subordinates are not met, they then see this as the misuse of power and undertake actions to redress their complaints.

The leader therefore must harness the power inherent in his followers. They can use their power destructively in a gross way, as in a mob action or a strike. They can do so in a more clandestine manner by damaging themselves or their machines, by sabotaging the organization instead of supporting it, and by failing to produce — whether goods or scientific papers. The power of a group of people can be dissipated in faculty politics, church schism, union jurisdictional disputes, or in an interdepartmental conflict. Power also can be harnessed as in productive work. The power of a work group is always used in some combination of four alternatives: (1) directed to the task; (2) displaced from the task to some other activity; (3) contained, or not invested in either task or some other activity; and (4) directed to the self as in sickness absence, accidents, the withdrawal behavior of low morale, or injury to the organization despite its cost to the people themselves.

The power available to the leader for channeling into the tasks of the organization can never be more than the energy left after subtracting that which is diffused or used for destructive purposes. A steam engine operates at about 35 percent efficiency. People probably operate at about 10 percent of their potential. Most organizations constructively utilize even less of their potential power.

All of these five loci of power — the public, sources of finance, management controls, competitiors, and employees — are interrelated. The leader is always dealing with them simultaneously even when he is confronting only one immediately and directly. They might be schematized as five interlocking cogs with the leader in the center. The way in which these sources of power are managed by the leader depends on the strength of any one of the forces, the competence of the leader, and the cumulative effects of their acting in concert and acting upon each other.

The experience of Ford with its Edsel serves as an example of how these forces combine to effect an outcome. Ford had the *power to serve,* the leadership, and the *financial resources* derived from its *stockholders* but failed in *competition* for customers. Meanwhile, the company was obliged to retain many *employees* and ease the burden of dealers to whom it had made commitments. The $250 million budget and the vast resources of a major international company were powerful forces, but not as powerful together as the single one of failure to interest the customers.

Often, new political or business leadership brings about drastic reorganization but the reorganization soon flounders on the resistance of the employees. Some companies go through periodic drastic reorganizations. They act on the assumption that any change is good, mistaking temporary increases in productivity for long-term gain, and they never recognize that the underlying resistance of employees is increased by the reorganizations.

Failure to effectively handle any one of these five forces will threaten the executive's position, and failure in relationships with any two will certainly cost him his job. Yet a man who heads an organization, even though he is supposed to be in control of it and presumably has the capacity to manage it, more often than not finds that neither of these assumptions is completely valid. However, others assume that he is actually in control of its detailed operations and even of those external forces which may affect its operation, and they therefore hold him responsible.

Expectations and Feelings About Self

Think again of the executive's expectations of himself. A man's expectations of himself and how he should use power have many origins — in the personalities of the kinds of men who seek positions of power, in the traditional conceptions of how power is to be used, in the modes by which power is acquired, and in the multiple sources of power already discussed. Unless it is seized in some fashion, power accretes like fat on a middle-aged man. Before a man realizes it, he has girth. Even when he becomes aware of his girth, it does not seem nearly as large to him as it is in reality and as it appears to others. Similarly, often before he realizes it, a man has power — power which seems larger to others than it does to him.

The head of an organization unwittingly assumes the responsibility of being all things to all men who are related to the organization. He must revere the past, predict and succeed in the future, make a profit, carry the burdens of people and operations no longer efficient, and enjoy himself besides. His whim becomes magnified into other people's law, try as he might to make it clear that his whim is not the same as law. His law is often treated as if it were whim, for few people want to recognize a law other than their own.

If he demands that people produce, he is exploitative. If he treats them with beneficence, he is paternalistic. If he is unconcerned about their worries, he is rejecting. If he opposes what he believes to be irrational, he is hostile. If he gives in, he is weak. He no longer knows with the certainty of his predecessors which way to turn.

In addition to more complex responsibilities within the organization itself, the contemporary executive is the pivot man of vast technological and social changes. He is expected to assume a major responsibility for training and employing the disadvantaged members of society — the dropouts, the handicapped, the aging, minority group members. He also is expected to arrange matters in such a way that as he increases the technological efficiency of his operations, he will not discharge those whose skills have become obsolete. Furthermore, he is expected to assume a leadership role in his industry and his community in their efforts to cope with social problems. Indeed, he expects himself to fulfill these responsibilities. He is frequently conscience-driven.

What goes on within him is the same turmoil with which every other man must live and, in some respects, a little more. The leader must never admit that he is frightened or that he does not know; his doubts become his subordinates' panic.

He is perennially vulnerable. He is sometimes like a blind man who must operate by echoes and soundings. He can never know all that he needs to know to make wise decisions. To complicate matters, there are always people at his elbow guiding him in this direction or that for their own purposes. His trusted secretary is no less manipulative than his lieutenant, not because they are dishonest but because each sees the world in his own way and wants to go that way. A man with a cause will more often tear at his heart or demand his help in mending the hearts of others because of the power he represents.

Rivalry is also a problem. To achieve his pinnacle, the leader must pass others by, some older, some seemingly more capable. He may have arrived at his position by dethroning a less successful predecessor. If he came from humble origins, each advancing step was also a step higher than his father reached and takes him further away from his family. For some, these experiences produce feelings of guilt and the anxiety of adapting to successively higher social roles. There is also the additional anxiety which results from the knowledge that others are competing for his place, which ultimately he will have to give up, and that the higher he rises, the more painful will be the fall if he fails.

However inadequate his efforts may be, an organization leader portrays omnipotence. In reality he only postures that Godlike quality. At best he constantly strives toward being only half as good as his inner aspiration. A baseball player is thought to be good if he gets three hits out of ten times at bat, but an executive on the way up has learned that he is allowed but one mistake. It is not difficult to understand why the leader, sitting atop his lonely summit, projects his inner disquiet. Often he sees these below him as incompetent, inadequate, or idiotic, and he distrusts what they might do or say, and despairs of ever making an organization of them.[6] It is a common psychological mechanism to deal with the intolerable anxiety of one's own despair by attributing it to others.

Although the power of executives has been decreasing consistently for the past hundred years, a man may delude himself into thinking he is powerful because he is someone else's boss. The responsibility of executives, on the other hand, has increased. The contemporary executive frequently continues to act as if the contemporary business scene were that of a century ago and as if he could carry on his task in much the same way as his predecessors. With less outright power to face greater responsibility, the executive can no longer function effectively by control and command. The Imperial German General Staff Plan, the organization chart of most organizations, is obsolete. The executive role has changed, too. Current executive practice is as radically different from nineteenth-century procedure as driving a stage coach is from piloting a supersonic airliner.

The implications of this change recall the earlier football analogy. A football coach needs a mode of management which permits him the broadest flexibility. He needs to be able to interchange players year after year without losing the vitality of the team. Therefore he must constantly be developing men. His plays must fit the changing skills of new men as they come along, and the yearly changes in rules as well as the varying characteristics of different playing fields and opponents. Plays which work brilliantly in the sunny, early fall may fail miserably in bitter cold and mud. Technological innovation, like the introduction of the forward pass, requires drastic reorganization of tactics and demands new player skills. A team which does not have weight in a given year must have speed and plays which call for speed. A team which has neither weight nor speed must have determination. Even in football, some coaches have turned to computers to analyze the myriad data which affect performance. As the players have become more educated, coaches have found it wiser to let them make more decisions on the field. The coach, too, must satisfy the alumni, the fans, the administration, and the players, as well as himself. His record is a lifetime score. He must be directed to survival.

The issue for the executive is the same: in what ways does he lead in order to ensure his survival and that of his organization? Chester Barnard argues that "survival depends on two general factors: (1) the effectiveness of the system of governance as respects the *external* relations of the organizations; and (2) its *internal* efficiency, that is its capacity of securing cohesiveness, coordination, and subordination of concrete acts."[7] These two factors are intimately interwoven. However, the survival of an organization ultimately depends upon its internal efficiency. It is this factor which is the focus of this book, and which should be of primary concern to the executive.

In many respects the modern large business organization has many of the powers and functions of the old feudal lord — and indeed many of the same kinds of obligations. Executives serve much the same conceptual function as the mercenary knights — their task is to ensure the survival of the organization.

2 / The Pillars of Survival

Ancient explorers spent centuries searching for the illusory Fountain of Youth which was to ensure their survival. Modern day executives have something of the same task, but theirs is more easily accomplished. If organizations are to survive their founders and if executives are to survive in their positions, they must build into their organizations the capacity for perpetual life. This can come about only by making it possible for people within the organization to act innovatively and responsibly toward it. From a psychological point of view, behavior is a product of a combination of *drives, needs, expectations,* and *external demands,* and the capacities of people to deal with these forces. Any program for survival must be based on these sources of motivation. These are, then, the pillars of survival.

For present purposes, consider two sources of needs and expectations: those forces within the personality which give it its basic direction and those external cultural forces, which, in interaction with internal forces, mold and shape attitudes toward power. Psychoanalytic theory provides a comprehensive basis for understanding intrapersonal forces. It is a theory which gives heavy emphasis to drives and capacities inherent in the person, and to the structures of personality through which the drives are expressed and the capacities brought to fruition.*

Intrapersonal Forces

Psychoanalytic theory conceives of three systems or structures within the personality.[1] The theory attributes to each one of these structures certain functions and energies by which it carries them on. One of these structures is called the *id,* within which, it is hypothesized, are two constantly operating drives. One is a *constructive* drive leading to growth, love, expansion of the personality, and integration of the personality with the surrounding world. The other is a *destructive* drive leading to hate, contraction and

* This discussion of psychoanalytic theory is deliberately brief because an adequate discussion would take several chapters, if not a book. For a more complete short discussion, the reader is referred to the first four chapters of my book, *Emotional Health: In the World of Work* (New York: Harper & Row, 1964), and for a good single volume discussion to Charles Brenner's *An Elementary Textbook of Psychoanalysis* (New York: International Universities Press, 1955).

constriction of the personality, alienation from the surrounding world, and death. These drives, often referred to as the sexual and aggressive drives, or love and hate, are derived from the biological forces of anabolism and catabolism. One of the major tasks of the personality is to fuse these drives so that the constructive drive is dominant. The id is also the site of repressed memories and experiences and primitive wishes and impulses. It is comprised of the uncivilized core of man which always struggles for expression.

The executive part of the personality is the *ego*. It is the ego's job to control, guide, and direct the pressures from the id. The ego is made up of the five senses, together with the abilities to concentrate, judge, attend, form concepts, think reflectively, recall, and learn, and the physical ability to act. The ego is in touch with the outside world and takes it into account when dealing with the id. The ego also seeks to master the outside world so that the person can survive.

The third structure is the *superego* or, more colloquially, conscience. The conscience is an internal self-governing agent which is made up of four component functions: the acquisition of rules, the evolution of values, the aspiration to an ego ideal, and self-judgment.

1. *Rules.* As part of the process of growth, a person identifies himself with his parents and other important figures in his environment. In doing so, he assimilates many of their rules for living. The rules which have to do with expressing aggressive impulses as well as with giving and receiving love are particularly imperative because of the strength of those drives.

2. *Values.* In addition, by the same process of identification, he adopts and evolves certain values which become the bases for his attitudes about important aspects of living. These values range from such firmly and universally established ideals as the sanctity of human life to the more specific ones which are part of a professional discipline, such as the values of privacy and confidentiality which govern the practice of medicine.

3. *Ego ideal.* Another aspect of the conscience is stimulus to attain an ego ideal. The ego ideal is an internalized image of oneself at his future best. This image is constructed from the expectations which parents and others hold of the child, from the aspirations the child develops for himself out of his recognition of his capacities and abilities, and from his identification with important figures in his environment. Concepts of "self-fulfillment" and "self-actualization" in part refer to a person's efforts to attain his ego ideal. However, the ego ideal is beyond one's capacities so

that it continues to serve as a distant goal toward which one is constantly striving. Various kinds of social models ranging from presidents, creative artists, military leaders, and saints on the one hand, to criminals and racketeers on the other — depending upon the cultural milieu from which the child comes — serve as the raw material for the ego ideal. Their function as models is reinforced by history, literature, religion, myth, and folklore.

4. *Self-judgment.* The fourth part of the conscience is an internal judging-policing function. This aspect of the conscience is most evident. Everyone has experienced pangs of conscience or twinges of guilt after having violated the rules or values by which he lives or when he has not met the demands of the ego ideal.

The superego acts upon the ego by the process of warning of or arousing guilt feelings as the latter seeks to express id impulses. The ego, then, must satisfy the demands of the superego as well as deal with reality as it channels the forces of the id. Reality places various kinds of pressures on the ego and also provides for a range of opportunities for dealing with them. For example, American children are stimulated to considerably more aggression than are children in Eastern cultures, or even in European subcultures. Murder mysteries and violence are highly popular in movies, television, comic books, and daily newspapers. Aggressive impulses are more likely to be stimulated by such themes in the environment. At the same time, the environment provides a range of acceptable outlets for stimulated aggressions. Participation in competitive athletics is widespread. Those who are unable to compete, watch these events, identify with the participants, and thereby vicariously discharge some of their aggressions.

Sexual impulses are likewise widely stimulated. Scanty clothing for women is acceptable as informal public attire. Highly erotic love scenes in moving pictures, nudes in popular magazines, and public expression of affection are common. Social practices complement this stimulation. Early dating, for example, is commonplace in the American culture. By way of contrast, it is forbidden in Latin American countries and India.

In the process of resolving the forces of id, ego, superego, and environment, as has been indicated, the person must deal with people in his environment who are more powerful than he — his parents and other dominant figures. Early in life he is completely dependent on his parents. Gradually he becomes increasingly independent. Becoming independent is in itself a struggle, for there are many gratifications in being cared for. It is the critical struggle of adolescence.

Freeing oneself from dependence on parents is not enough to form the adult personality. A person must decide for himself who he is. He must consolidate and organize the myriad experiences of his young lifetime into a consistent, coherent pattern in keeping with the demands and expectations of his ego ideal. He accepts certain values and rejects others. He adopts favored ways of behaving which are consonant with his picture of himself as an adult. In a society which does not specifically define a person's social role based on his position or that of his parents in the society, a person chooses his own vocation. This task of self-crystallization is part of the problem of identity formation.

Each person, therefore, must deal with three major psychological problems or conflicts: (1) the twin drives and repressed memories; (2) the conflict between his wishes to remain dependent and his desires to become independent; and (3) establishing his identity.

Since each person must resolve these core problems, he has enduring needs for help in their solution. To fulfill some needs he requires other people to do something to or for him. Such needs might be called *ministration needs*. To satisfy other needs he requires a congenial environment. The unfolding of a person's intellect, for example, requires a stimulating atmosphere. These needs might be understood as *maturation needs*. A third set of needs, those related to integrating the various facets of his personality and coming to effective terms with his environment, could be called *mastery needs*.

A person's favored ways of solving these problems and fulfilling these needs become the characteristic traits of his personality. Personality traits may be viewed as coping mechanisms or styles of behavior. They might also be regarded as economical practices, the most efficient and effective ways a person has of managing his inner impulses and external environment. Some people are gregarious, devil-may-care. Others are more diffident and reserved. Still others are impulsive and erratic, now conservative, now extravagant. Some take responsibility seriously; others do not know what the word means. Each in its own way is a method of dealing with these ever present problems.

This conception of personality has two implicit assumptions, among others. It assumes that personality is a genetic phenomenon, evolved continuously from a changing physical matrix and shaped by experience. Earlier experiences, as in childhood, have considerably more impact on the shaping of personality than later experiences because the person is more malleable earlier in life. This conception assumes further that personality is a dynamic phenomenon; that it is a result of many different forces and seeks to maintain its equilibrium. Disturbances in the equilibrium of the personality are what clinicians call mental illness.

These assumptions about the personality underlie two propositions:

1. *A man brings attitudes, expectations, and modes of behaving to his work which have evolved from his life experience.*

2. *A man brings his continuing efforts to maintain his personality equilibrium to his work.* To use a homely analogy, like a Diesel railroad engine, he always has his motor running.

The Meaning of Leadership

Consider the implications for leadership of attitudes and expectations toward power. As a result of extended experiences with people who have wielded power over him when he was small and unpowerful, a person has expectations about how he should relate to others who have power and how they should behave toward him. He has a posture toward authority, derived from his relationships with the only authority figures he knew as a child — his parents and parent surrogates. These attitudes were somewhat modified as a consequence of experiences with teachers, ministers, scoutmasters and other authority figures, but fundamental attitudes toward power are derived from the earliest and most intense experiences with authority figures.

These experiences vary from family to family. They also have a strong common element in any given culture. As a result, there are generalized expectations about how authority is to be wielded, how the more powerful people should act toward the weaker, and what kinds of behavior the latter might expect from the former. Essentially, these expectations are that one will use his social strength according to culturally established norms. Therefore, when one acquires control over others, he also incurs the effects of these expectations about power figures. In short, a person who becomes authoritative in direct relationships to others will be expected to act in much the same way, as in that culture, a father acts in the family. This does not mean that he is expected to be a father or consciously recognized as such. It is to say only that inasmuch as people develop their expectations of and attitudes toward power from their earliest experiences with it, they will tend to carry these same attitudes unconsciously in their every encounter. If a superior fails to conform to these expectations, then he will be seen as an inadequate, unfair, or unjust leader.

Manifest management practices vary according to the more obvious aspects of the family structure in a particular culture or subculture. For example, Germans speak of Germany as "the Fatherland." The father's role in that country is authoritarian and directive. The style of business management is also authoritarian and directive. Britain, by contrast, is referred to as "the Motherland" and historically its queens are more widely known by name than its kings. British boys, compared with American boys, have relatively less contact with their fathers.[2] Lower-class fathers until recently did not help care for the children. Upper-class boys historically went off to public school as soon as they left their mothers' knee. Britannia, who rules the waves, is a royal feminine figure. British business executives are frequently criticized as being "old maidish." American executives allege that their British counterparts prefer the economic comfort of protective arrangements to open competition.[3]

Russians speak of Russia not as "the Motherland" or "the Fatherland" but as "the Homeland"; alternatively they refer to "Mother Earth." Here there would appear to be little identification of the state as the surrogate of the family, despite its all encompassing qualities. Rather it is as if only the land is important. For the Russians who have always had to struggle to fulfill the most primitive needs, the land takes on an especially poignant meaning. With land one always has something to eat, a place to hide, and a space to be buried. Professional management in the American sense is very poorly developed.

Further corroboration comes from a study of business organizations in Turkey.[4] There, employees tend to be evaluated in terms of loyalty to the manager rather than on the basis of objective criteria of job performance. Authority within the business organization is highly centralized and even routine decisions are referred upward for approval. "The relation of superiors and subordinates is highly particularistic and mirrors in many respects that of father and son in the Turkish family," writes Norman Bradburn, the social psychologist who did the study. Patterns of relationship within the business organization parallel those in the Turkish family, which is characterized by close family ties with strong emphasis on family loyalty and by the dominant role of the father. Luigi Barzini describes the same phenomenon in Italy, and John Fischer reports that in Japan business and other organizations have taken over the role of the ancient clan.[5]

Projection of the family model into other forms of social organization is not limited to businesses. Sociologist Daniel P. Moynihan points out that the political structure of large cities in which the Irish were dominant was patterned closely after that of the old country Irish family.[6] The Irish politician was *supposed* to grant favors, for his was the personal relationship drawn from the Irish village life. "Village life was characterized by the preeminence of formal family relations under the dominance of the stern father. Substituting 'party' for 'family' and 'leader' for 'father,' the Irish created the political machine."

Americans have no such parental image of their country. The culture of the United States is said to be child-centered. Parents are often the servants of their children, who have considerable freedom. The American concept of governmental power is a benign Uncle Sam who may from time to time "want you," as the World War I and II recruiting posters indicated. More often his task is to help his wards better themselves. The American tradition is one of being free and equal. Government is to do only those things which people cannot do themselves or which they must do in concert. Its powers are derived from the sovereign states and from the people at large. It is not presumed to be, like the crown in Britain, the source of the power which it then delegates to others. With such a tradition it is not surprising that concepts of human relations in business and industry have spread more widely than elsewhere. This cultural conception of power is reflected in the Horatio Alger myth. The commonly accepted moral of the myth is that hard work will bring success. However, there is another character in the Horatio Alger stories about which few people have heard: an older, kindly, wealthy, helping person who boosts Horatio along.

That there are similar expectations of the executive is verified repeatedly in American morale and motivation studies.[7] These show that a good superior gives recognition to his subordinates, helps them grow in the job, represents their interests to higher management, looks out for their interests, corrects them justly and in private, and does not exploit them for his own gain. In this country the major objective of parents is to help their children grow to independent responsibility. The executive implicitly is expected to do the same in the course of fulfilling the objectives and goals of the organization.

A distinction should be made to clarify the difference between paternalism and the father-figure concept of leadership. In paternalism, the leader acts *as if he really were the father* and treats his subordinates as if they were children. He does things for them that they might better do themselves, like providing recreation programs.

Thus, business leadership comes to have an important psychological role for those who are subordinate to that leadership.[8] Although analogies must not be taken too literally, it is important to recognize these often unconscious expectations as realities with which each leader must deal and from which there is no escape so long as one holds power.

The Meaning of Work

The second implication of the assumptions about personality was that a man brings to his work continuing efforts to maintain his personality equilibrium. What in psychological terms, is work?

For all of man's preoccupation with work over thousands of years, no one has yet proposed a satisfactory definition of work. To understand the paradoxical meaning of work is no simple task. It is simultaneously a curse and a blessing. Man cannot free himself from work, nor would he do so if he could. A man works when he is hungry; it is equally obvious that he still labors when he is so satiated with material goods that he cannot even use what he has. Some men's work is other men's play; some make work out of play, and some make play out of work. There are those who gird themselves relentlessly to take lives while others struggle desperately to save them. A few men spend their adult years trying to escape work; more escape into it. Some sing of working to pass the time away; and some, in a more anguished vein, of being oppressed by barges and bales. A man devotes nearly half of his waking hours to his job. It is said that he both works to live and lives to work.

When Morse and Weiss asked a national sample of 401 employed men whether they would continue to work if they inherited enough money to live comfortably, 80 percent said they would. The researchers were particularly impressed with the vividness of the responses: "It was almost as if they had never consciously thought what working meant to them but now that they were presented with the imaginary removal of it, they would see for themselves and verbalize to another person the feelings which had really been there implicitly all the time." [9]

Nowhere does man do without occupation; in the West, occupation is synonymous with work. With this conception, the occupational millennium which automation promises is not freedom from work, but rather freedom from being a substitute for a machine. Man will always find and always have work.

Realistically, most people need to provide financially for themselves and to protect themselves against possible emergencies as well as the realities of aging. Work, then, as a medium for survival, has a fundamental economic meaning. Bare subsistence rarely satisfies anyone. The need for money is a basic reason for working but not the only one. When a person is able to earn enough to meet his fundamental financial needs, then other reasons for working become proportionately more important to him. Thus many people prefer white-collar jobs at which they earn less than they might as skilled technicians, or prefer to work in a more elite downtown business district than in a factory area.

Money is an important incentive to some, not for its own sake, but because its acquisition represents power, achievement, success, safety, public recognition, and many other things. In recent years, studies of motivation to work frequently have emphasized the importance of factors other than money, leading some managers to think money was of little importance, with unfortunate consequences.[10] Many businesses today suffer from inadequate leadership largely because they allowed men of initiative to be attracted away by higher financial rewards.

A study of the motivation to work indicated that dissatisfaction with salary in middle-management ranks can make a man discontented with his work.[11] However, satisfaction with salary alone is not enough to make him satisfied with his job. For some people, particularly managers and unskilled workers, money remains the important incentive. Managers enter business rather than the professions because money more than service or function is an incentive.

From a study of executive views of management compensation the researchers report that the higher the level of management the less satisfied the executive was with the amount of his pay, regardless of the amount he was receiving.[12] Unskilled workers have few other sources of gratification in their work than the money they earn, since their lack of skill deprives them of both esteem from superiors and sense of accomplishment from skill itself.

Work also has many social meanings. When a man works he has a contributing place in society. He earns the right to be the partner of other men. The fact that someone will pay for his work is an indication that what he does is needed by others, and therefore that he is a necessary part of the social fabric. He matters — as a man. To have a skill, trade, or occupation is to be a "who" and "what." That is, a man is identified in his own mind and to others by what he does. His work defines the nature of his partnership with others and the value of that partnership. In most cultures, the healer, the holy man, and the arbiter traditionally have been the most valued partners. A man's work, therefore, is a major social device for his identification as an adult. Much of who he is, to himself and others, is interwoven with how he earns his livelihood.

In Western societies, work enables a man to meet another definition of manliness: the head of the family. Most men take this role for granted and most can do so until they have no work. Then the meaning of work for this aspect of being a man becomes all too painfully clear.

During the extended depression of the 1930's a number of studies of the unemployed provided us with considerable insight into the meaning of work for a man's place as head of the household. One of the classic studies was conducted by Eli Ginzberg.[13] This and other studies disclosed that when a man lost his job and was on relief, often his whole family's picture of him changed. Not only did he feel himself to be less a man outside his family, but also within his family he was often regarded as less a man than he had been.

Frequently, for example, the children of the unemployed men would no longer accept his discipline or listen to his advice. After all, he was demonstrating to them by the fact of his unemployment that he was not successful or powerful. Relief, not he, was supporting them, and they would flaunt this fact to him. His lack of a work position in the community deprived them of status among their friends whose fathers held jobs. Sometimes, in his desperation to be doing something useful, a man turned to cleaning or cooking or making toys, as many men did. These activities further vitiated his role as the strong masculine identification figure for his children that every father ideally should be.

It is pointless for boys to try to be like unsuccessful fathers. They have to turn elsewhere for models. It is painful for fathers to feel that their sons do not want to be "chips off the old block," that they have no fundamental respect for their fathers. It is equally painful for the boys not to be able to consolidate their schooling, aptitudes, and interests around a central core of identity, which usually comes from identifying themselves with their fathers. Girls, too, need to be able to see their fathers as competent masculine figures, as the measure of a man, because such a positive experience with their fathers gives them a better basis upon which to make a choice of a husband.

Unemployment created problems for their wives, too. Some mothers, of course, would try to "pump up" their husbands in the eyes of their children, and to support the fathers in their positions as head of the family. Others used the occasion of their husband's economic defeat to emasculate them even further. Under the combined stress of being without work and losing some of their masculine self-respect, the sexual demands of the men tended to increase. Those wives who had merely tolerated sexual relations while their husbands supported them, rejected the advances of their now unemployed spouses. Thus, a man's work not only makes it possible for him to provide financially for his children as befits the head of a family, but equally important, to provide for them psychologically as a man should. Furthermore, his work is an essential ingredient of his ability to hold his place as a man in his family. Every manager of men, therefore, would find it wise in his own self-interest and in the interest of his men, to look carefully at what it takes to be a man among the friends and families of his employees, and to encourage, support, and give public recognition to the socially acceptable aspects of that behavior on the job.

Most people are guided by a personal governor and guide: the superego or conscience. Therefore much of a person's behavior is an effort to appease or alleviate the pressures of the conscience. The traditions of being "fair and square," of doing the right thing, of being our brother's keeper, are strong in the American culture. Among these traditions is the almost conscious belief that a man must earn the right to be alive.

Philosophers and theologians have debated for centuries about the purpose of man's existence. Ordinary men do not usually debate such questions in so many words, but they do make certain assumptions about their purposes in life and act accordingly. A man who reads meters for an electric utility company whose basic function is service and who devotes every spare moment to Boy Scout work, assumes, among other things, that a fundamental reason for living is to render service, to give something of himself to others. An English teacher who also makes furniture assumes that, in addition to communicating knowledge about language, it is important to use a part of one's life to create enduring items which increase comfort. A landscape gardener tacitly assumes that it is important to create beauty and thereby to enrich living.

Sometimes man justifies himself by his aspirations. He may aspire to a certain position in life, to "arrive," to provide a better social and economic springboard for his children, to protect himself from adversity, or even to make the world better. Sometimes a man's justification is a matter of trying to be loved, which he assuages by seeking popular acclaim or prestige. Often he is uneasy because he does not have a justification. That leaves him dissatisfied with himself because no achievement provides any lasting internal satisfaction. Work goals and achievements can become both temporary and enduring justifications.

Work helps man to live with his conscience in another way. Through work he tries to achieve his personal goals and to live up to his aspirations. He feels inadequate when he is not doing quite as well as he thinks he can or should. Even though he may not yet have fulfilled his aspirations, so long as he is working toward them, he tends to feel more comfortable with himself.

A finding by J. Stacy Adams of the General Electric Company provides an interesting sidelight to the function of work as a mode of dealing with conscience.[14] In the course of an experimental study, he made some hourly workers feel that they were overpaid and others that they were being paid fairly. Those who felt that they were being overpaid increased their productivity to justify to themselves the greater pay they were getting.

Work provides a means of reinforcing the conscience. Usually a person has to be at his job regularly at a given time, and produce goods or services of a certain quality. The task itself makes demands on him for a level of performance, stimulating and reinforcing his internal desires to do well. People such as artists and commission salesmen who have no externally imposed schedules or demands often have a difficult time motivating themselves to produce. Those who become successful usually have had to discipline themselves to work consistently so that it seems as if the work itself is making demands on them. An interesting sidelight to this phenomenon is that people who are unemployed seem to lose a sense of time. It is as if work, work schedules, and work demands become measures of time. Time is irreplaceable. When people devote significant amounts of time to anything, implicitly they are assuming that it is important to do so. They are justifying to themselves why they exist.

The need to justify oneself is so strong that many people have difficulty accepting relief, welfare, charity, even social security or hot lunches in public schools. Yet all these forms of assistance are intended to help people overcome and prevent family disintegration. If the purpose of the work is in itself not worth living for, if it does not meet the implicit assumptions of those who do it, if it does not make reasonable demands on people, then it should be no surprise if employees are apathetic and need constantly to be bought off with ever higher wages and fringe benefits. Recent trends in business and industry toward participative management, such as the Kaiser cost-cutting program, are one step toward increasing the responsibility of employees.[15] Responsibility as adults for the success of the business helps many people meet the demands and expectations of their consciences.

Freud once said that in order to have mental health, a man had to be able to love and to work. Work, he pointed out, was a consistent and fundamental means of staying in touch with the world and of mastering it.

Almost everyone has had the experience of being sick in bed. Before long the patient begins to lose touch with life beyond what he can see from his window. People whom he ordinarily saw every day at work, he now sees only occasionally. The longer he is sick, the less frequently he sees them. The sick man is desperate to *do something,* to use himself. In the museum of The Menninger Foundation there is a large ball of string, perhaps two feet in diameter. A state hospital patient plaited bits and pieces of string together over a period of years — because he had nothing else to do. It is painfully eloquent testimony to a sick man's need to master some part of his environment.

A layer of apathy insulates a man from his own problems, as well as those of a city or the nation. This is one reason why it is difficult to arouse interest in impoverished countries about the possibilities of Communist threat, and to motivate the chronically unemployed to seek retraining. People who are not working seem to lose some of their motivation to try to solve their own problems. It is as if they had lost both their skill and their confidence to contend with reality. The longer they are unemployed, the more afraid they are of going to work. Most people dread being helpless. When man works, he demonstrates to himself that he is not helpless. To be without work is to increase the feelings of helplessness.

In addition to being a fundamental medium by which an adult adapts effectively to his world, work is also a major medium for mastering himself. Each person has the continuous psychological task of controlling, fusing, and channeling the twin unconscious drives of love and hate. Work is a central psychological device for this task. The woman who pounds the typewriter is not only discharging her aggressions but also rendering a service to others. The carpenter who hammers nails builds shelter by doing so. The salesman who persuades a customer also provides employment for those who make his product.

Work helps a man master himself in another way. People frequently say, "I'd go nuts if I didn't work." By this they usually mean that two things would happen: they would become increasingly tense and restless, and they would have many fantasies ("I would think and worry too much."). In fact, in the Morse and Weiss study, one third of the men gave such reasons for wanting to continue working, even if they could afford not to. By concentrating on his task, a person pushes out of consciousness many thoughts and ideas he would just as soon not have. In some prisons there is a punishment cell called "the hole." Neither light nor sound penetrate "the hole," and meals are shoved into the cell through an aperture. Few prisoners want to talk about their experiences in "the hole," because, without stimulation from outside themselves, their own thoughts become "crazy" and frightening to them.

Work, then, is a way of being "on top." To work is to be in control of oneself and some part of the surrounding world, to have some idea of what the future holds and to be prepared for it. It is also to be in touch with the changing world, and to grow more competent and secure in it. The motivation to work is strengthened with increasing opportunity of the employee to master and control his work in keeping with the task to be done.

Many people find a means of socialization in their jobs. The work activity which people share requires interaction and communication. It is not unusual to find people who live lonely lives after working hours, particularly those who do not make friends easily. In fact, in the rehabilitation of the once mentally ill, often the most difficult problem to be surmounted is not quality of performance but the loneliness of the after-work hours.

Work has another social meaning, too. It is a psychological truism that people tend to recapitulate their early family experiences in their subsequent activities. In fact, people often speak of their work group as being a "family."

As in the family, working with others usually involves a certain amount of friendly give and take, and sometimes not so friendly exchange. There are relationships to people who, like parents, have more power. Fellow employees can have greater, equal or lesser power, depending on their seniority, experience and skill; thus, a man's relationships with them may be similar to relationships with brothers and sisters. Hiring and firing is psychologically similar to the parent's giving or withholding of love. To be hired is to be valued and to be discharged is to be rejected.

As the family fostered social activities among its members, so does the company. Coffee breaks, lunch together, evening entertainment in each other's homes, all encourage social relationships among people whose basic tie is that they work together. Golf, fishing, hunting, and other group activities often stem from work associations. It is not uncommon for men to head for a bar as they leave the plant, to have a few beers together, and to continue their discussions of the job and sports.

To understand some of the deeper meanings of work to his employees, an executive would do well to know the kinds of families from which they come. If the work process can recapitulate the style of family relationships typical of his employees, so much the better. If it is radically different, he is likely to have difficulty keeping his people. Conversely, he would be wise to select people whose family experiences fit the kind of work process he must use. A highly mechanized work process in which people cannot talk to each other because of the noise level or the distance between them will hardly meet the needs of people who are accustomed to close family relationships. In addition, work is one of the most constructive modes for transforming impulses, derived from the constructive and destructive drives, as well as for resolving problems of identity and dependency. In work, a man channels his aggressive drive, adequately fused with the constructive drive, into creating products, rendering services, and competing with others.

If work serves these many purposes, it is apparent that a man who finds gratification in his work has attained a harmonious coordination of experience, interests, capacities, skills, drives, and conscience. Thus work is essential to achieve and maintain one's psychological balance. It should be no surprise, therefore, that one of the indications of emotional disturbance is a man's inability to find gratification in work. For some men this means an inability to hold a job. Others seem unable to be happy no matter how much they change jobs. Still others are never able to find themselves or to realize their potential. Some manage to fail no matter what the opportunities.

The most trenchant evidence of the importance of work to psychological balance is a common clinical phenomenon. Psychologists and psychiatrists often see mentally ill persons whose friends and relatives are disturbed by their symptoms at home, symptoms which either never occur on the job or become evident at work long after they have become an old story at home. The alcoholic, for example, will rarely come to work drunk. Work becomes a fundamental resource, something to hold onto as long as it is possible to do so. It is at the same time a psychological glue which often holds a man together. Folk wisdom says that to work is to live, and those who do not work seem to die — literally and psychologically.

The Meaning of the Organization

Work has thus become an important social device for resolving the three major psychological problems previously specified (unconscious pressures, dependency, and identity). Therefore, the organization within which a person works and the leadership which represents the power in that organization are both important aspects of the environment of that person. They define the modes within the organizational structure through which aggressions may be expressed and affection obtained or given by promotion, demotion, transfer, reward, assignment, job definition, and other methods of control. The organization and its leadership have an important bearing on how a person feels himself to be as an adult, whether he fulfills the aspirations of his ego ideal, whether he is held in esteem or whether he judges himself a failure.

The psychological importance of the organization to the individual who works in it has increased in the last two generations. Radical changes in contemporary Western industrialized society have altered many of the ways in which people could satisfy their economic, social, and psychological needs. These changes have required people to find new ways of obtaining job security; new social devices for protection against injury, sickness, and death; modes of developing new skills, new forms of recreation, and new sources of support. Increasingly, people have found new devices for dealing with their reality problems through employment in organizations.

These changes also have diminished the possibilities for certain kinds of relationships between people and increased the numbers of people who have ties to organizations, as well as the strength and range of such ties. For example, the movement of people from towns and villages to cities, and the more frequent transfer of people from one community to another have made the conception of the "hometown" almost obsolete. The neighborhood and the hometown are no longer the psychological anchorages they once were. Those to whom such a point in space is an important element of their identity, experience a loss. "I miss the mountains (or the plains, or the sea)," they will say with deep feeling.

Increasing mobility, both social and geographical, has made it more difficult for people to establish relatively enduring friendships. Many who anticipate further moves from one area to another are reluctant to involve themselves deeply in friendships to avoid the later pain of separation. Thus they lose some of the impetus to consistent ties with others, and therefore opportunities to give and receive affection.

The extended family unit is less likely to be found living in the same geographical area where family members can turn readily to each other for social activities and mutual aid. Family elders in many cases are too far away from their grandchildren to become models for identification and sources of psychological support. This means both fewer sources of support and less sense of family continuity. People who turn to professionals for help with some form of stress frequently speak of being without support when they say, "I have nobody to turn to." Children, seeing other children's experiences with grandparents, express regret because they have none or theirs are far away.

Services to people have become progressively more institutionalized. Social services, voluntary health agencies, hospitals, nursing homes — these and similar organized efforts have taken the place of the more personal services and charitable acts characteristic of a previous era. "More personal" means that people believed there was more affection and concern in noninstitutional services. The change therefore represents a perceived loss of certain sources of love — "nobody really cares."

Even in work some sources of gratification are being lost. Rapid technical changes have altered the composition of work groups and work tasks. Occupational and status achievements are somewhat tenuous when skills can readily be made obsolete or when their social value can depreciate rapidly, as occurs with technical changes and new industrial developments.[16] Many of the services formerly performed by small entrepreneurs are now carried out by larger units of production and marketing. For those who are members of work groups, these changes taken together contribute to the loss of a sense of group purpose about work and of group solidarity. When skills become obsolete, they not only lose their meaning as instruments of economic security, but also of psychological security, for a man loses an important method of mastering some part of his world. Movement from a small business to a larger enterprise usually means some loss of personal freedom.

Affiliation with an organization in which a person works seems to have become a major device for solving the problems resulting from these economic, social, and psychological changes.[17]

Organizations have recognized and fostered the intention of people to seek financial security in the organization by means of long service, even though college recruiters may be impatient with young college graduates who ask about company retirement provisions. Seniority advantages in union contracts, vested rights in pension funds, and the tendency to promote people within a given organization rather than for them to move easily upward by going from one business to another have encouraged long-term affiliation with one organization. Often, a man enters a work organization before he marries and remains in it long after his grandchildren are grown.

Instead of geographical orientation, many now have corporate orientation. They identify themselves with an organization — whether a company, church, university, or government department. In a man's movement from one neighborhood or community to another, the work organization is his thread of continuity and may become a psychological anchor for him.

Frequently, as already noted, his social friendships arise from his work associations. Old navy men have long had a ready bond for friendship and two strangers who work for IBM already are likely to have much in common. In the course of our own research in a public utility my colleagues and I encountered a number of men who had moved from one electric generating station to another in the same company. On their days off, these men frequently would drive long distances to visit their old work buddies in the plants from which they had moved. They did not mention visiting others in their old communities.

The fundamental quality of the giving and receiving of affection in the work organization has been overlooked by those who would see a business as only a place to earn a living. Kenneth Boulding has pointed out that the

Christian concept of fellowship is an important component of business organizations.[18] Without fellowship there can be no organizations; without organizations there can be no fellowship.

It is not unusual for the company, both by means of its staff services and the personal interest of an employee's associates and superiors, to come to the assistance of the person in emergency circumstances. The "kitty" for emergencies is a ubiquitous phenomenon in organizations, whether raised by contributions or profits from coin machines. Fellow workers mobilize for blood transfusions as well as cash, and in some instances the organization continues a man's salary beyond sick leave provisions until he can return to work. When his colleagues mobilize to help him, a man sees this support as personal giving by people who are his friends because of their common interest as organizational members.

If changes are required in the task which a person does, often the company will retrain him to do a new kind of work, thereby helping him to adapt to technical change and assuring him of long-term job security. Recent contractual innovations in the steel industry provide for cushions against job displacement as a result of technological obsolescence. Organizations recognize obligations to help their employees, particularly those of long service, to cope with change.

Custom reflects another aspect of the psychological meaning of affiliation with the work organization. At one time a man was introduced to others by his name or by identifying him with his trade. Now a man is more likely to identify his place in society in terms of his organizational affiliation. Today he is identified to others not merely as John Smith, but John Smith, foreman in the Midland Utilities Company, or more simply as being "with Midland Utilities." This, together with the movement from small businesses to large organizations, means relatively less recognition of the person as an individual and relatively more of him as part of an organization. It gives added importance to the relationship between a man and his work organization as a way for him to gain social power. Within that relationship, however, the individual seeks support from his supervision to obtain increasing individual recognition, consideration and responsibility.[19]

Affiliation seems to be as important to executives as it is to people on hourly wages. A far larger number of graduates of business schools go into companies than start their own businesses. A 1963 Bureau of the Census report indicates that salaried men now outnumber self-employed professional and businessmen in the top 5 percent income bracket.[20]

Managers and salaried professionals, according to the report, account for half of those in that bracket while the self-employed number only one-fourth. These figures are a reversal of those of 1950 and reflect the growth of corporations and the increasing number of executives in them. Moreover, executives hold social and economic power only so long as they wield power in organizations, which is one reason many give for not wanting to retire. To such men, to retire means, as they put it, to become a "nobody."

Organizations have important social functions to perform: to produce goods or render services. They also provide means of earning a livelihood. These are basic functions of organizations. Because of the fundamental quality of these functions, organizations become important psychological devices as well.

Elliott Jaques has observed that, in addition to serving the many economic, social and psychological purposes already referred to, organizations are used by their members to reinforce individual defenses against unconscious anxiety.[21] In this he follows the conception of Melanie Klein, the late British psychoanalyst, that infants respond to early frustration by experiencing the outside world as hostile and potentially harmful.[22] For example, if the infant is not promptly fed when he is hungry, or if food is taken away before he is satiated, he reacts to a deprivation and learns of the possibility of further deprivation. This experience then leads to two kinds of anxiety, which Mrs. Klein called paranoid and depressive.

Jaques suggests that as people mature, they are on guard against recurrence of these anxieties and use social institutions as modes of warding them off. For example, the phenomenon of "splitting" or dividing people into the "good" and the "bad" is commonly observed in clinical practice. This is one way of handling paranoid anxiety. The "bad" impulses of people in an organization may thereupon be projected onto a "bad" figure or figures. Jaques calls attention to the way in which the first officer of a ship is commonly regarded by the crew as the source of all trouble, permitting the men to idealize the captain and identify themselves with him. There is often a similar polarity in the army between the executive officer and the commanding officer or "old man." Executives will recognize another phenomenon of the same order: the tendency of people to see those in other divisions of a company or certain key figures as the "bad" ones who cause all the problems.

Depressive anxieties can be dealt with by identifying with an organization which "does good" and by working hard at its activities, thus relieving inner guilt. After the 1936 hurricane that devastated New England, employees of a major public utility came from many parts of the country to work long hours under dangerous conditions in unfamiliar territory to restore service. In their six weeks of intensive work there was not one accident. The work in itself was sufficiently guilt-relieving that accidents were not necessary.

A psychologically interesting phenomenon, which illuminates these considerations, is the characteristic American college tradition of "Homecoming." Former students return (as many do year after year) to the alma mater; there they regress or revert to more infantile forms of pleasure — getting drunk together and recalling old exploits. The whole college turns out for the traditional football game with the historic opponent. There the sons of the alma mater do battle with the threatening foe, egged on in their aggressive exploits by scantily clad girls. All this is carried on in an atmosphere of gaiety. Usually the campus is decorated with large crêpe paper displays; each fraternity, sorority and independent house tries to outdo the other in the imaginativeness of its decorations. All, however, have one theme: murder. The sons of the alma mater are urged to destroy the enemy. The illustrations in the crêpe paper murals are of bombs dropping, tanks rolling, or other forms of mayhem. Recently, at one midwestern university, whose opponents were called the Gorillas, enterprising students made a papier-mâché gorilla. They mounted it on a Jeep to parade it before the assembled football crowd. In keeping with contemporary mores, the accompanying sign read, "Rape the Apes."

This example demonstrates how the organization provides an arena for the operation of the kinds of psychological defenses under discussion. The alma mater is the good mother; the opponent alma mater is bad and to be attacked. Hostility is drained from within the group and directed against the opponent. At the same time, the alumni relax in the figurative arms of the good mother, indulging themselves in the bottle.

The clustering of aggressively manipulative people in loosely structured organizations which provide large incomes but no guarantee of continuing employment is another example of the way in which the organization is used as a reinforcement of individual defenses. Some advertising agencies are a case in point. In such settings people deny their wishes to be dependent on any organization, thereby maintaining their personality equilibria. Simultaneously, they serve the purposes of the organization whose fluid structure requires such people.

Granted, the work organization is used by the people in it to serve their individual psychological defensive purposes. However, it could also be justifiably argued that the organization is only a legal fiction and therefore cannot have relationships with people. But there are two reasons for speaking of man-organization relationships. First, phenomena with typical features of transference are commonplace. Second, many people, in their relationships with other people, act as agents of the organization and thereby convey the feeling that the organization lives and acts.

Transference, as used here, means unconsciously bringing past attitudes, impulses, wishes, and expectations, particularly those usually experienced toward powerful parental figures, in exaggerated form, into present situations.[23] Transference phenomena occur subtly with great frequency in everyday life. When people are close to each other for a long time, their continued closeness creates conditions in which reality tends to merge with fantasies of the past. It is not unusual, for example, for a wife to call her husband's attention to the fact that she is not his mother, or for someone to say, "He is like a brother to me." When such feelings are strong, they tend to obscure the real identity of the respective persons, thereby distorting judgment. To avoid such problems, physicians do not treat their families and lawyers do not take theirs as clients.

Transference occurs with respect to organizations and institutions just as it occurs with individuals. People project upon organizations human qualities and relate to those organizations as if they were human. They generalize from their feelings about people in the organization who are important to them, to the organization as a whole, as well as extrapolating from those attitudes they bring to the organization. This phenomenon makes it possible to use a hospital as a therapeutic device because patients believe it to have therapeutic powers.

Philip Selznick, a sociologist, argues that organizations quickly become invested with psychological meaning by their members.[24] In fact, he makes the point that organizations cannot endure for very long unless this does happen. The pioneer psychoanalyst, Ernst Simmel, discussing the management of a psychiatric hospital, spoke of creating "a positive attachment to the institution as such . . . so that the patient may be thus secure of a firm foundation." [25] Norman Reider, carrying this one step further, reported that patients maintained ties to a psychiatric outpatient clinic which served them rather than to the therapists who treated them. Reider says "as soon as a medical institution achieves a reputation, it is a sign that an idealization and condensation of the magical power and the benevolent greatness of parental figures have been posited in the institution . . . The phenomenon is widespread and *touches upon every type of institution which has any characteristics of benevolence* [italics added]." [26] Reider sees such transference as a way of gaining power to deal with reality by participating in a great organization.

Another psychiatrist, H. A. Wilmer, gives added support to Reider's thesis, speaking of transference to a medical center as a cultural dimension in healing. He points out, "One cannot understand staff-patient relationships in any institution without an appreciation of this important psychologic [*sic*], social and, particularly cultural dimension of its healing powers. Physicians, just as patients, are enmeshed in transference feelings toward the institution, while the physician must cope with the additional countertransference feelings toward both patient and institution." [27] He adds that the institution can stand as the symbolic parental surrogate, and the positive or negative attitudes of the person toward the institution may well be, in part at least, transference reactions. This phenomenon is an old story in relationships with other institutions. In this country some men seek to enroll their sons in their alma mater as soon as they are born. In England there is a similar attitude toward some clubs. In both countries some men look upon the army as others would upon their college or club.

Describing the elements of an institution which contribute to transference feelings, Wilmer observes that a medical center is a great institution which occupies many large and impressive buildings and has certain institutional rites of introduction, examination, and treatment which gratify the dependent and narcissistic needs of patients. The personality of the physician is endowed with the power of the center. The institution endures beyond and transcends the individuals who work there. The more famous the institution, the greater the anonymity of the individuals representing it. "The very name of the institution is a cherished and sacred title, a powerful symbol to which much transference feeling is attached." Then Wilmer adds a critical element: "It is in *affiliation* — to take a son — that the whole phenomenon of transference to a center takes on new meaning and new members."

The contemporary organization in which a person works has some of the benevolent characteristics Reider talks about. It is a medium for recouping psychological losses in a rapidly changing society. Moreover, in an organization the actions of individual people are viewed by them, by the objects of the action and by observers, as actions of the organization. For example, if a local manager of Midland Utilities cuts off someone's service for non-payment, that action is seen as the company cutting off the service. There are many reasons why this should be so. The organization is legally, morally, and financially responsible for the actions of its members as organizational agents. The organization has policies which make for great similarity in behavior by agents of the organization at different points in time and in different geographical locations. These policies are supplemented by precedents, traditions, and informal norms as guides to behavior. In many instances the action by the agent is a role performance which will have common characteristics throughout that organization regardless of who carries it out; e.g., personnel officer. In addition, selection processes in an organization tend to result in the clustering of people whose personality structures have much in common and who would therefore tend to act along some personality dimensions in the same general way. These factors result in what is sometimes referred to as a "corporate personality." There also tends to be a consensus of perception of a given person by others in an organization as a result of discussions with each other about their experiences with the man, and review of his actions. This is particularly true if there are systematic and periodic appraisal and decision processes in the organization.

As a legal and group entity, the organization has power independent of that of its agents. Often it also has financial and other resources which can be used on behalf of people. The organization's capacity for aggressive and benevolent power can be perceived by its members, particularly when it is used either against people or to support them in emergency situations. Furthermore, it is often difficult for a person to know who in the organization has done what to him. There is much talk of an undifferentiated "they" who make decisions and take actions. Vague organizational policy permits people to form and express such thoughts. And finally, those who act within the power structure can often act out transference feelings which are well rationalized. The executive who complains that his subordinates are too dependent may be treating them as children, using the product of his behavior as a rationale for continuing it. Another might justify his sadistic behavior with that time-worn rationalization of parents, "It hurts me more than it hurts you," or "It has to be done."

In *The Devils of Loudun,* Aldous Huxley offers an example of such rationalization: "partisanship is a complex passion which permits those who indulge in it to make the best of both worlds. Because they do these things for the sake of a group which is, by definition, good and even sacred, they can admire themselves and loathe their neighbors, they can seek power and money, can enjoy the pleasures of aggression and cruelty, not merely without feeling guilty, but with the positive glow of conscious virtue. Loyalty to their group transforms these pleasant vices into acts of heroism." It was this thesis that permitted men of the church to torture a victim to death, all the while crying, "Dicas" (confess). Huxley adds, "When Grandier criticized the monks of Loudun, it was, we may be sure, with a sense of righteous zeal, a consciousness of doing God's work. For God, it went without saying, was on the side of the secular clergy and of Grandier's good friends, the Jesuits." [28]

The generalized mode of behavior characteristic of organizational agents as they act on behalf of the organization, together with the demonstration of the organization's power, make it possible for transference phenomena to occur. This gives the organization a psychological reality in the experience of the individual member.

The very circumstances which are necessary for the existence of transference phenomena in one direction are also conducive to their presence in the other. Those who act on behalf of the institution or organization have power and use it in the manner of parental surrogates, according to the folkways of the organization. A mental hospital, for example, is in the business of getting patients well. If a patient is so "recalcitrant" as not to improve, the staff may reject him. In a typical state hospital, he is consigned to the back wards. In a more enlightened institution the rejection takes place informally, as happened in one West Coast short-term treatment center which admitted only acutely ill patients and placed heavy emphasis on psychotherapy. The psychiatric residents (physicians in training to become psychiatrists) scribbled informal notes to the officer of the day which were appended by paper clip to his official log book. Each resident was officer of the day in turn and at the same time was also the admitting officer, so each had before him the notes of all the others. These unofficial notes instructed the officer of the day in no uncertain terms not to readmit certain patients who, in the judgment of the residents, would not profit from treatment. The residents naturally would prefer to work with those patients who would be most responsive to their efforts. Economics alone would make this a reasonable point of view. This, however, does not explain their strong feeling about those whom they were not able to help and the subtle way they chose to keep them away, even when the hospital had no formal policy of rejection.

In industry, there is a similar phenomenon. For example, the management of a major heavy manufacturing industry believes that employees should want nothing from their jobs but their salaries. Management complains that though it pays its people relatively well, they do not understand that the stockholders need a return on their money, and they keep demanding more wages. "Look at all that we give them in fringe benefits," the management says. "Look how good we are to them. Why don't they understand our point of view and not keep demanding more money?" The parallel between this attitude and that of many parents is obvious. The industrial culture is replete with such examples.

In these illustrations of what psychoanalysis has called transference phenomena, that is, bringing attitudes from one period of life to experiences in another, those who have power in the organization perceive the individual as a member of the organizational family and react to him as such. Although an employee may be a complete stranger in the personal sense to other persons in the organization, he is often something more to them than just another person who draws a salary from the same company. At the very least, what the person does reflects on the organization and its members. The major underlying reason for the appearance of transference phenomena from the organization to the person is the importance of the person to others in the organization, who, taken together, comprise the organization as it relates to the person.

This relationship is important to contemporary business organizations because the major concern of most top managements is not today's profitability, though that is important, but the long-term survival of the organization. With larger capital investments which must be amortized over longer periods of time and with an emphasis on organizational growth and creative innovation as a means of surviving in a competitive economy, corporate managements encourage personnel to remain in the company. Permanent employees presumably will be more loyal, productive, and willing to assume increasing responsibility. Their psychological investment in the organization will be likely to stimulate creativity. Legal decisions relating to workmen's compensation and labor relations, pressures from labor unions, and concern about the company's public image, all tend to foster company interest in the individual, transcending the interest of any given management group.

There also is a growing sense of social responsibility on the part of business executives, which arises partly from the fact that contemporary business leaders have higher levels of education than their predecessors and partly from the recognition that the corporation, in its own self-interest, cannot afford to be irresponsible. Taken together, these forces make the person-organization relationship highly important to people in the organization.

The person-organization relationship is vital because it meets certain needs of the person. In addition, the individual uses the organization to replace certain psychological losses, to reinforce his psychological defenses, and to serve as a major object of transference. The relationship is important to people who comprise the organization because of the reverse transference phenomena present in many decisions and actions which have to do with organizational members, and also because of the organization's need for survival.

The employer-employee relationship is not simply a two-party arrangement. It is not without good psychological reason that one speaks of paternalism in industry and that some companies are referred to by their employees as "Mother [name of company]." It is an important psychological fact that those companies which are called "Mother" by their employees are benign and kindly and have either no union or a relatively nonmilitant union. In fact, some of the kindliness is an effort to head off unionization. This defines one psychological meaning of the union, namely its mothering function. The dual loyalty studies by Theodore Purcell point up this aspect of the union.[29] Purcell shows that employees expect the union to protect them and obtain security provisions for them. They look to management to run the business, and have loyalty to management for doing so.

When the union plays its mothering function well, it enhances the employees' relationship to the organization. An example is the way in which the Scanlon plan, conceived by a union leader, involved employees in the survival efforts of a company and saved the company from failure.[30] This plan is the basis for the present Kaiser Steel pact.

When, however, the union does not serve this function well there are two problems. It either inadequately replaces the organization or deprives the worker of significant psychological ties to his work. Some of the major industrial unions are examples of the first problem. They are highly militant, define the company as an exploitative enemy, and, with unwitting cooperation from a too aggressive management, encourage the worker to identify with them. The union even under the best of circumstances cannot provide the worker with the gratification that ideally he could and should be getting from his work because the union does not manage productive processes.[31]

In some industries the employment pattern is a temporary one. Employers hire workers from among those who gather daily at the union hiring halls. The worker's basic loyalty is to the union. As a result, he may be deprived of significant psychological ties to his work because, without a consistent relationship to any single producing organization, most of these men work primarily for immediate monetary return. They are among those criticized for featherbedding, for failing to use their skills to produce high quality work, and for their seemingly exhorbitant wage demands. They do not seem to have much interest in their work. This is not to be construed as an argument against unions. Rather, it illuminates some of the psychological meaning of the union and the ways in which union-management relations can affect person-organization relationships.

In a Menninger Foundation study of mental health in industry, my colleagues and I observed transference phenomena and people's efforts to fulfill various psychological needs in their relationship with a company.[32] It was apparent that, in a large measure, the relationship arose out of and constituted efforts to fulfill expectations (only part of which were conscious) of both parties, person and organization. This process of fulfilling mutual expectations and satisfying mutual needs in the relationship between a man and his work organization was conceptualized as a process of *reciprocation*. Reciprocation is the process of carrying out a psychological contract between person and company or any other institution where one works.[33] It is a complementary process in which the individual and the organization seem to become a part of each other. The person feels that he is part of the corporation or institution and, concurrently, that he is a symbol personifying the whole organization. The public image of the organization is displaced onto the person and vice versa.

For example, a middle-management man in a medium-sized company, perhaps unknowingly speaking for all middle-management men, talks about this phenomenon: "After all, in this locale I *am* the company. Anything I say reflects back on the company." Another man at the same level in the same company observed, "You can't divorce your position from yourself. Various social groups catalogue you." He then recounted all of the community activities, and specific jobs within those activities, which he had been asked to assume because he was a manager in his particular company.

This same phenomenon can occur at any level in the organization. Even a foreman in the same organization has a similar experience, as do many line employees. "In your neighborhood, you are [the company]. The neighbors think if you weren't the right sort of a fellow, you wouldn't be with them. Most people think our salaries are above average, so you have to keep your place looking half way decent and your kids in shoes."

Among the ways in which reciprocation fulfills the needs of both individual and organization are these:

1. Ministration needs. Some of the defensive potential of the work organization for the people in it has already been discussed. It is relatively easy to see defensive phenomena and how the organization may support the individual when he is experiencing stress. It is more difficult to see how the individual supports the organization under similar circumstances. A case in point would be the spontaneous mobilization of employees to help a public utility company keep its franchise in a community, though the employees would have had no difficulty obtaining other jobs if the company lost its franchise.

2. Maturation needs. Reciprocation fosters psychological growth in several ways. When the person feels as if he is an integral part of the organization, he is identifying with his superiors. This means that he is incorporating as a part of himself some of the skills, experiences, points of view, and knowledge of those who are more successful in the organization than he. By making multiple identifications and reorganizing them in keeping with his own personality structure, a person grows more skilled and occupationally mature.[34]

When reciprocation is functioning well, a man finds advice, counsel, and guidance from his superiors. These, too, contribute to growth, and their importance is recognized by executives. If one interviews executives about their work, sooner or later most will mention spontaneously some older person in an organization who took a special interest in him and "was like a father to me." Rarely do first level workers spontaneously make the same comment. This suggests that the presence of such a person can make a significant difference in career progress.

Reciprocation also contributes to growth by opening up opportunities. Where the relationship between a man and organization is a good one, the man is more likely to move to greater responsibility than if reciprocation is not taking place. Peter Drucker cites the different degrees of progress made by comparable young management trainees in two different parts of the Sears organization where the psychological contract was fulfilled differently.[35] The important variable seemed to be more opportunities present in one situation than in the other.

The organization contributes to the growth of the person in the demands made upon him which stimulate him to new learning. Technical innovations, varied problems to surmount, and the changing functions of the organization stimulate the person to grow. The growth of the person contributes to the character of the organization. A man may identify himself with his superiors, but he also brings something of his own personality to the organization. Therefore, as he becomes more experienced, others will identify themselves with him. He leaves something of himself in the organization and thereby contributes to its development.

The organization is stimulated to growth by the collective demands of its employees which may force it to greater efficiency, as in the coal industry; by the determination of its employees to take on new challenges, as in the Scanlon Plan; and by the behavior of its employees as they seek to use the organization for their own psychological purposes. A case in point is the contemporary trend toward more flexible and innovative management. This direction, in part, stems from the increasing rejection of autocratic leadership by employees.

3. Mastery needs. A person has not only the psychological task of maintaining the equilibrium of id-ego-superego forces in their interaction with his environment, but he also has the task of mastering enough of his world so that he can survive in it. His job is a major way of attaining and sustaining that mastery. Work which serves all of these purposes might be looked upon as creative adaptation, a process much like that of a ship or an airplane which must move forward, retaining its balance despite the variable currents of water or air, or the turbulence of storms.

Sometimes these efforts take the form of indirect controls. This is especially true when there are inadequate channels for more constructive mastery and shaping of the organization. For example, one company supplied its men with new shovels of a type they did not like. These "inadvertently" were left in the field, run over by trucks or disposed of in other ways. After that the men were consulted on the tools they wanted. Another group of men were dissatisfied with the failure of the manager to obtain better physical facilities for their equipment repair shop. To the chagrin and embarrassment of higher management, they managed to scrounge enough surplus paint and other items to refurbish their shop. There are other methods of indirect control. Every company knows the problem of subtle empire building and the *fait accompli* which commits the organization to actions never intended by official policy formulations. That people in organizations resist change and avoid responsibility by means of passive resistance is widely recognized.

Knowledgeable leaders are aware of how the organization tries to make itself the master of the man. This has been the focus of much recent research. The company requires that task demands be fulfilled, that some people accept the direction of others. It also controls the ways in which employees may behave on the job by its allocation of financial and production resources. It even may require certain behaviors off the job. Earlier reference was made to men who spoke of how they were expected to behave at home because they were employees of the company. They were not told they had to behave that way, yet they felt obligated to do so. Employees are not usually told they must believe in the free enterprise system or that they must give to the United Fund, but there are powerful informal forces in the organization which influence them to do both.

While some people deplore the fact that the organization, to some extent, shapes the man, in reciprocation it is inevitable and not always damaging. The shaping process can promote individual growth. Moreover, the man is not merely a Pygmalion in the hands of a commercial behemoth. He, too, makes demands. If the organization does not meet his needs, he can leave it. No department wants to be known for having high turnover or absenteeism. He and his fellow workers establish informal production norms. Work groups frequently control work processes and thereby production schedules, profitability, and other factors which presumably are under the control of management.[36] The ultimate direct control technique of the employee is the strike.

In most organizations there are those employees who have learned what threats, hints, and complaints move the company. Most companies formulate policies to deal with only a small number of problems. It is impressive to observe how much executive time and expense a company will devote to a recalcitrant employee, how often he is appeased, and how long it takes an organization to confront an inadequate employee. In these instances, the employee clearly exploits the organization and forces it to adopt certain formal courses in its own defense. In other instances, as in the Scanlon Plan companies, employees have a more direct influence on shaping organizational processes and products.

In the context of reciprocation, to speak of the alienation of the employee from his work means that he feels he is not making an impact on the organization by his presence.[37] Conversely, if the organization feels it has little possibilty of shaping the employee, it feels itself to be at his mercy. Then organization leadership takes a hostile view of him, as is common in a number of industries. If reciprocation facilitates meeting the needs for ministration, maturation, and mastery of both the individual and the organization, it should then have a significant relationship to the mental health of the employee and the effective functioning of the organization. When the process does not operate well, both suffer.

Those who go to work in organizations have two tasks. Presumably, they are always working on the organizational task, whether it is to produce goods or render services. Invariably, they are also working on personal psychological tasks. In addition to its other social functions, the work organization is always an arena for the resolution of psychological problems.

3 / Leading by Following

The psychological dynamics of the individual are an enduring mainstream of human motivation; although obscure, they underlie most of the consistency of human behavior. They might be likened to a water table which, though invisible from the surface, is of critical importance for human survival. Their relationship to work and to the employing organization comprise one set of forces which must be understood if the executive is to effectively manage the problem of organizational survival. To fail to take these emotional forces into account is like planning for a community without thinking of its water supply.

Closely interrelated with intrapersonal psychological factors, and equally important for the purposes of this book, are the social and historical forces which create the context for individual behavior. Education and cultural modes for solving problems, particularly those of love and hate, become devices for forming the ego. Traditions, aspirations, and values become dimensions of the superego.

The Concept of Freedom

Probably the most deeply imbedded and cherished American traditions, aspirations, and values are those related to the concept of freedom. No other nation in recent history has grown from so many diverse fragments of people, each seeking either freedom of conscience or freedom of opportunity. And they found the freedom they sought, not without struggle and not without imperfection, but freedom nevertheless. For nearly a century and a half mobility was the concrete embodiment of the concept of freedom. The open frontier is still vivid in the minds of the grandchildren of those who trekked westward. People moved freely as need and opportunity motivated them. Even now, one out of five American families moves each year, many for greater economic opportunity or greater personal freedom.

The combination of geographical and social mobility comprise one important basis for the dominant theme of hope which characterizes the American ethos: "If at first you don't succeed, try, try again." A man may not have absolute freedom, but so long as he lives in a society in which freedom is its central thrust, he can still have hope. What for him may be only theoretical freedom can become real for his children. The most depressed and oppressed segment of the population, the Negro minority, found a basis for hope in its migration to the cities. This is a reverse twist on the historical frontier tradition, which resulted in making theoretical freedom a real possibility.

While in many respects an overgeneralized myth, the Horatio Alger concept that each could succeed by dint of his own hard work still is true. It inspires sufficient hope that individual success stories are to be found in every community. Many did make something of themselves by themselves, and many continue to do so.

An American psychiatrist, riding in a British train, overheard two British soldiers talking about what they would do when they were demobilized. They talked about various kinds of jobs they might take. Finally the psychiatrist could curb his impatience no longer and he intruded into the conversation. "I'm curious to know," he said, "why neither of you has mentioned the possibility of going to college." "Oh," replied one of the soldiers, "we weren't born to it." There is no concept in this country of "being born to it," of stationary social position. Rather, each child is told that he, too, may become president. In effect, he is "born to" individual opportunity for he is the political equal of every other person.

Americans have a strong egalitarian tradition which has its roots in the concept of freedom. Sociologists Seymour Lipset and Reinhold Bendix argue that "Americans may esteem the attainments of a man and recognize his high position, but they will not kowtow to him." [1] Many people do defer to people in higher positions. Most, however, dislike doing so; they do not want to be seen as submissive.

Leadership as Consent

The idea of political equality has a significant influence on the meaning of leadership in this country. With less need to take into account a man's social status, one is more likely to become a leader because of the skill and talent to lead specific groups under given circumstances. A man is not automatically a leader because he is born to it, or because of wealth or position. He may temporarily hold a leadership position because he inherits ownership of a corporation or because he is the scion of the dominant family in a community. If, however, he does not operate the corporation as others expect he should or if he does not exercise responsible community leadership, he will lose his power. Leadership arises out of expertness and is thereby leadership by consent. He can be dethroned in many ways. If he is a business executive he may be rejected because people will not work for him on his terms. This is what happened when workers organized themselves into unions. The function of collective bargaining is to *collectively* define the terms of work. The leader also may be unseated if others who have financial ownership distrust his leadership. For example, Howard Hughes was displaced from his control of Trans-World Airways by banking interests. If the leader abuses leadership, he may be shorn of his holdings and power by governmental action. Holding companies which controlled American railroads and public utility companies were broken up by antitrust actions because they abused their power. The railroads and public utilities are still regulated by governmental commissions in order to prevent recurrence of such abuse.

Consent by his followers constitutes much of the leader's power. He leads so long as he has followers. He has followers so long as he leads the group effectively toward solving their problems. In *A Stillness at Appomatox,* Bruce Catton describes with painful vividness the demoralized state of the Union armies in the middle of the American Civil War. As Grant took charge, his gradual tightening of controls communicated to the men that he meant business and that he really was going to fight a war. Though no one wanted to die in battle, the men did want to have the war over. If the only way to have it over was to do battle, and the leader proposed to do just that, enough of them were willing to follow him to put an end to the war.

In much of American business and industry, consent is limited and, therefore, power is correspondingly curtailed. In manufacturing, for example, rates of production in many cases are lower than necessary because of informal agreement among the employees to limit productivity. The employees do not consent to produce at the rate at which the leader wishes. They deny him the power to require such production, even when their failure to grant him that authority is against their own long-term self-interest.[2]

Consent is temporary. Although the leader may operate by consent, he must continue to earn his position. If he does not, he will lose it. Displacement of political leadership is the most conspicuous example of that fact.

The adage is contained in the cynical question, "What have you done for me — lately?"

Without voluntary consent, the leader can remain in power only if he can coerce consent by rigid control of his organization. Today that is less possible. The American economy is no longer based on the twin pillars of ownership and scarcity. It is an economy of plenty. In effect, people can now rent a wide variety of goods and services when the "cost" is a pittance "down" and so much per week. Rank and file employees, therefore, cannot so readily be compelled into submission as a condition for obtaining goods and services. Furthermore, there are multiple social devices ranging from public welfare to social security, to counteract the possibilities of compulsion.

Labor unions arose primarily to deprive the leader of unwarranted control over his followers. As Eli Ginzberg points out, "the major thrust of trade unionism must be seen not from the viewpoint of wages and hours, but in terms of control of work in the shop. This reflects the determination of workers in a democracy to control their own lives as much as possible and to reduce to a minimum the authority of others over them. This is the nub of the issue; it helps to explain the reach of democracy into the industrial area." [3]

The labor union as a social device has now been reinforced by various laws and mediation agencies to avert expensive or disruptive labor disputes. Contemporary political pressures against the use of the strike as a weapon of social power are so strong that major nationwide strikes like that of the airline mechanics in 1966 immediately produce pressures for legislation to forestall and control them. Already the steelworkers and steel management are engaged in continuous talks rather than periodic bargaining sessions.[4] The leader, therefore, will be less likely to "take a strike" as a means of maintaining control over his followers, even though automated and mechanized processes might permit him to do so more readily than in the past.

With increasingly widespread public ownership of business, leadership must constantly take stockholder relations into account. This consideration limits arbitrary use of power. The compulsory retirement age of sixty-five is an offshoot of public ownership and another way of limiting leadership control. For example, lending institutions will want to know that a business organization will have an alert and continuing leadership before they will commit large sums of money over long periods of time. Much the same is true of institutional investors in corporate stock.

The leader is less able to coerce consent for another reason. With American egalitarian traditions there are different forms of leadership, each based on varied group needs. A corporate president may be a company grade officer in the military during war time. His commanding general could be his own chief accountant. The political ward leader may be looked upon with disdain by some of his more sophisticated constituents, but they could not fill his leadership shoes. Various kinds of leaders are required at different times. It has been said, for example, that the Catholic Church alternates between religious popes and political popes, first an "inside man" and next an "outside man" as it were.[5]

In the electric utility business, after the holding company days, the first generation of presidents were generally engineers. For the most part, the present presidents are attorneys. It is not yet evident whether the next generation will be engineers or specialists in financing. Early utility leadership had to deal with constructing electric generating and transmission services. The present leadership has had to concentrate attention on governmental regulatory bodies and financial institutions. The next generation of leaders will have to contend with radical changes in engineering conceptions; e.g., nuclear energy generators, and consequent interrelationships among utilities. Leadership varies with the circumstances which demand different capabilities and qualities of leaders at different times. Such flexibility is possible because leadership in this country increasingly means leadership by consent.

American traditions and circumstances foster widespread leadership potential. The proliferation of voluntary associations, "causes," educational institutions, community services, and many other organizations is testimony to the concept that many can lead. When a company says it will need many new executives for future leadership responsibilities in its rapidly growing structure, it assumes that there is widespread leadership potential. When company recruiters go to college campuses to find potential executives, they make the same assumption.

Coercion by the leader is limited further by the accepted notion that each person, at voting age, achieves democratic responsibility. In some democratic countries the people leave politics to the politicians. They do not have the proliferation of voluntary associations, which carry on so many civic enterprises in this country. In the United States the citizen is often an active agent of his citizenship. If he is not individually active, he probably belongs to one or more organizations which are active on his behalf.

In effect, the citizen becomes a member of the national board of directors. It is he, by his vote, who determines what national, state and local policies will be. He determines what his political leadership will be conceptually and who it will be individually. He believes himself to be powerful in this sense; his belief is reinforced by the manner in which candidates for public office seek out his opinions and his handshake. Some would argue that he has no essential power, that his consent is engineered, that he is manipulated by political forces beyond his control, and that he takes no active part in political events.[6] Such critics describe the effects of his political behavior, not the underlying reality. From the displacement of Tammany in New York to the rise of antidiscrimination legislation, from the Taft-Hartley Law to foreign aid, the consent of the citizen is more than assent.[7] It is active involvement. He exercises responsibility. This is because Americans implicitly hold the conviction that an informed electorate will make wise decisions. The trend of legislation has been toward making the individual more politically capable of responsibility. Negro registration drives in the South, supported by federal legislation, and recent court decisions requiring reorganization of state legislatures are steps to diffuse power among citizens.

Kenneth Boulding has pointed out that the fundamental political problem is that of power and its distribution, sources, and use.[8] The problem of freedom is essentially the same. When a man is free, he has power. If he is not free, another has power over him. Power in this country is widely distributed. It is reinforced in its individual distribution by the continuous refinement of the ideal of equal justice before the law. It is in equality before law that the heritage of freedom of each man is preserved. It is in man's continuous potential to lead that the reality of freedom is validated for him.

The American citizen is a political adult. He is, in the full political sense of that word, a free citizen as no other man before him has been. He delegates power to those he permits to lead him. He also takes that power away. His leaders must perforce listen to him. This fact is as valid for industry as it is for government and the church. It is nowhere better illustrated than in the contemporary metamorphosis of the Roman Catholic Church. Recent events in that institution, long thought by many to be monolithic and unresponsive to its adherents' opinions, reflect the feelings of its followers. The elections of Pope John XXIII and Paul VI and the subsequent ecumenical movement found particular popular support in the United States. It was argued in the *Wall Street Journal* that American Catholics helped to impel the Roman Catholic Church along a more liberal path.[9]

Another device for countering possible coercion by the organizational leader is the trade or professional organization. Despite the proliferation of such organizations, almost nothing has been written about them as social institutions. Companies spend an estimated 1.2 billion dollars annually to support 18,000 of them, although they are an important instrument of modifying and directing leadership power.[10]

Professional and scientific organizations have always had a communication, educational, and vested interest function to perform for their members who were, for the most part, in individual practice or university research. Labor unions had their origin in the medieval guilds of Europe. Their function was essentially a protective one. Contemporary professional and trade associations have taken over a combination of these functions. The job of such an association is to inform, to protect, and to serve as a vested interest. In addition to the professional and trade organization, today there are formally organized associations for almost every division and job in a work organization. There are associations for institutional housekeepers, purchasers, personnel men, training directors, safety men, finance men, salesmen. No one knows how much time and how many millions of dollars are spent in support of these organizations. While some executives complain that such associations serve little purpose and bemoan the amount of money spent to send people to these meetings, organizations of this kind continue to proliferate.

The rational functions of such associations are self-evident. They usually have formal programs devoted to communicating new information about a given field, insights from experience and research, and exhibits of various kinds. There is considerable cross-communication at meetings, as well as entertainment and job-seeking. Less evident are the subtle control aspects of such organizations and their function as instruments for counteracting organizational pressure on the individual. In some respects they serve the same psychological purposes as adolescent peer groups.[11]

An adolescent joins a group of fellow adolescents as one way of breaking away from his parents, asserting his independence and warding off parental strictures. His association with his peers provides him with acceptance, amusement with those who share common interests, opportunities for greater sophistication, and the leverage of group mores as a pressure on his parents. If, for example, his parents refuse him the family automobile, he can always argue, "Everyone else has a car." The adolescent establishes certain standards for his and his parents' behavior, derived from the in-group pressures of his peers, and he demands that his parents behave in these ways.

The trade or professional association serves as the same device for the organizational member. He reports to his organization what other organizations are doing in his field and demands that it do likewise, whether his concern is a safety program, a nursing program, or a personnel program. And he goes a step further. In his professional or trade association, he sets up inspection and accrediting services, or establishes criteria for effective functioning in his given field. His association may give awards or other recognition for meeting its standards. With such devices he uses his association to exert leverage on his own organization as a way of protecting his function. The effectiveness of such maneuvers is readily evident. For example, a mental hospital superintendent or a state director of psychiatry may make little progress with his own governor and legislature. When he allies himself with his colleagues in a professional organization, sets up standards and presents them to a governor or to a legislature, they carry a certain official weight. Individually the men who formulated these standards have equally little influence in their own state legislatures. Collectively they are in a position to tell the powers-that-be how to behave. They do so with some success. The same phenomenon is seen in diverse forms in business organizations.

The adolescent uses his peer group as a mode of discharging hostility. In such a group he may complain about his parents; the group may go to a football game where it takes sides and expresses its hostility to the other team by cheering for their own or deprecating the competence of the other; the group may become delinquent and express its hostility directly and destructively to the embarrassment of the parents. Much the same kind of thing goes on in a professional or trade association. Here people often talk about how bad things are in their own companies, what terrible bosses they have, or the lack of support to get a job done. For many people, the association meeting is an opportunity for them to safely criticize the organization to which they belong.

In his peer group, the adolescent becomes something of a "cosmopolitan." [12] He develops loyalties and values which may be different from or other than those of his parents. He sees the world through the eyes of the peer group in ways his parents cannot perceive it. This sometimes creates conflicts between the values of the peer group and the values of the parents since the adolescent wants to be approved by both. The same kind of phenomenon occurs in professional and trade associations. Members of these associations, and simultaneously of business organizations, must balance the values of both. The safety engineer wants to be identified with his own organization, but at the same time, he would like his organization to maintain safety standards such as those his professional colleagues champion. He is more sophisticated about these standards for having taken part in meetings where there was exchange of opinions and ideas as well as factual information. He is not as narrow and as naive as he might be if he did not attend such meetings. Therefore the professional association serves to make him more "cosmopolitan" and less "local."

As the adolescent escapes the coercive control of his parents in his peer group, so the organization man makes of his association a similar escape device. There is a tendency in association meetings to drink more freely than one might at home and to partake of the best in restaurants while on the expense account. Few people return from conventions without having had a good time, or at least without saying they had a good time. It is commonly recognized that a major function of such meetings is to provide a good time. This is why so many communities try to attract conventions and why they are unhappy about conventions whose participants are not interested in having a good time. There is much conviviality, and, depending on the kind of meeting, sometimes sexual gratification.

Like the adolescent peer group, the professional or trade association provides an avenue toward power. Just as one can become a "wheel" in his adolescent group by being president of his class or a star athlete, so a man becomes a "wheel" when he assumes official responsibilities in a professional organization or trade association, though in his own organization he may be low on the status totem pole. In fact, he may become more important in his work organization because he has become important in his trade association. His work organization may welcome his participation in the trade association for less complimentary reasons: it may be a way of getting rid of him while, at the same time, deriving some incidental benefit. The trade or professional association, just as the adolescent peer group, offers the participant approval for his activities at his own level. His association of peers approves of and encourages a man in his work however unimportant that work may seem to his superiors, however little they agree with his ideals and standards for his work, and however little encouragement they give him.

As an adolescent can move from one peer group to another when his interests change or when he finds one group more satisfying than another, so a person can move from one professional or trade association to another. To illustrate, a man at one time may have been particularly interested in management development and therefore became a member of the American Society of Training Directors. As he moved up the ladder or became more involved in other forms of personnel work, he joined a personnel society. A person tends to outgrow a trade association as he acquires more power in his work organization.

The professional or trade body, in addition to its apparent functions, serves to counter the possibility of coercion by the leader. Often its power is so great that an organization must be on good terms with the association if it is to recruit competent personnel or otherwise carry on its activities.

The Expanding Middle Class

Because of both limited education and economic resources, the concept of freedom for many people in this country has been almost academic. They have not been close to power or identified with leadership. Freedom, and its accompanying power, becomes real when it becomes functional. From generation to generation, larger numbers of people are attaining economic security and higher levels of education. They are becoming middle class. As of 1963, one fifth of American families had incomes of at least $10,000 annually, up from 9 percent in 1947.[13] There are now more white-collar workers than blue-collar workers (approximately 30 million versus 24 million). White-collar workers increased 34 percent between 1950 and 1963, while blue-collar workers increased only 4 percent. The Bureau of Labor Statistics estimates that white-collar workers will form 54 percent of the work force by 1975 and the blue-collar sector will shrink to 33 percent.[14]

The direct impact of this shift from blue collar to white collar is most evident in the California aircraft industry. In 1941, when the United Auto Workers were first certified as the bargaining agent at North American Aviation, 85 percent of the employees were covered in the contract. By

1962 65 percent of North American's 100,000 employees were outside the bargaining unit. This reflects a shift in the aircraft industry from airframes to missiles, from production lines to electronics. From 1957 to 1962, 100,000 workers were displaced from the Southern California aircraft companies, but 150,000 more were employed by the same companies and by new electronics industries mostly for more highly skilled jobs.[15] White-collar jobs are expected to increase twice as fast as blue-collar jobs in the decade ending in 1975.[16]

The functional increase in freedom is shown by Herman P. Miller, of the U.S. Bureau of the Census: the rising standard of living; the increasing numbers of working women; the growth of ownership of vacation homes, second cars, television sets and radios; the increasing demand for personal services and the expanding market for discretionary items as contrasted with survival items (food). In middle-class thinking, he adds, " 'needs' stem not so much from what we lack as from what our neighbors have." [17]

Reports on the status of working women echo this thesis. According to the U.S. Labor Department's *Handbook on Women Workers,* women comprise 34 percent of the American work force.[18] Furthermore, in nearly one third of all married couples in the nation, both husband and wife are now holding paid jobs. Only 11 percent of all married couples worked in 1940. National Industrial Conference Board figures support Miller's observations.[19] They show that the average family with two breadwinners spends about 40 percent more than the one-earner family on alcoholic beverages, clothing, house furnishings, and appliances. It spends a third more on recreation and automobiles and 20 percent more on food and medical care, but about the same for shelter. Perhaps there is no more significant indicator of the transition of large numbers to the middle class than the fact that Sears, Roebuck has begun to sell original works of art.

An interesting consequence of the rise to the middle class by way of the two-breadwinner family is observed by Eli Ginzberg: "The question of whether a man will change his job depends increasingly on whether his wife must also change her job. The issue is no longer the optimization of a man's income and career opportunities but of the family's." [20]

One subtle but significant indicator of the rising numbers in the middle class is a recommendation of the American Medical Association's Council on Drugs that pharmacists print the name of the prescription on the label to protect patients. Editorializing on this recommendation, the *Journal of the American Medical Association* said that the rising level of education of

Americans, plus other factors, "have all contributed to the patient's expectation that his illness will be explained to him and that he will be told about the proposed treatment and what to expect from it." Another is the change in advertising to advertisements which are "fun to read." [21]

Another outcome of having a larger middle class is that more people have stronger feelings about their ability to manage their own lives. Professor Ginzberg, long noted for his studies of manpower, comments, "This is the first time in the history of the world that the masses have options, somewhat similar to those previously known only to the wealthy, about the kind of life they want to lead. They can decide whether they want to throw the major part of their efforts and energies into the job or into activities unconnected with the job." [22]

The transition of large numbers to the middle class has several implications of importance for leadership. The family and school experiences of people at this level give added impetus to concepts of equality and individual responsibility as well as a sense of personal power. Both nursery and public schools have emphasized heavily the values of initiative and participation in the last two generations. Teaching has become more intensive and television has opened a wide range of new stimulation. Greater social freedom for adults extends to earlier personal freedom for adolescents in dating, possession of automobiles, travel and personal responsibility. Rensis Likert observes that the more education a man acquires, the higher is his expectation about job responsibility, authority, and income.[23] In addition, the longer a man is in an educational environment which emphasizes individual initiative and participation, the greater the possibility he will carry these values into his working situation.

Middle-class families devote more attention to caring for their children than do lower-class families; they are more concerned about reputation and obligation.[24] They are also more concerned about themselves and their futures, particularly about the possibility of greater realization of their individual potential. Never before have so many people consciously sought to attain psychological well-being and to conduct themselves and their social institutions in a way that will be conducive to mental health.

What are the correlates in the work organization? A study by Floyd Mann and Richard Hoffman, comparing two Detroit Edison electric generating plants, emphasizes the Likert thesis.[25] One was an old plant, the other a new, automated one. The men in the older complex had worked in it a long time. They were drawn from the metropolitan community. They were unionized and Democratic in their politics. They expected little by way of human relations consideration from their supervisors. What they wanted most from their supervisors was technical competence. In the new unit, farther away from the metropolitan area, the employees were younger men, many from farms and small towns. They were better educated, more conservative, more often Republican in their politics, and not particularly union-minded. They valued human relations competence most in their supervisors and, unless the supervisor was not competent in human relations, his technical ability carried little weight with them.

This demand for consideration by superiors in the work situation is evident in repeated surveys of what people expect from their bosses. A dominant feature of each survey, as in the Mann-Hoffman study, is the desire for consideration by the superior.[26] However, such consideration has no meaning to the subordinate unless the superior has power.[27] A powerless supervisor is a supervisor in name only.

Another correlate of middle-class concerns and child-rearing practices is seen in an observation by the sociologist Daniel Bell.[28] Bell points out that middle-class and white-collar people have greater expectations of job security than do blue-collar people. The blue-collar man expects to be laid off from time to time. He is the first to become unemployed or displaced by new equipment. Bell notes that in the several economic recessions which have occurred since World War II, those who were laid off from their jobs were almost altogether blue-collar people. White-collar people in the same companies which laid off large numbers of blue-collar people continued to work. Thus, the experience of white-collar people is that they have greater job security because they are middle class and white collar. On the basis of this and similar experiences, they are more likely to assume that they are of greater value and held in higher esteem by management and therefore will continue to have job security. In elementary emotional terms, they have more reason to assume "the boss loves me more than those others."

A labor organizer, discussing the problems of unionizing white-collar workers, points out that being middle class the white-collar worker wants to be loved and accepted.[29] He does not want to be viewed as an "odd ball" or as a deviant. He wants to find and maintain a secure place in his group. An obvious consequence is the increasing concern on the part of business leaders about their employees, their reputation, and their social obligations. A major topic of contemporary business leadership discussion is the image projected by the organization. This is a middle-class preoccupation personified in corporate form. Another aspect of middle-class orientation is the greater effort devoted to self-control, particularly to control of aggression. Middle-class people establish elaborate forms of self-control, manners being one of them. They are far less direct in their expression of aggression than are lower-class people. In addition, middle-class men tend to regard themselves more as partners with their wives in the management of their families. When wives go to work, the distinction between male and female tends to become somewhat blurred.

Greater control over aggressions and diminution of the masculine role also have implications for the work organization. From 1947 to 1957 the size of the manufacturing work force in the United States increased approximately 17 percent. The number of nonproduction employees in the manufacturing industries increased from 2.4 million to 4.3 million, approximately 79 percent.[30] D. W. Dobler, who analyzed this growth, comments that there are proportionately more "chiefs" than "Indians" in manufacturing today than there were fifteen years ago. The more chiefs, the more energy is devoted to controls and the less to direct action.

Organizations also evolve control characteristics which are akin to sexual characteristics. In *In-Laws and Outlaws* C. Northcote Parkinson points out: "A male corporation is to be identified first of all by its rough exterior. The layout is more practical than pleasing, the machinery unconcealed, and the paintwork conservative and drab. Combined with this rugged appearance is an assertiveness in advertising, a rather crude claim to offer what is at once the cheapest and the best. The organization is extrovert, outgoing and inquisitive." [31] Few large American corporations meet this standard of masculinity. The rough exterior has given way to the multi-colored, decorator-designed plant or office building calculated to disguise its utilitarian functions. The executive's office is likely to look more like a living room than an office, and it often contains a hidden kitchenette. For several years the cosmetic industry has been repackaging its female products for the booming male market.

When Albert Porter studied 428 graduates who had received master's degrees from the Stanford University Graduate School of Business Administration, he found no correlations between a student's "masculinity-femininity" score on an interest test and his success as an executive.[32] He then sorted the graduates into three groups: those in large organizations, those in medium-size organizations and those in small organizations. He found that in smaller organizations a "masculine" pattern of interests was positively associated with executive success; in larger organizations, a "masculine" pattern of interests was *inversely* associated with executive success. Thus, the larger the organization, the more control people must exert over their feelings, the more they must abide by formal and informal codes of conduct, the more middle-class values govern.

Other sociological studies confirm these findings. They show, as do these observations, that people who rise to the middle class are more conservative than those who are born to it, which is why suburbs of large cities tend to be more Republican than Democratic. They are also the group in society with the most emotionally intensive drive for success. As a result, they have greater identification with management and management values and with the organization in which they work. However, emulation alone is insufficient to satisfy their aspirations. One consequence of the concept of freedom and equality is that people do not feel free unless they also feel equal. Therefore those who seek to fulfill their aspirations naturally want to be partners with others who have already attained leadership.

Middle-class, white-collar people, technicians, and middle management are therefore likely to be concerned about their relationships to top management. They also tend to have more intensive expectations in their relationships with their leaders than lower-class, blue-collar people. Lower-class people have long since been alienated from the executive echelon top management. They have withdrawn much of their consent from top management and given some of it to labor unions to exercise power on their behalf in dealings with managerial leadership.

All these phenomena comprise a revolution of rising expectations. Although this term has been used with respect to changing economic expectations in underdeveloped countries and in the movement from the lower class to the middle class in this country, it is even more applicable to changing psycho-social expectations in the United States. Taken together, these considerations make it increasingly clear that he who would lead must follow. That is, he must understand the values and expectations of his followers. Unless he does, he will be unable to win their consent. Without consent, he cannot lead.

4 / The Executive's Denials

There is little recognition among leadership in American business and industry of the idea that expectations of how power will be used are derived from a person's early experiences with authority; it follows that there is limited awareness that these expectations must be met if leadership is to function effectively. The typical American executive seeks personal power and fears relinquishing any part of it. The "father-figure" concept of leadership by consent is only dimly perceived and even then in a paternalistic sense. As a result there is widespread denial in practice of the leader's psychological obligation to his followers.

There is also little or no recognition of the deep psychological meaning of the work organization to the people in it. Although some companies have been concerned about the welfare of their employees to the point where they are described as maternalistic or paternalistic, these concerns tend to be of a material kind. Such provisions — good wages, hours, and working conditions, support in emergencies, recreation facilities, educational opportunities, and so on — are in effect fringe benefits. They are rewards which are to be obtained *off the job* in payment for loyalty, consistency, reliability, and time spent in the organization. The assumption is that the good employee will do as he is told; if he does so, he will find a pot of gold at the end of his occupational rainbow. Some rainbows have a short arc — the recreation program after work. Other rainbows have a much larger arc — a pension at sixty-five.

The assumption that the good employee is the willing-to-be-controlled-and-rewarded-employee is implemented by elaborate job descriptions, position classifications, and salary schedules. These in turn are supplemented by policies and procedures whose major function is to delimit the area of individual freedom, thus centralizing control and standardizing operations. This philosophy is clearly illustrated by the following comparisons, which appeared in the employee publication of a large organization.

Times Have Changed Since 1872

Office Regulations for a New Jersey Carriage Manufacturing Firm — 1872

1. Employees will daily sweep floors, dust the furniture and shelves.
2. Each day, fill lamps, clean chimneys and trim wicks. Wash windows once a week.
3. Each clerk will bring in a bucket of water and a scuttle of coal for the day's business.
4. Make your pens carefully. You may whittle your nibs to your individual tastes.
5. The office will open at 7:00 A.M. and close at 8:00 P.M. daily, except on the Sabbath on which day it will remain closed. Each employee is expected to spend the Sabbath by attending church and contributing liberally to the cause of the Lord.
6. Men employees will be given an evening off each week for courting purposes, or two evenings a week if they go regularly to church.
7. After an employee has spent his hours of labor in the office, he should spend the time reading the Bible and other good books.
8. Any employee who smokes Spanish cigars, uses liquor in any form, gets shaved in a barber shop or frequents pool and public halls, will give me good reason to suspect his worth, intentions, integrity and honesty.
9. The employee who has performed his labors faithfully and without fault for a period of five years and who has been thrifty and attentive to his religious duties will be given an increase of five cents per day, provided a just return in profit from the business permits it.

Fortunately! We have come a long way since those working conditions of yesteryear. In comparison with the carriage manufacturing firm, ——— expects much less of us and offers us so much more.*
In return for working a 40-hour week, we the employees of ———
receive the following:
1. Paid vacations.
2. Stock option plan.
3. Paid holidays.
4. Workmen's Compensation.
5. Sick leave or other paid absences.
6. Group life insurance.
7. Retirement plan.
8. Medical insurance.
9. Social Security.

10. Unemployment compensation.
11. Social activities.
12. Time not worked.

* All the extras — beyond payment for time worked — will cost the company on the average of about $1,000 per employee (this year).

The assumption of the employer has not changed since 1872 — namely that the superior is giving rewards for services rendered. The argument is that the superior is much kinder, his rewards are more comprehensive, and he demands less in return. The organization is seen as meaningful to the employees only because it provides these rewards. No other psychological significance is recognized.

Behind the widespread belief that a man should do as he is told lies the distorted image that those who have power hold about those who have less of it. Middle- and upper-class people typically have such an inaccurate image of lower-class working people. When, for example, a group of college students were asked to rate the personality characteristics of five occupational groups, they attributed the least favorable traits to factory workers. They saw the factory worker as the least reliable, the most excitable, the most frivolous, the most blunt and the most easy going.[1] If college students hold such an uncomplimentary image, it is likely that those in higher levels of management, most of whom have been to college, also have such views.

This assumption becomes stronger when research results indicate a negative view of the managerial subordinate by his superiors. Although every executive knows that a good manager must keep his subordinates informed, make the most of their talents, and bring them into decision-making, he has doubts about the capacities of his subordinates for initiative and leadership. Ideas dealing with management practice have been persuasive, while the basic conviction about the nature of people remains unchanged.[2]

More subtle cues reflecting negative assumptions about employees are evident in these statements: "The key to improving employes' 'Will to Work' is locked in innovation, rather than improved administration, according to the majority of 237 top industrial relations/personnel officers interviewed by the National Industrial Conference Board," reports the *Industrial Relations News.* "Respondents generally agree that the 'do-gooder' type is becoming extinct in the industrial relations/personnel field."[3] In another issue of the same publication, a leading industrial relations practitioner is quoted as saying, "Most of them (industrial relations graduates) seem to be indoctrinated with a too liberal, organized labor, impractical philosophy. They stress the welfare concept and couldn't care less about the need to make a profit." [4]

In statements like these management demonstrates that it cannot really be concerned about people and their feelings. To think of people in other than mechanistic terms often is synonymous with "welfare" and being "impractical." All the average manager wants to do is to get production out or sales up and for him that means two things: "sell them" and "sweeten the kitty." The selling emphasis is heavy, but people know when they are being "sold" and their massive resistance is a major management problem. The usual selling activities fall on deaf ears. How many employees are motivated by the argument that the stockholder needs a greater return on his investment and that therefore he, the employee, should work harder? The employee also knows when he is being given a "snow job." When the question is raised with managers, "What about looking deeper into human motivation?" the usual response is, "I haven't time to do that." However, they continue to deal repetitively to the point of frustration with the same problems without solving them. This in itself is so preoccupying that it often leaves relatively little time to scrutinize what is actually happening.

Such behavior is most often avoidance and rationalization; managers are reluctant to look at underlying motivations. This is partly because so many managers are trained in fields which are essentially objective, whether engineering, finance, or distribution, where training and focus have been on the specific and concrete. The concern of such managers is with those things which can be controlled. To try to deal with more complex problems frightens many people.

An important executive in a large company was taking part in a management development seminar. After the seminar group had spent most of the first day talking about human problems, he interrupted the discussion with a painful and plaintive protest. He said, "But I don't want to have anything to do with people." When he entered industry he had not anticipated having to supervise others. That was not part of his psychological contract. He knew engineering and he wanted to use that knowledge. Yet there is not much choice if he is to manage an organization, as there is so little choice for most executives.

"The term 'organization,' " Philip Selznick points out, "suggests a certain bareness, a lean, no-nonsense system of consciously coordinated activities. It refers to an *expendable tool,* a rational instrument engineered to do a job." [5] The resistance of scientists to scientific discoveries is an old story.[6] Resistance of management and leadership to contemporary knowledge of human motivation is no less striking.

A Closer Look at Management's Assumptions

Because these assumptions, perceptions, and social forces go largely unrecognized, their implications for leadership and for the survival of innovative and flexible business organizations are never clearly examined. A whole range of data crucial to the survival of organizations never comes into consideration. For example, there is almost no mention in the management literature of unconscious motivation in conceptions of motivation, in incentive plans, in the way work groups are organized, in the way leadership functions. Instead there continues to be a heavy emphasis on engineering or rationalization methods. The pursuit of simple answers, methods made concrete and measurable regardless of their validity, leads to more system, larger bureaucracies, widely extended control efforts, and repetitive administrative failure.

Problems tend to be perceived as a series of isolated events that can be dealt with individually. This situation is analogous to palliative relief in medicine. For example, managerial publications are disproportionately preoccupied with communication and communications problems. Most writers assume that when there are failures in communication it is because superiors have not made their words clear enough for subordinates to understand. They contend that if the subordinates really knew what the superiors were talking about and the logic behind the superiors' thinking, they would accept both and act accordingly. Large expenditures of money to improve communications, with few demonstrable results in productivity, is testimony to the widespread acceptance of this belief.

There is considerable scientific evidence to indicate that how messages are received depends on the values and attitudes of the receiver.[7] A man who had disliked a book in manuscript form saw it a year later in print. He asked if this were the same book or whether it had been rewritten. As it happened, the two versions were the same. Seeing much of it for the first time, he approved of what he now saw because the differences which had existed between him and the author a year before had been resolved.

Now he could look at the book more objectively. The words were the same; the relationship between sender and receiver was different.

Psychologist William Schutz has pointed out that the emphasis on and discussion about communications in management circles is essentially superficial because many of the phenomena which become barriers are unconscious.[8] He notes that there is too much communication, that there are too many cues of threat and attack and depreciation, and that people have to protect themselves against the dangers they perceive. To this end they must distort the messages they get — deny them, avoid them, forget them.

The emphasis on the relief of symptoms by better communications is part of a generalized focus or pressure on those who are at the lower end of the hierarchy. This becomes apparent in both executive development and supervisory training in industry. One of the most frequent requests which comes to psychologists from top management is that psychologists train first-level supervisors in human relations. Rarely does top management understand that the way those supervisors handle people is a reflection of how they and their subordinates behave.[9] Although management often seeks to solve it problems of relationships among people by training, the manner in which it sets up its training programs frequently is self-defeating, and, more important, produces even greater difficulty.[10] No amount of training will undo the influences and examples set by higher management.

The emphasis on symptomatic relief in management circles is widespread. For example, it is common experience that industrial engineers can only approximately and arbitrarily decide on production quotas, and that these are always below what the work group can ideally achieve. Yet, there continues to be extensive use of engineering or rationalization methods. This is true despite the fact that when employees are given responsibility for meeting task obligations, the results attained are better than when quotas are set by engineers.[11] Furthermore, when the producers set their goals, there is no attempt to defeat the engineer and his quotas as there is when management relies on industrial engineering alone. With the advent of automation, there has developed an increasing reliance on accounting methods as regulatory measures. Such methods are useful as controls, but as motivators they have the same negative impact as a stick has to a donkey.

Thus the focus is both on symptom relief and on "them" — those below who are supposed to be responsible to those above and who therefore must change. In addition, efforts to ameliorate the symptoms by various forms of human engineering are themselves inhuman because they fail to deal with the core of human problems, people's feelings.

When the focus is on "those below," the executive's initial impulse is to try to force them into a mold. When such an intention becomes an in-grained attitude, this posture is much like that of the parent who intends to spank his child into being good. Furthermore, a philosophy which assumes that management alone is responsible for making the decisions and resolving the problems of the business presents an adult employee with an unadultlike situation. He is merely told what to do and paid for doing it. He is exhorted to be responsible and to invest himself in his work, but it is often made impossible for him to assume any real or important respon-sibility for what he does.

From his point of view, he is a free man who is legally responsible, and who, as a citizen, serves as a member of the Board of Directors of the U.S.A. Yet he is free only from 5 P.M. to 8 A.M. During that time he can voice his opinions, go and do as he pleases. He may be a leader in his union or the local commander of the Veterans of Foreign Wars. He may influence the school board by a protest or help build character by leading a Boy Scout troop. However, at 8 A.M. he loses much of his freedom.[12] Major decisions about his work are likely to be made by someone else. If he is a blue-collar worker, the way in which the work is laid out, the specific movements he makes in doing it, and the amount of time allotted to it may be determined by an industrial engineer. Furthermore, the lower in skill and socio-economic level, the more likely he is to be controlled by mechanical or automated pace and processes, and the less consideration he has come to expect from higher management.[13] The assumption underlying this rationalization of the work process is that he is another form of machine. He contributes little to solving the organization's problems or even those of his work unit, whether they be production, marketing, or finance. There seems to be a tacit assumption that he has little to offer the organization beyond his own limited task and that his ideas, judgments, or observations are of little value to the organization. He rarely is asked for them despite the proliferation of morale studies and suggestion systems. All the responsibility is held above him, and those who hold responsibility spend much of their time exhorting him to do more. He is never confronted with the realities of the organization's survival in such a way that he can help directly with these realities. Success or failure in dealing with them is always management's success or failure. Sometimes, after going along for the ride for twenty years or so, he finds that he is no longer necessary to the organization: *A machine can do better what he has been doing for a working lifetime!* He is abandoned like an obsolete piece of equipment.

The authoritarian traditions of business leadership in the nineteenth century have been only slightly modified to a more benevolent but little less authoritarian style of management in the 1960's. The underlying assumption of the organizational leader might be stated as: "We hire you, we pay you, do your job. We will control and direct you. If you obey these controls and directions, our operation will survive and you will have income. Furthermore, we will provide you with fringe benefits so that you may have your pleasure off the job." Such an assumption requires a continuous spiral of buying the other person off. Part of the repetitive round of the increasing monetary demands which are the product of labor negotiation stems directly from the "buying off" psychology of leadership and is inherently self-defeating. Management complains that increases in wages do not result in corresponding increases in motivation to work. The management which operates on this psychology, and almost all American managements do, not only fosters dependency by arrogating to itself the responsibility for the success of the organization, but also is much like the parent who buys off his son with presents because he does not have time for meaningful relationships with the boy.

In the years since World War II this problem has been accentuated by what has been called the "paper curtain." [14] More companies are seeking young management trainees directly from college. There are fewer opportunities for a man to rise from the work bench through the ranks to the presidency of a company. A class of working people has been created who themselves will have little opportunity for advancement. The paper curtain accentuates the alienation of the lower-class working man from his higher-class executives and from the organization as a whole, leaving him with the feeling that no one really cares much about him; not only is he replaceable by any other person like himself, but more likely, he will be replaced by a machine. What a sense of utter uselessness and hopelessness such a person must live with! Not surprisingly, there is a higher incidence of psychosis, or serious mental illness, among people at the lower socio-economic levels than among those in middle and upper classes.[15] Mental health is poorer among those alienated from the processes of work, the work organization, and its leadership.

The consequences of management's failure to take into account the psychological and socio-historical considerations discussed earlier are readily evident. One of the major consequences has been the withdrawal of power from business leadership and its transfer to labor leadership. Management, failing to confront its own mistakes, long attributed the rise of labor to the manipulation of the masses by unscrupulous agitators. Psychologically, the behavior of labor leaders in any industry is a mirror image of the style of management in that same industry. A rough, tough management group will spawn a rough, tough union leadership. Even where there is corruption in union leadership, it should not be forgotten that often the corruptor is a manager. Labor power is one of the managerial consequences of ignoring psychological data.

A second consequence of the failure to recognize the implications for leadership of the underlying psychological, sociological, and historical trends is the feelings of resentment, fear, anger, and disillusionment which so often characterize the relationship between executive management and both middle management and line-level employees. As long as top management assumes that its power is its own, it tends to operate unilaterally. No matter how well intentioned, unilateral action is seen as threatening by those who are affected by it. To whatever extent people are subject to the action of someone else, they are less able to predict their own future and to exercise control over it. Furthermore, if unilateral action of a benevolent kind can be taken, then there is always the possibility that destructive unilateral action can occur. There is a large body of evidence about employee sabotage of unilateral management action and the subsequent guilt of the saboteurs.[16]

In addition to these feelings of resentment, fear, anger, and disillusionment and the behavior which results from them, a more serious problem is the impaired relationships with the work organization. A reciprocal relationship with the work organization is an important asset to the mental health of a person. If that relationship is impaired, it becomes a source of stress and tension, rather than a source of support and personal enhancement. From the company's point of view, the impairment of this relationship undermines the employee's identification with the company and its goals. There is already tacit recognition of this lack of identification in the existence of many programs to "sell" economic education to employees. If the relationship between a man and his work organization were as strong as it could be, and if he, as a member of that organization, had some direct responsibility for contributing to the resolution of its problems, then he would be getting economic education in practice. He would learn firsthand the realities of business. Instead, seeing himself as an expendable and manipulable appendage, he has little interest in economic education or whatever might be said about the effectiveness of the system for him. While it may produce income, it also produces feelings of anger, helplessness, and defeat.

The emphasis on selecting and promoting people who will do what they are told, and do it with a smile, has a predictable consequence in the behavior of young executives. Much of middle-class, middle-management psychology is an effort to sell oneself, to put oneself across, to be liked by those who are more powerful. In such circumstances a man responds more to what is demanded by external forces rather than to internal ones. This is what David Riesman has called "other directedness" and Erich Fromm, the "salesman personality." [17] Under such circumstances, a man sells not only himself but also his wife and his children. If, for example, a man moves repeatedly for the benefit of the corporation, then he and his family are adapting repeatedly to demands which come from outside themselves. The process of adapting to external demands often occurs at the expense of *being*. One follows another's decisions about where he will live and what he will do rather than doing what he and his family want.

In turn, the notion that one must behave in ways which are marketable impairs relationships with colleagues and subordinates. The person must look out for himself first rather than for the common interests which he and the organization have together. He must compete with his peers, although often that competition in the long run may be injurious to the organization because under competitive circumstances it is difficult for people to cooperate toward their common goals. Furthermore, the executive who is bent on selling himself must control his subordinates in such a way that he is always presenting the best possible image of the collective performance of his unit. This creates pressure toward suppressing conflicts and differences, disguising errors and inadequacies, and making for pretense and show rather than candor. Anything other than honesty about the nature of problems leads to efforts to deal with symptoms rather than with the difficulties themselves. If morale is low, a common device for trying to improve it is to make communications better, which usually means redoubling efforts to persuade or exhort people. The problem is not that communications are unclear; so much of the time they are altogether too clear. People get the message. It is the message of cover-over and manipulation which often destroys morale.

A common example will clarify this issue. Retail stores advertise to entice customers. Some stores use fake loss leaders, subtle wording in ads intended to mislead people, and manipulative selling efforts to divert prospective customers from the product for which they have come to the store to something more expensive. The merchandiser may regard this as nothing more than smart salesmanship. His position is that the customer should watch out for himself — *caveat emptor.* Some customers, alert to the tricks of the trade, do watch out for themselves.[18] The salesman who is required to be a part of the manipulation knows that he is using *tricks* and that he is manipulating the customer. Many will feel that they have been given license to steal and see themselves and their employers as being dishonest. If a man believes his employer is dishonest and that he is expected to be that way, it follows that to steal from the employer is little different than stealing from the customer. In fact, if he is sufficiently angry with himself for stealing, he may act out his anger against the company which has encouraged him to do so. The employer who then believes that he is going to stop stealing in his organization by catching people who steal and firing them deludes himself. As long as he keeps teaching people to steal, and all his employees perceive him and themselves to be thieves, they will have psychological reasons to steal from him as well as from customers. The employer's efforts to catch and fire the thieves deal only with the symptoms, not with the underlying problem.

The impairment of relationships with the organization and with colleagues in the organization contributes to a generalized feeling of loneliness. It is commonplace among young men moving upward on the hierarchical ladder that they not take part in political or civic enterprises which might be controversial. They are to stay neutral lest what they do come back to haunt them years afterward. "You can make only one mistake in this company," a vice-president said, "and it will be held against you thereafter." It is also part of the folklore with which the young executive lives that he should not make too many friends among his colleagues for he might one day be the boss of one or of all of them. Presumably, if he is too close to some people, he will have difficulty supervising them. And, assuming an authoritarian structure where power is thought to be granted from the top and fought from the bottom, this is true. A man need not keep such distance from his subordinates when there is joint responsibility for problem-solving. If a leader is selected of whom the followers approve because he brings the leadership skills they need, the issue of closeness will be less relevant. The leader will have enough strength in his skill so that he need not stay aloof to hide his humanness.

The generalized denial among executives of the meaning of power in our culture, the psychological meaning of the organization to those who work in it, the egalitarian tradition, and legal responsibility at twenty-one years of age constitutes a denial of the importance of the twin drives of love and hate, dependency needs, the problem of identity, and the need for mastery. Often it is as if management says to its people, "These things which you need psychologically and which are so important to you really are all in your mind. They are only figments of your imagination. We can't care about these things. All we want to do is buy your services for a given number of hours. Now be nice and go along with us." Employees, then, give up much of their sense of responsibility for, in most cases, there are no avenues in which they can participate with management to improve products and services. The only avenue open to them is to adapt, to be nice, and to be paid not for dealing with the realities of the business situation, but for being agreeable. The outcome of this is increasing selfishness with the repetitive, but often unasked, question, learned from management, "What's in it for me?"

Reacting to these and similar problems, C. S. Lewis comments:

> The greatest evil is not now done in those sordid "dens of crime" that Dickens loved to paint. It is not done even in concentration camps and labour camps. In those we see its final result. But it is conceived and ordered (moved, seconded, carried, and minuted) in clean, carpeted, warmed, and well-lighted offices, by quiet men with white collars and cut fingernails and smooth-shaven cheeks who do not need to raise their voice. Hence naturally enough, my symbol for Hell is something like the bureaucracy of a police state or the offices of a thoroughly nasty business concern.[19]

As the series of pressures, social forces, and cultural cross-currents has begun to ferment in the last two generations, it has become increasingly difficult to motivate and to manage people from a position of power. Authoritarian methods no longer work consistently and, even if they did, they are unfashionable. Some of the human relations methods which have been advocated have turned out to be extremely superficial ("increase communications," "take an interest in the men") because they failed to take unconscious motivations — drives, defenses, problems of identity, mastery, dependency, attitudes toward power — into account. Various people in management, sensing the difficulty in traditional modes of management, have tried to eliminate these problems in different ways. Some have taken the easiest defensive road by denying the reality of underlying psychological needs and saying in effect, "My job is to make a profit and to make this organization survive. I'm not going to be concerned about how the people feel. They will do what I tell them or they won't be around here very long."

Others have struggled in more painful ways. One company president has unwittingly abandoned the leadership of his organization. He has become so concerned with some aspects of the psychology of his situation that he has forgotten he is supposed to be a manager. In this particular case he appointed a vice-president to carry on one of the major organizational functions. He was surprised when people in the organization soon began to look to the new vice-president, not as a vice-president but as the executive vice-president. As a matter of fact, the man was not the executive vice-president, and the president could not understand why so many people turned to him in this way. What the president did not see was that in his preoccupation, he was not leading. Furthermore, he was so taken with what he considered to be democratic leadership, but what was really nonleadership, that he thought an organization could run itself if only it were sufficiently democratic. There is a difference between a laissez faire, nonleading leadership and a leadership which makes believe it doesn't lead while it still retains the effective power to manage. So long as the power is centralized, there will be expectations for its use in leadership. When the power is not being used by the nominal leader, people will turn to someone else, for they have no right by the very structure of the organization to use the power themselves.

When he started his company, another president had determined to give special attention to the motivation of his people; he would give them something to work for. He intended to accomplish this by working with his men on the line, by showing them that he was democratic and that he was not going to dictate to them simply because he owned the company. He still does not know why he is having so many difficulties in the organization and why there is so much bickering among the top management group. A general cannot lead by being an infantryman.

Another company president took a different approach. He would have no trappings of business in his office — no desk or the equipment that went with it. Instead, his would be a living room suite so that anybody who wanted to do so would feel free to come in and talk with him. This, however, was strictly a gimmick because he quickly made it plain that he did not want to talk with anybody. He would call meetings and then not appear himself, and he would keep people waiting indefinitely. He would assign a group of men to a task; after months of work they would return with a set of plans to which he would say, "But anybody would know this plan isn't good for anything." In his eyes, he was challenging and stimulating his men. He did challenge them — never again to open their mouths. Yet another chief executive resolved the problem very effectively. He has only one chair in his office — his. This means that nobody can talk to him for more than a few minutes and all who come in must stand up. He effectively cuts himself off from his people and manages to deny the reality of his power position. In another company the top management for many years did not want to relate to subordinates in any way except to give them orders, despite its protestations to the contrary. Thus a stranger walking down the hall of the executive suite of the company would see no names on the doors. Subordinates who wanted to talk to any of the vice-presidents or the president had no way of knowing who was behind which door. This keeps subordinates from questioning or discussing their problems except on call.

Leadership perquisites are so emphasized and the executive suite is so well furnished in one engineering design company that those who do not share it speak of it as "peacock alley." When subordinates see top management as strutting and showing off in this way, it is not hard to guess what kinds of communications go on in that organization. These adaptations are stances of frustration. They reflect withdrawal from or exploitation of the leadership function. Although they are extreme cases, each illuminates a facet of the conflicts of leadership which most executives experience.

5 / The Pressures of Technology

Business leadership still operates on questionable assumptions about human motivation. These assumptions have the effect of denying many of the needs and expectations of people who affiliate themselves with organizations. To the increasing frustration of the executive, problems of managing people who are already in the organization tend to proliferate.

Three major social problems, arising from increasingly sophisticated technology, compound the pressures on the executive. These problems are (1) residual unemployment and the continuing high level of poverty amid prosperity; (2) the personal and social impact of automation; and (3) the implications of automation for the middle class and middle management.

Why are these problems for the executive? Robert W. Austin summarizes the reasons succinctly:

> Business is responsible today for incredible technological change.
> Technological change will continue to cause social change.
> Social change brings demands for action to meet or mitigate the effects of social change.
> The job of top management today must be broadened to include an awareness of the social change it causes. And that awareness will place new responsibility on business management for intelligent, carefully thought-out decisions as to the basic responsibility for meeting such change.[1]

Austin's argument is one of conscience and responsibility. There are others which have their own validity. A major one is that businessmen who believe in the free enterprise system should seek out and help solve difficulties, rather than leave them to the government to resolve and then criticize the growth of "Big Government." [2]

Residual Unemployment

Much has been said about structural unemployment — the numbers of people who are out of a job because present production processes make them superfluous. Some have argued that these people are only temporarily out of work, that by retraining and by the requirements of new products and expanding markets, there will be more than enough jobs in the future.[3] Others contend that it will be fruitless to create additional jobs — more present work will be automated; instead, different mechanisms for distributing wealth will be required.[4] Both of these positions oversimplify the situation. The fact remains that as long as the superego or conscience is a necessary psychological device for civilized living, some form of behavior which people experience as work will continue to be necessary as a mode of meeting superego demands.

The problems of unemployment and poverty have been dealt with as if they were minor ones. Procrastination, awkwardness, and waste have characterized efforts to resolve them. When such ineffective actions failed conspicuously, then more comprehensive programs were evolved. Even then the antecedent factors were never fully examined, leaving the programs as monuments of futility and the chronic problems relatively untouched.

The United States has not had the same vast gaps between the abject poor and the princely rich which characterize some other countries. But it has always had a pressing problem of poverty, although today much of the problem is not apparent to those who are not impoverished. A welfare system provides submarginal income sufficient to hide the indigent. "Nobody knows the trouble I've seen," goes the old Negro spiritual. It might well be the theme of the inconspicuous poor. So obscure have they become that the decline in charity cases in public hospitals poses a problem for the training of physicians.[5]

The statistics of poverty have been widely discussed.[6] It has been argued that these statistics do not accurately portray the poverty problem, since many students, servicemen, and farmers who live well on small cash incomes are included in these figures.[7] Nevertheless, whatever the figures, enough people are out of work or impoverished to constitute a major social problem, despite the fact that more than 72,000,000 are employed. In addition, the welfare load is growing. Most of the increase is for people who, under present circumstances, cannot work. In 1964, eight million people were public aid recipients, one-third more than in 1955, despite a population increase of only 15 percent. Much of this was accounted for by the 78 percent increase in aid to dependent children and their mothers. The average ADC family consists of a mother and three children; the mother is thirty-five years old and has completed only eight years of school.

Some 25 percent of ADC recipients have been receiving welfare aid five years or more.[8]

Seen from another perspective, the problem looks like this. In 1944 the highest fifth of American families in annual income had 21 percent of the total income.[9] Today's proportion is substantially the same. The lowest fifth of American families received about 5 percent of the total income in 1944 and 1963. According to census figures, the lowest 20 percent made less than $2,800 per year. Real incomes have risen primarily among middle-income people. The greatest relative gains in average income during the past decade have been made by craftsmen and by professional and managerial workers. Although incomes have risen during the postwar period, there has been no narrowing of the gap between the bottom and top income groups.[10]

Nor has there been a narrowing of the gap between whites and Negroes. The unemployment rate for Negroes is still twice that of whites and they earn about half as much. While family incomes for both groups have risen proportionately since 1961, and unemployment for both has dropped proportionately as much, there has been a significant decline in the Negro's economic status in specific areas. This has resulted in a piling up of concentrated and explosive misery in the Negro ghetto.[11] Efforts to increase the employment of minority races and other unemployed will be self-defeating unless they include corollary efforts to upgrade those who are least skilled. There is no point in training large numbers of unemployed for jobs which will be the first to suffer from advances in technology.

Despite the debate about whether more sophisticated technology has or will result in increased unemployment, certain trends are obvious. Though management representatives have often argued that there is a total increase in the number of employees in a given business despite technological innovations, there is no denying that many businesses are more efficient with fewer employees. There continues to be substantial increases in the number of white-collar employees, working women, skilled groups, professional and technical workers, and those holding two jobs. These increases and the potential for their further expansion are little help to the unemployed who are the least educated, least skilled, and least in demand. In fact, they can only fan the anger of the unemployed and those threatened with unemployment, who see the widening gap between where they are and where they must be to attain economic citizenship.

The effects of that anger and fear have been evident in the recent riots in the Negro ghettoes and in repetitive stubborn strikes like those in the newspaper industry and among stevedores. The important point here is that many of the rioting Negroes in Detroit had jobs and that the typographers and stevedores are comparatively well paid. They were stirred not by present unemployment but by the threat of future unemployment.[12]

Rather than becoming preoccupied with an effort to provide employment, necessary as that is, and with retraining for individual jobs which are likely to be quickly obsolete or are remote from the education and skills of most of the presently unemployed, we need a national policy of continuous upgrading of skills and capacities at all occupational levels. People will then be able to see themselves as part of a continuous upward-moving process in which they can participate step by step. Otherwise we shall be faced with ever increasing numbers of displaced unemployed.

One political implication of unemployment and displacement is the possible rise of radicalism as larger numbers of people become dislocated, lose hope, and seek political solutions to their problems. Radicalism, however, has never been a major political trend in this country, and it is more likely that people may withdraw from active involvement in the events that take place around them, as happened to so many of the unemployed during the depression. Many of the presently unemployed, barred long ago by the paper curtain from upward mobility in business organizations, turned to labor organizations to compensate for their feelings of powerlessness and inadequacy. Union membership did not adequately assuage their anxieties because often they felt that nobody really cared about them as individuals in the massive unions; they felt that they had already lost some of their identity as unique human beings. Furthermore, when they lost their jobs, the unions proved powerless to keep them from being displaced. Even the powerful United Mine Workers had to close its hospitals and cut its pensions. It is easy for many of the chronically unemployed to feel hopeless and helpless, and for boredom and lethargy to take the place of active participation in living.

Those who have been displaced and have no meaningful part in the economic system can become hostile to that system — as the metropolitan racial riots have shown. So long as they are unemployed and angry with the system, they constitute a continual implicit threat to it. If these people are to have a commitment to the economic system they must be incorporated into it. No amount of economic education will undo their feelings of uselessness and resentment. Products of pent-up hostility toward the system, the riots have an interesting corollary. When the anger of those who feel aggrieved is directed to the larger society which they believe constrains them, the incidence of crimes against each other decreases.[13]

More social upheaval of this kind is likely because little significant and permanent progress is being made against a continuing economic abscess. The impoverished proportion of the population threatens to grow with increasing technological change. John W. McConnell calls for "developing a national culture in which something other than work is the cement which holds our life together and gives it meaning . . . a positive program of education in the arts and humanities for the young and old." [14] He further recommends joint government, business, and labor planning for change, and educating people to be willing to use and pay for new and beneficial social services. In the context of the earlier discussion of the meaning of work, the first recommendation is dubious. The second is long overdue. As for the third, people have little problem taking advantage of services when the services are available and they have the money to pay for them.

The major present effort, combining to some extent the joint resources of government, management, and labor, is focused on training, retraining, and elevating people to middle-class, white-collar jobs. That will not be enough. A systematic national upgrading program must come next. The executive and his organization there will increasingly become the means through which large numbers of people will advance to responsible citizenship and fulfill their psychological needs. Even if this effort proves to be reasonably effective, two major problems remain. One is the psychological and social effects of improved technological processes on those who are already in the organization; the second is the implication of more efficient technological processes for middle-class, white-collar people.

Personal and Social Impact of Automation

According to the World Health Organization's report on Mental Health Problems of Automation the "human impact of automation will be of a twofold nature. It will affect the physiological functioning of the individual, thus influencing social structures; it will also induce a number of social and cultural changes which will have a repercussion on the individual . . . Where mental health is concerned, it is the effect of technological change on interpersonal relations in the smaller units of society — the family, the working group, the recreational group — which is likely to be of particular importance." The report distinguishes two types of reaction to the introduction of automation: first, emotional reaction to new methods and the possible consequences of innovation; second, reaction to new working conditions. The report cautions further that ". . . when certain fundamental psychological needs are not met, there is a likelihood that unreasonable hopes will be placed in machines which are represented as capable of rapidly improving standards of living." [15]

Already some observational and research evidence indicates that there is significant impact of automated processes on the nature of work itself. One more readily observable impact is the reduction of materials handled by people. A piece of steel placed at the beginning of a machine tool system comes out of the other end as an automobile block, ready for its components to be mounted. Knit goods can be guided from thread to finished suit by automated processes. Newspaper copy can go directly from reporter to automatic type setter and editor. Much of the dirty, back-breaking work of the world and much of the detail are now handled mechanically, electronically, and automatically.[16]

If the materials or the work process are handled automatically then the individual has far less control of the work pace and often can feel that he is an extension of or mastered by the machine. He must respond to the machine's pace and to the demands of automatically controlled processes, rather than have them respond to him. This negatively alters his self-image.[17] At the same time he has a greater feeling of responsibility for the production process. Errors are more costly and disrupt the flow of an entire system. When even simple mistakes or minor breakdowns occur, they are likely to bring down on the employee inspectors, repairmen, supervisors, and sometimes executives. The feeling of greater responsibility is stimulated further by the mystery of the automated process and the eerie quality of its almost human functioning at a speed many times that of human beings.

Greater responsibility means a demand for constant attention. Instead of handling and manipulating goods, the employee observes dials and signals. He must constantly observe them, for, with processes operating so quickly repercussions can spread ever more quickly. (Witness the 1965 electricity blackout in the northeastern states.)

People who before more sophisticated technology were somewhat more casual in their work are now required to be more alert, more ready for danger or error. A group of men in a manually operated electric power generating station, for example, handled big boilers and observed their dials firsthand by walking from boiler to boiler, looking into the mouths of furnaces and making adjustments by hand. Following automation, they did the same work by observing the furnaces on closed circuit television and the control signals on an illuminated board. Their pace was less strained before because they now must pay exquisite attention to all of the lights, dials, and screens in front of them. Furthermore, as the World Health Organization report points out, subliminal attention is also required of them. That is, they have to be sensitive to cues of which they may not be entirely conscious. Such vigilance contributes to insidious fatigue, particularly when it is combined with a decrease in motor activity. According to some reports, this degree of alertness is one factor in tension and can place a strain on the heart.[18]

The repetitively perfect operating of the machine, assuring tolerances and quality control far beyond those of which people are capable, together with its seemingly apparent capacity to do almost anything, leaves the man who operates it or who is not yet replaced by it with a frightening sense of being replaceable. Sometimes it seems as if there is almost no process which cannot be mechanized and ultimately automated, ranging from picking cotton to flying a man to the moon; from composing a song to directing other computers.[19]

Alterations in work processes and in materials handled make for changes in work relationships. Work which previously had meaning because of the nature of the social groups involved loses its meaning altogether if people are more widely separated from each other and have fewer opportunities to come together. Some people will thrive on greater isolation. Many will not. In addition, automation often destroys the hierarchical structure which previously governed production and administrative processes. The programmer becomes a new boss, directly or indirectly. With larger systems involved, people in one part of the system may have to obtain the cooperation of others over whom they have no authority; sometimes they will be evaluated by people who never see their work. This is especially true of specialists from one company who must work with those of other companies on major project sites distant from any of the firms themselves, as is the case at Cape Kennedy.[20]

Increasing isolation from others, greater distance from supervision, and diffusion of administrative responsibility all tend to contribute to resentment and to the use of the psychological mechanism of projection.[21]

Under such conditions it is easier for people to criticize and blame "those others" who are neither visible nor palpable.

With less physiological work, less handling of materials, and less action for some people the function of work as an atonement device may be lost. In Western cultures there is a feeling of obligation about work. People who are not working feel guilty. If work seemingly makes fewer demands on them, that makes them uneasy. In work man expresses his aggressive feelings in a constructive way and he also taxes himself with the yoke of work to relieve some of his guilt feelings. With less of such work, what will happen to the guilt feelings of many people? Behavioral scientists do not yet know. One possible consequence might be greater incidence of depression both from feelings of uselessness and from feelings of guilt. It is bad enough that one can already be displaced by the machine; it is worse that one cannot even get sweat on his brow, literally or figuratively, to show himself that he has done an honest day's labor. A man in such a situation has a sense of being lost and deserted by his company. After all these years he is nothing.

Left untouched so far are the questions of how machine tending will be evaluated and how opportunities will be upgraded. James Bright argues that there will be no substantial upgrading of the work force, that training for automated jobs has often been over-rated, and that high rates for automated jobs are frequently unfair when compared with conventional work.[22] He found some upgrading in early stages of mechanization but as mechanization approached automation, the reverse took place. He concluded that many key jobs requiring experience and training will be reduced to easily learned machine-tending jobs; many traditional contributions of employees will be of lesser or no economic value. Even the promise of automation pales.

These conclusions are echoed by Albert Kushner, a management consultant who specializes in data-processing installations.[23] Computer processing, he says, may require a different type of clerical employee than was employed previously. He reports that of five hundred people involved in a conversion to a computerized billing system in one company, 21 percent of the employees were reassigned to a higher level, about 60 percent remained in the same grade, and 19 percent were reduced in level. The people most affected by the large-scale change were often employees with the longest service. Furthermore, the changes resulted in fewer opportunities for promotion since many of the senior or technical clerical jobs had been eliminated.

Reporting another study, sociologists Bernard Karsh and Jack Siegman observe that prior to the introduction of automated processes in the company in which they conducted their research, it had been possible to advance by increased skill. With the computer, work performance was no longer the sole criterion or even the relevant criterion for advancement, nor was understanding of the organization's routines of value. Intellectual skill now required by the computer became correspondingly more important. Similar observations are reported by other sociologists.[24] A corollary finding is reported among airplane mechanics who were moved to a more technically efficient overhaul base. Many found that their jobs had been more constricted and curtailed, and that supervisor-supervisee relationships became more formal, resulting in a loss of status and impairment of their self-image as trained, skilled mechanics.[25]

Such examples, of course, are the inevitable concomitant of technological change. They serve to indicate that technological change, despite its economic promise, holds many headaches and dilemmas. The problems are not only those of individual employees but also will be of increasing concern to the executives who are responsible to them and for their occupational well-being.

Technological changes are occurring in a social context of declining property ownership and an increasing abundance of goods and services. There is not only greater flexibility of operations within a plant or office, but greater possibility of individual movement free of the anchor of property. Work may come to include many activities which have not been considered to be work and for which people were not paid in the past.[26]

The projected flexibility of production resources, the possibility of locating them more widely than present requirements of personnel permit, and the greater mobility of individuals means that people must be prepared to adapt to constant change. They will necessarily require new modes of relating to organizations to replace those ways which were possible by being in one place or one structure for an extended period of time. Young people can no longer expect to learn a trade and follow it for the rest of their lives.

Even the nonwork implications of further mechanization raise questions. What will people do with the shorter work week and more leisure? Some, of course, will take another job or "moonlight." Others will be bored. As more wives enter the labor forces the image of a man in our society will change. Women are increasingly becoming the occupational equals of men, particularly as there is less need for the physiological strength of men. Those wives who do not go to work may be bored at home since much of what they have done also has become mechanized. The rising incidence of alcoholism among women suggests such boredom is already a problem. If a husband with more time on his hands stays around the house, he is likely to get in his wife's way. One has only to read the advice given by newspaper columnists to people who have retired to see how often new frictions arise between old couples because they are together too often and too long.

Implications of Automation for the Middle Class

By 1970, every second person entering industry will have attended a university and will expect to reach managerial-professional-technical status.[27]

But for all of the growth attributable to expansion, certain realities remain. Despite an increase of 250,000 employees in the postwar period, the Bell system, for example, has six thousand fewer telephone operators. The rate of increase of white-collar jobs has slowed down as companies effect efficiencies by automation. New York financial institutions report hiring fewer employees despite increases in services and business. The Bureau of Labor Statistics predicted that banks will increase their employees by 400,000 in the next ten to fifteen years, despite the introduction of automation. This is 200,000 below the number which would be required if there were no further automation.[28]

Automation has produced considerable dislocation of white-collar people. The Bureau of Labor Statistics estimates that the average computer abolishes thirty-five jobs and changes the kind of work for about one hundred other workers. More than 10,000 computers are being produced each year, meaning that 350,000 clerical jobs are abolished and a million others require retraining. In the study of twenty companies, on which the Bureau of Labor Statistics based its argument, nearly half of 2,800 employees affected by the installation of computers were removed from their former assignments. Although 80 percent of the employees given new positions in electronic data processing were selected from within the office, only 6 percent were selected from among employees whose work had been directly affected by computer installation. Older workers were not hired as trainees or promoted to newly created positions to the same extent as were younger workers.[29] One observer suggests that reassignment may become as much a part of the life of the office worker as periodic lay-offs are of the factory worker.[30]

Reports are beginning to demonstrate that it is now no longer possible to advance from a lesser skilled job to the most highly skilled by worker performance alone when electronic data processing has become the basis for technical change. Furthermore, bringing in outside computer specialists identified with the process rather than the organization creates a split between the old work group and the new. The major stimulation for the computer specialist comes from organizing and developing the basic computer programs and the organizational structure required to support them. When that is done, the computer specialist finds nothing left to his job but routine. He begins to look to other horizons, probably in other organizations. Meanwhile, previously independent activities have become dependent upon computer operations and directives; operating responsibility and decision-making have gravitated to the programmer. This creates political problems within the organization. It poses particular problems for subordinates who cannot "see" the skills of the people to whom they are responsible, and who are caught between the demand of loyalty to the organization and the literal fact that loyalty has not won them the security and advancement which originally were such an important part of the psychological contract they made.

Albert Kushner reports that there must be an appreciable build-up of personnel to do the necessary programming and conversion work, incident to the adoption of electronic data processing. There is a period of duplicate work while parallel efforts are being carefully checked to insure that the new method is completely satisfactory. He then adds, "A different type of employee may also be required. Those added to the payroll for the computer program are generally quite different from the usual clerical force, and this creates training problems as well as possible problems of morale." Furthermore, with the tight processing schedule required, "There is little latitude for delay in the availability and preparation of the data that are to be fed into the system. This imposes on personnel inflexible deadlines and new pressures for performance." [31]

All this contributes to growing restiveness in white-collar groups. Just as had previously happened to the blue-collar group with mechanization, automation brings with it alterations in organization structure, new kinds of white-collar occupations to impinge on the old, changes in age and education requirements, and increasing job mobility. These trends indicate that there is no return to the "happy family" concept characteristic of many managements in dealing with salaried employees in the past.[32]

Howard Jacobson concludes that the nature of white-collar work is becoming more like that of the assembly line. As this happens, the white-collar worker is changing his ideas about social identification, loyalty, and job security. Jacobson's study indicates that management is complacent about the effects of technological change on white-collar workers. "It would be a costly mistake for management to go on believing that all white-collar workers can be made to feel close to management again. You cannot convince a white collar employee that he is part of the management team if he has no decisions to make and is completely isolated from the decision makers." [33]

Despite changes in the nature of white-collar work, 67 percent of the executive respondents in Jacobson's survey did not think salaried employees were sympathetic to unionization. A study among 85 Michigan firms by the Bureau of Industrial Relations of the University of Michigan, 10 of which had all or part of their white-collar workers organized, indicated that 57 of the 85 managers queried believed their white-collar workers to be basically different from blue-collar workers.[34] By implication, they were not likely to be further organized, these executives believed. White-collar workers were thought to be more individualistic and independent, more loyal, more intelligent and better informed, closer to management in thinking, and more aggressive. A labor organizer echoes this thesis. Writing under the pseudonym Dick Bruner, the organizer says, "not only does the average office worker look to management for social models and advancement, he is often repelled, even frightened, by the idea of getting involved in union activities, chiefly strikes." [35]

Many union leaders think such views today are but pipe dreams. According to Albert A. Blum, "They are convinced that automation and technological change are so altering the nature of white-collar work that the white collar is now grey and will soon turn blue." They believe the white-collar worker will be ripe for organization. Howard Coughlin, president of the Office Employees International, points to cutbacks in white-collar employment and the likely increase of more as the basis for his aspirations to organize them. In the 1963 negotiations between Westinghouse and the

Federation of Westinghouse Independent Salaried Unions, protection against automation was the major demand. "The production and maintenance employees have been clobbered by automation, but our turn is coming," said Leo F. Bollens, president of the federation. The United Auto Workers, responding to what they saw as both a need and an opportunity, formed the Michigan White Collar Advisory Council in September 1963. While white-collar employees do better on fringe benefits than blue-collar workers, in one survey a fourth of them judged pay, fairness in promotion, merit-rating administration, and handling of complaints in their respective companies to be poor. "We've had something like 90% success in organizing offices where computers are about to go in," says Coughlin. Yet from 1962 to 1965 the office employees union added only about 15,000 members. Furthermore, a miniscule 7.4 percent of the white-collar workers in 8,486 companies in one survey are organized, little changed over the last few years.[36]

Management will take little satisfaction in the fact that the attempt to organize white-collar workers is not limited to business and industry. For example, the legendary David Dubinsky, former president of the International Ladies Garment Worker's Union, was reported to have been in a steady rage at the May 1962 annual meeting of the union. He criticized the "enemies" of the union who wanted to "undermine us, degrade us," who used "sneaky ways" and "machinations" against the union. The traitors were members of the ILGWU staff who had organized a union of their own. Reflecting a feeling management sometimes has, Dubinsky was said to have felt like a father whose children turned on him.[37]

The problems are evident; the possibilities present. White-collar people are hard pressed for better social mobility and greater consideration from management. Their pressure seems destined to conflict with current organizational directions. When people as individuals can no longer surmount their problems, sooner or later they organize. There is little reason to think white-collar workers will not follow this pattern. Unionization of engineers, for example, is already an old phenomenon. The reasons why engineers join unions are much the same as those which may have similar effects on other white-collar people. According to a study by Bernard Goldstein and Bernard P. Indik, the differences in social background and political orientation between unionized and nonunion engineers is negligible. Engineers who become union members do so in an attempt to remedy present dissatisfactions in the face of a generally conservative orientation. The dissatisfactions continue to grow with frequent and rapid changes in engineering demand and utilization.[38]

Some writers project the same problems for middle management, following technological innovation, as exist for nonmanagerial white-collar employees. Historically, the argument runs, the function of middle management has been to assemble and interpret data and to exercise controls along lines already established for them. Automated processes gather the data far more quickly and, because of the programming required and the rapidity of feedback, exercise controls far more rigidly. There is therefore likely to be less need for middle management to do these tasks. Furthermore, when the major functions of control and monitoring errors pass to the machine, there is less room for initiative and judgment. Some authorities say that as much as 80 percent of middle management activity is information handling. It then follows that many present middle management tasks will be downgraded, just as has been true of white-collar and production tasks; some will be upgraded to the technical specialist level.

This is what Harold Leavitt and Thomas Whisler have called "the champagne glass phenomenon": broad base, narrow stem, broad cup, indicating that the traditional hierarchical structure of business organizations will give way to a newer structure in which there will be only a narrow middle management range. They point out that in automated systems, the boundary between planning and performance moves up in the hierarchy; planning is directly in the hands of specialists. The specialists have relatively direct contact with the producers of goods who operate equipment, thus eliminating much of what historically was middle management. With greater access to more complete information and with equipment-controlled production and performance, top management is likely to be less dependent upon middle management because there are fewer areas of experience and judgment in which middle-management people are specialists. The line between the top and the middle becomes more clearly drawn. Automation makes for controls by the top of the middle, just as industrial engineering made it possible for middle management to control the bottom by specifying the nature of work performance, the production rate, and process of production. If that occurs, what happens to traditional apprentice systems of management and management ranks? Will the average middle management man have to satisfy his personal needs off the job? [39]

How realistic the Leavitt-Whisler prediction will be is hard to judge.

Charles Silberman contends that no company is so automated that its managerial people do not have to make important decisions. It is true, however, that there have been severe cutbacks in middle-management ranks in some companies. Some of these cutbacks have resulted from the need to streamline operations, others from the changing directions of given industries. Still, executive search firms report requests for specialists — forward planners and operations research people — as contrasted with generalists, with consequent effects for those who are not specialists. It is also true that there is increased job hopping by junior executives, partly as a result of what seems to them to be limitations on promotion.[40]

There may be forces other than automation at work. Peter Drucker argues that there are not enough places for all of the bright young men to move upward. Psychological studies suggest additional factors. "Lower levels of management (as opposed to upper levels) seem to have definitely more unrealized fulfillment of the esteem, autonomy and self-actualization needs," reports Lyman W. Porter. "These needs are frequently cited as being relatively unsatisfied at the worker level, with the assumption that they are fairly well met at the management levels. This study casts doubt on that assumption." In Hjalmar Rosen's study, staff personnel were less certain than other levels of management that their work would be fulfilling. All levels of management were found to base their predictions about their occupational futures upon their current job experience rather than upon their personal desires. As managers experience it, what *is* in this company, *will be*. The managers in this study indicated by their responses that they see themselves relatively powerless to effect desired change in their work environments. In their eyes, the organization calls the tune.[41]

Data relating to the impact of automation on the middle-manager's job are sparse. One interview study of fifty-three middle managers who had had at least two years' operating experience with an electronic data-processing system disclosed that they worked longer on planning than they did before the system was introduced.[42] This was, they said, because of the increased volume of data, the speed-up in the flow of information, and the demands of their superiors for more detailed analyses and greater output from the system. All these pressures were compelling these managers to plan more intensively and make more decisions than they used to. They reported little change in their organizing activities. They also said that higher caliber managers were now required to fill the same positions; they felt that their jobs were expanding and that their status was raised.

If the predictions about the impact of technological change on middle management are correct, they project a severe problem. The pressure by middle managers for consideration, identification, esteem, and security is even more severe than that of white-collar salaried employees.

In discussing the growing distance between management and line employees, sociologist Robert Merton has commented that not only has the progress of workers through the ranks progressively diminished, but also relations between executives and workers have become increasingly formalized and depersonalized. He points to increased insulation of managerial personnel from the outlook of the workers because of this depersonalization of contact and changes in career patterns which limit the advancement of line workers. Merton adds that these circumstances make for a polarization of the social origins of workers and executives which may be one source of increasing tensions between them.[43]

If a consistent trend toward limiting the role of middle management as a result of automation does evolve, Merton's point could be raised anew with respect to middle management. If the middle manager's relationship to the organization becomes further impaired, and if he is less able to identify himself with top management, he will have an increasingly difficult time defining his own identity. He, too, may come to think of himself "as a standard, replaceable element in a pattern whose creation he has played no part. In short, he is less a man than a perforated IBM card, missing only the legend DO NOT FOLD, MUTILATE OR SPINDLE across his chest, as it is across his neatly punched and programmed soul." [44]

Despite improvements which provide him with an ever more hygienic and attractive workplace, the middle manager may well experience a sense of loss as a result of repeated change and disruption of personal and organizational relations. The rewards of excellent job facilities and more efficient work processes are no substitute for intrinsic satisfaction and opportunities for identification. With respect to mental health, it should be noted that "significant life events, associated with unresolved feelings of loss and followed by the experience of 'giving up' (affects of helplessness and hopelessness) form a pattern that is frequently reported by the patient as occurring prior to the onset of a disease." [45] Losses which presently are long-range threats to middle management conceivably could produce an increasing incidence of illness.[46]

There are additional implications. Although the middle manager is presently the backbone of voluntary political, social, and community action, if he withdraws in anger from a work situation in which he feels deprived, he may also withdraw from community responsibilities. Furthermore, like the blue-collar employee who often no longer expects much satisfaction from his job, the middle manager, while withdrawing, may be counted on to resist the change which threatens to defeat him. It is not much help to say that the average middle management man may have to satisfy his personal needs and aspirations off the job. He is the one who is making the most of his leisure in the form of hobbies, travel, or sports. His aspirations have to do with his image of himself as an executive, not with his golf score.

The possibility of no longer being "part of the family," as has already occurred with many white-collar workers, and long since with blue-collar workers, is more threatening to people who have aspirations of high upward social mobility, strong identification with management, and who even more intensely need the organization to serve their psychological requirements. If the threat materializes in any significant way, it can produce a new form of alienation and hostility which will have economic, social, and psychological consequences. Such alienation and hostility are not limited to management. During the past several years, angry younger lieutenants have rebelled against national union chiefs. This rebellion has reflected not only their own ambitions but also the restlessness of the rank and file. To the average member, union leadership often seems distant, arbitrary, and unconcerned.[47]

Even if the projected threats to middle management do not materialize, there is still an important problem, as both turnover rates and studies indicate. *Dun's Review* editorializes that, "The greatest and most persistent problem for top management is middle management. The continuity of growth, the preparation for change, and the latent power of competitive vision and action of any company rest on middle management resources." [48]

The middle-management dilemma is the paradigm for the major personalized social problems of technological change. It is in the solution to the middle-management dilemma that a new style of management will be found, and with it, ways for resolving the additional pressures of the unemployed and impoverished and of the impact of technological change on those in organizations. The problems of management following upon technological change are also the avenues for the creative development of leadership.

Part Two / Redefinition

Once the psychosocial terrain has been at least partially mapped, the executive task becomes less illusory. What is the executive expected to do in contemporary society, what is his organization to do, and with whom are they to do it? In this section some of the major dimensions of both the executive and organizational tasks will be sketched. The mode for doing so is based on a common business technique.

The question is often asked, "What business are we in? What is the broadest possible conception that will enable us to retain maximum flexibility yet not dilute our efforts?" This section addresses itself to a similar but more comprehensive question: "What is the broadest social function of the business institution? How can it be conceived of so that it retains its basic economic purposes yet adapts itself flexibly to social evolution?"

To answer these questions does not mean abandoning the historic role of the business organization or trying to substitute other purposes. Rather, it calls for shifting emphases to those aspects of the managerial role and organizational effort which heretofore have been largely regarded as secondary. The discussion in this section reconfirms the fundamental importance of human relationships for economic as well as social purposes by showing that what is often considered dross has become the heart of the contemporary business matter.

6 / The Tasks of Top Management

What is it that those who are responsive to the guidance of the business leader want him to do? The discussion thus far proposes three major leadership tasks for him: he must manage the business; be an effective social engineer; and maintain democratic values.

First, he must manage the business. His fundamental task is to make the business survive. Furthermore, in addition to the returns paid to investors and the monetary and psychological rewards to employees, the business provides the underlying financial stability for such varied social institutions as colleges, hospitals, research institutes, and even federal, state, and local governments.

To make the business survive, as Thomas J. Watson, Jr., has noted, requires bringing out "the great energies and talents of its people." [1] This, Watson says, is the most significant element in the difference between success and failure. He argues cogently that neither size nor present demand for the company's goods and services is an indication of capacity to survive. The capacity for survival lies in continuous regeneration. Contemporary behavioral science research has shown us that there is indeed the possibility of a "fountain of youth" in organizations. It is possible for organizations to create social and psychological climates which are conducive to the growth of people and thereby to the creativity and flexibility of organization.

Second, the leader must be an effective social engineer. Already he directs numbers of people and organized systems of service or production. He manages them in communities and therefore wields considerable civic power. He exerts his personal and his organization's influence on many things for good or evil, ranging from good schools and better social services to depletion of natural resources and air pollution. He influences vast segments of society. He is now called upon to help manage them, to assume responsibility in circumstances where he has long exercised his authority and power.

Peter Drucker insists that large scale organizations must be limited to whatever is necessary for the fulfillment of their social functions. "All around us," he says, " 'responsibilities' are being asserted by large scale organizations — businesses, unions, universities, military services, and what have you — which are simply not grounded in the necessary function of the institutions. Let us not forget that 'responsibility' always carries with it 'authority;' whenever any institution asserts its 'responsibility' it must have authority in the area . . . The job our large-scale organizations have to do is so big that they need a great deal of authority; and the impacts they make, of necessity, are so great that they carry heavy responsibilities. But let us make sure that they do not go beyond this, no matter how well-meant, how attractive, or even how badly needed such action may be." [2]

Yet the business executive has no choice but to see himself increasingly as a social engineer. Business leadership is already required for many governmental tasks. Increasingly it will have to be called upon for the management of other social institutions. This new demand may put the executive into conflict between his obligations to the corporation and his obligations to the community. Frederick Pollock observes that planning ahead with respect to social responsibilities is a difficult task because anyone who assumes responsible executive functions in a large business organization today must be prepared to identify "body and soul" with the organization he serves.[3] Can men who must necessarily have such obligations to their organizations also assume societal responsibilities? Yes. The business executive has a dual responsibility because a business is a "profit center" for a community. Unless it produces economic, political, psychological, and other "profits" for a community it has no business there. If, as Thomas J. Watson, Jr., has pointed out, the executive cannot synthesize these two obligations, then ultimately society will itself increasingly restrict and govern the corporation.

Since he serves by consent, the executive is in many ways an elected leader. As time goes by, judgments of *all* those who are affected by his power will be heard more frequently in his selection. In turn, this means that people will expect that he extend his leadership, not merely control, to wider ranges of their daily lives. They will expect that he use the power delegated to him to help them expand and integrate the psychological rewards they can get from their work and those which, with rising standards of living and rising middle-class expectations, are to be had in the broader society.

Much has been said about the sense of deprivation which people experience because they can no longer make a complete product. Some even go so far as to say that since the worker is divorced from his product, he sees no particular significance in his contribution to productivity and, as a result, his sense of purpose in life is diminished. They would then argue that if the employee is to recover a sense of worthwhile achievement, he must look elsewhere than to his work for his greatest satisfactions. This is a misconception. Historically, few people ever were creative. Most simply struggled for a livelihood in the most primitive fashion until the industrial revolution made it possible for large numbers to have a higher standard of living. The deprivation lies less in the loss of the experience of shaping some *thing* than in the experience of shaping one's own world.[4] It is the loss of responsibility and the failure to utilize adult capacities which makes one feel childlike, useless, inadequate, and incompetent. It is particularly these loss experiences which have resulted in having a large group of socially immobile people from whom the chronic unemployed have come. It is also such experiences which, because of technological change, now threaten middle-class, middle-management people. The task of the executive is to do something about that loss experience in the interest of the survival of the organization and of a democratic society.

The third task of the executive is to take the lead in developing and maintaining those social forces which preserve the American democratic heritage and, conversely, in combating those which threaten that tradition. The business leader has talked much too much about returning to by-gone eras, has opposed every major protective innovation from child labor laws to social security and has made a fetish of attacking governments while simultaneously seeking government money and protection. He has too often allied himself with the past instead of the future. As a leader, the executive cannot drag; he must lead.

Society will increasingly expect such executive leadership for three reasons: the cultural conception of the authority figure; the tremendous amount of power which the executive has and which he will add to; the changing conceptions of the growing numbers of people rising to the middle class. He will be expected to manage his business and that aspect of society which relates to his business in ways which will sustain those beliefs Americans hold dear. Everyone lives with what he had yesterday in history and its extension into today and tomorrow. Americans will neither relinquish democratic values, nor tolerate increasing authoritarianism, the effects of which are so vividly remembered from recent and contemporary experiences with Nazis and Communists.

Values of freedom, opportunity, and democratic decision-making are the core of American initiative, vitality, and way of living. As a nation, Americans will not let them be threatened from the inside. If the executive does not take the lead in sustaining them but instead appears to be an instrument of threat, then ultimately, as Watson noted, society will constrain the corporation to the point of taking it over.

If it is demanded of the leader that he insure organizational survival by creating processes of regeneration within organizations; that he assume some of the burden for social engineering by raising his sights on the nature of that responsibility and sharing decision-making more effectively; and that he take the lead in *actions* to preserve democratic values, then guidelines must be erected to assist him in successfully carrying out these demands. Such guidelines can take the form of specific ideas and delineation of forces which militate against the accomplishment of these goals.

The shoals must be kept in mind throughout the piloting process. Consider the negative forces first. There are two major ones: increasing trends toward mechanistic-statistical thinking and toward centralization of power.

Forces Restricting the Executive's Tasks

The trend toward thinking of people and problems in terms of numbers, percentages, norms and mass, makes it increasingly difficult to conceive of social problems in human terms. Thinking solely in computer terms tends to eliminate or ignore those problems which cannot be computerized — in particular, people's feelings. Management cannot deal with problems it cannot "see." If it can conceptualize only computerized problems, others are likely to ferment until they explode in some fashion. Among these may be the psychological problems of the middle class and middle management which result from technological change.

The issue is the same in science, industry, and government. With the pressure for publication, and especially for statistical documentation, scientists turn more frequently to studies which lend themselves readily to "yes-no" answers and tests of statistical significance. There is, therefore, a tendency to lose sight of the richness and complexity of issues, to think not about the dimensions of a problem but the dimensions of experimental design.[5] Simple scanning of scientific journals demonstrates this trend. Reflective, integrative articles, let alone comprehensive theoretical books, are comparatively rare in scientific circles. Even in the humanities, which are supposed to be concerned with human feelings and values, there is repetitive complaint about computerized doctoral dissertations which yield little that is new and less that is insightful.

One dimension of the cost of focusing on problems which can be computerized is the failure to anticipate problems which are likely to arise out of people's feelings. To take a few straws in the wind of current events: No sociologist, to my knowledge, predicted the race riots of the last several years. A throughway in San Francisco lies uncompleted in the center of the city because no one thought to ask about it. In my own experience, literally dozens of consultants' reports gather dust on executive office shelves because, despite the weight of their evidence, they have stopped short of the human problems of introducing change. I am sometimes amused by the efforts to computerize medical diagnosis: I keep looking for the place in the computer programs where the patient's mother-in-law is entered. It may indeed be she who precipitates his heartburn.

It was the fear of narrow thinking and lack of consideration of non-measurable matters which led Norbert Weiner to point out that the computer might produce a victory, if used by the military, but at the cost of "every interest we have at heart, even that of national survival." [6] This is not to say that we should abandon or ignore the contributions of computer technology. Some problems need only the weighing of objective facts for their solution. Traffic control is a simple example. Others require the consideration of esthetics, values, stereotypes, prejudices, and opinions, in conjunction with facts. It may be more economical to run electric transmission lines through an expensive residential area, but what will the residents think about it? Should a highway be put through a redwood forest if it is cheaper to do so than to skirt the forest?

Questions of judgment about human social problems must take into account something more than easily arrived-at facts. A critical question has to do with who is responsible for social decisions.[7] Given masses of facts and cost-efficiency decisions based on those facts, it is relatively easy for a deliberative body to avoid responsibility by saying in effect, "The computer said so." A number of noted physicists who were involved in the development of the atomic bomb have continued to raise the question of responsibility for the consequences of what they wrought. Do they have a responsibility for the results of their technology? Does a chemical company have any responsibility for how people use pesticides? Who does? Before or after people are maimed or poisoned? The same questions arise with respect to computer-derived answers to social problems.

But issues of judgment and responsibility are increasingly harder to cope with as the average citizen feels less and less knowledgeable. Even the Congress complains it cannot critically examine what the executive branch proposes. This means people are compelled to trust someone who presumably knows the answers. They themselves are more likely to feel helpless about solving problems (as is already evident with respect to the cities, racial conflict, and such involvements as the Viet Nam war). Therefore they are likely to look for paternalistic heroes, as the French did in electing Charles de Gaulle president.

The problem of mechanistic-statistical thinking is not just a problem of the data-processing machinery available to us. It has a more complex background, related to the American drive for power — economic rewards, materialistic achievements, political position. Psychological evidence indicates that high power motives and high achievement motives taken together not only produce both wealth and power, but also a high incidence of isolation, insecurity, and stress.[8] High achievement motivation in a culture is correlated with such psychosomatic symptoms as ulcers and high blood pressure; high power motivation is correlated with increasing rates of murder, suicide, and alcoholism. More important is the fact that material achievement — wealth and productivity — is purchased at the expense of original thought. People who "strive" hard all day want only light entertainment afterward and seem to have neither the energy nor the interest to think deeply when they feel they must *act* rather than think. In this kind of a culture there is strong pressure toward simplistic, statistical thinking, computers aside.

The development of science in the United States has followed a parallel trend. Scientists in the United States have been heavily oriented toward experiment rather than theory. While they have produced a dazzling array of technical contributions ranging from a cure for infantile paralysis to flights to the moon, a disproportionate share of the fundamental theoretical contributions from which these achievements have been made have been derived from European scholars.[9]

These two trends — the shallowness of thinking which is correlated with the drive for power and achievement, and the technically oriented style of American science — only make more vivid the varied forces pressing toward mechanistic thinking in the business world. This pressure is further increased when both forces are joined, as in the fact that "38% of approximately 1,000 top officers of the nation's 600 largest nonfinancial corporations had degrees in engineering or natural science, or equivalent on-the-job experience." [10] Furthermore, the strength of this combination of forces is increasing. The proportion of top executives with engineering or science degrees jumped from 7 percent in 1900 to 20 percent in 1950 to 38 percent in 1964. Business schools which emphasize scientific management orientation — the combination of computer-based technical thinking, engineering orientation, and high achievement motivation — may be preparing executives for the world in 1985, but it will be a world in which human feelings are systematically denied.

The crucial questions then are "What kind of world do we want?" and "Are we to use the facts, or are they to use us?" Will our society serve the mechanistic and statistical processes we have evolved or will they be mobilized to serve us? [11] The basic arena in which this issue will be fought is the business enterprise.

Centralization of power is the second major force which militates against the leader's meeting the goals and expectations society holds for him. This takes two forms: constriction of access to leadership roles, and a network of interrelationships among those who hold power. These two issues occur both at national and corporate levels. Both themes have been the subject of considerable discussion in the scientific and public press. The national picture has drawn more attention as a socio-political problem, but the issues are no less important within a given corporation: To what degree is power surreptitiously centralized and access to it narrowly circumscribed? At what price?

Despite the historic upward mobility of people from lower socio-economic levels, an increasing proportion of those who have moved into the business elite during the last two generations have come from well-to-do families of high economic but low social status.[12] While increasing numbers of people have been moving upward, more people from higher socio-economic levels have gained greater control in management hierarchies than those of lower-class parents. A large proportion of the people in top management ranks still tend to come from the highest economic levels in our society. The chances of a man becoming president of a major business organization in this country are considerably higher if he has graduated from one of the Ivy League schools or come from a wealthy family.[13] The reasons for this are obvious. Such men have contacts, social advantages, and an educational edge.

Of three high status groups — scientist-administrators, United States senators, and corporation presidents — the last group has almost twice the percentage of Ivy League graduates than either of the other two. It is well established that "educational milieu is an important source of members of the administrative elite groups in our society." [14] Andrew Hacker's study of presidents of one hundred corporations with the highest sales indicates that presidents of these corporations and United States senators tend to be "grandsons of 'old American' families," with 60 percent of the presidents belonging to high status Protestant churches. [15]

This does not mean that vertical mobility has been severed, particularly since at Harvard, Yale, and Princeton the wealthy are being edged out by better qualified students. [16] Rather it suggests a different route for many who come from lower-class families. As already indicated, an increasing proportion of those who have risen into business leadership in the last two generations have come from well-to-do families of high economic but low social status. When one generation became affluent but did not achieve the prestige to go with its money, its children were able to use their economic position as a springboard into higher executive positions which also carried prestige. The American business aristocracy is still disproportionately derived from white, Anglo-Saxon, Protestant, well-to-do families; nevertheless, others are able to make headway in it. If there are to be fewer middle-management avenues, those who are not well-to-do may be less able to do so in the future.

Rather than move up through the managerial ranks, a possible alternative is that people may be able to achieve greater independent success either financially or in some specialized function, and then be brought into the top management hierarchy. This is what is being done in some government circles. While there is a well-established civil service equivalent to middle management, top management people are politically appointed, with rare exception, at top levels for their specialized knowledge and contributions. Perhaps it was with this idea in mind that Leavitt and Whisler have argued that the business organization of 1980 will look something like the family-dominated organizations of Italy. [17] In such oligarchic organizations, the road to position for the outsider is marriage into the family.

As a result of the greater tendency both to mechanistic-statistical thinking and the more rigid class lines based on education and managerial position, it becomes increasingly difficult for people who have not come from lower-class levels to understand what lower-class and middle-class people experience, know, and feel. It is precisely this barrier toward knowing and feeling what the other person experiences which becomes a threat to social consensus and a democratic society as well as to the management of organizations.

Frederick Pollock contends that in an age of automation these social trends may be expected to continue in an exaggerated form.[18] He takes the position that a new kind of society based upon authoritarian or military principles might well be evolved. That is, there may be something like a general staff of people who have power and information (which also becomes power), and could conceivably command the rest. Although day-to-day operations might be carried on by specialists — engineers, administrators, public relations men — they will be the equivalent of military officers. In his view, a homogeneous class of executives is evolving who hold great intellectual and material power and are superior to the vast mass of the population. Such a social class, according to Pollock, will control the mass media. With larger businesses and larger power at hand there will be an increasing tendency toward authoritarianism.

There is a striking parallel between these predictions and the events which occurred in Nazi Germany as described by William L. Shirer in *The Rise and Fall of the Third Reich*. When media of communication provide only certain kinds of information, even the most critical of thinking people have great difficulty forming judgments on the basis of any other data than those which are presented to them. Only with a massive range of information can there be flexibility in thinking and democratic interchange.

Lipset and Bendix echo this theme by commenting that American society seems to be moving steadily toward a social order in which the relations of persons will be summed up in the hierarchial regulation of official duties.[19] Donald Michael, a social psychologist, elaborates the same theme with the observation that privileged information, resulting from automatic data processing and specialized knowledge, will lead to an authoritative unelected ruling class.[20] If the public does not have access to data on which to develop informed opinion, this will limit their capacity for political judgment. If such data become the paramount basis for decisions, there is likely to be a shift in emphasis from concern with people and problems related to people, and from leaders who understand these matters to leaders who can do computer thinking. The greater the concentration on efforts based on those data which come from automatic data processing, the more difficulty there will be in coping with the ambiguous and less logical aspects of society; people who will place their dependence on the data which can be quickly gathered and lend itself to statistical interpretation will be less likely to be patient with and encourage the slow, illogical, emotional processes of democracy. There will be a tendency to deal only in the mass, with little consideration for the individual. Of the problems of the mass, those which can lend themselves to statistical treatment will get priority attention.

Michael's thinking coincides with Pollock's thesis: that the general public will be alienated from its own productive and governmental processes and will be less sensitive to human dangers. As the population becomes more isolated from national and international realities, it becomes ever more the victim of insecurity, ennui, and increasingly mismated to the occupational needs of the day. It will be less able to contribute to the mastery of intergroup and social problems. This may lead to a withdrawal from productive and governmental processes and reorient life to private recreation with a corollary indifference to public responsibility. Such an attitude, Michael argues, plus centralization of authority, might not only lead to a governing elite, but an even more versatile, intelligent class of slaves.

There are evidences of Michael's point of view in the proliferation of engineering and technical advances as contrasted with the relative impoverishment of advances in the social sciences. Furthermore, the same man who will applaud advances in technology which require a constantly critical attitude toward what is happening today, will object if the social scientist takes the same constantly critical attitude toward society and suggests how society could do things differently. As a result there is not the same enthusiasm, support, and recognition of the value of social criticism as of the value of technological criticism.

Former President Eisenhower raised the same issue in his farewell address as president, cautioning the public against an alliance between the military and the manufacturers of military equipment which could become a controlling force in American society simply because others could not know what was going on. That this threat need not be as great as it has seemed is indicated by Robert McNamara's work as Secretary of Defense. It was apparent that the Secretary, not the military officers or the equipment-makers, had the major say in defense decisions.

The argument about a "power elite" has been a long-standing one in American economics and politics. Certainly there are trends which, if followed to extremes, could create such a class. But any trend, if carried to extremes, could be destructive. True, it is difficult for people to start new businesses which require a major amount of capital. Therefore, most of the new businesses which are started are service businesses. The older, more heavily capitalized businesses are well entrenched and constitute important vested interests. But even these decay. Neither the railroads nor the public utilities are as powerful as they were a generation ago, for example. Despite the tremendous power which large organizations exert over channels of communication, there seems to be no dearth of information about all kinds of ideas and events, not a little of which is devoted to criticizing and "exposing" those powerful organizations which presumably control the very media in which such information appears.

Reconception

If the executive is to manage the business for survival, be a social engineer, and maintain democratic values, he must act in certain directions and avoid known pitfalls. Historically, management incentives have failed to motivate employees beyond certain minimum levels in any significant degree. Rationalized engineering methods have failed to produce quantities of goods at anywhere near the level people could produce if they wanted to. Political action by management has traditionally been viewed by the public as being against the public interest, and therefore the management position usually has been the minority position.

It cannot be taken for granted that present trends will ultimately destroy society or that all problems will ultimately be solved if no one gets too excited about them. Both extremes leave man manipulated by external forces rather than in control of them. However, there is a danger in equating gimmicks with control.[21] For example, the problem of the trend toward a power elite and alienation of middle management from top management will not be solved by building small scattered plants to maintain a personal touch between levels. With more centralized control, such a solution is only a gesture. Unless real power lies at the plant level, relationships will be tenuous so long as the people in the plant know that the power lies elsewhere. There is little reason for people to identify with a manager or an executive if he is powerless to do anything for them, or on their behalf, or to seek their help in the solution of mutual problems.

These trends must be seriously investigated in the context of demands on leadership. More effective ways must be evolved for assisting leaders to meet these demands and to avoid the pitfalls. One implication of these new demands on leadership is that stockholders, boards of directors, and other vested financial interests will have to permit the executive to focus on developing the regenerative capacity of the organization. This is not to imply that today's profits are unimportant, or that lack of profitability is to be excused on the basis of some fuzzy concept of the future good; rather, the pressure for today's results cannot be allowed to impede the building for tomorrow.

Ultimately there will have to be a different kind of long-run accounting, in which the costs of the various styles of management can be computed. For example, how much does it cost a company to manufacture shoddy products and market them in high volume, only to have them returned repeatedly for maintenance and service? There will need to be ways of recognizing and paying for those actions which contribute to enduring survival as well as momentary profitability. One such way, as an illustration, might be to ask men who have been promoted rapidly to identify those superiors who had helped them most effectively toward increased responsibility.

There are already some efforts at "survival cost-accounting." These suggest considering employees as assets, and applying the analytic and conceptual approaches designed for the management of physical or monetary assets to the management of human resources.[22] No doubt other efforts will follow.

In creating such social devices to encourage and support more expansive and longer range thinking, the business will become an institution of problem-solving and learning. In doing so, it will continue to remain the social ladder on which new generations have the opportunity to rise.[23]

7 / The Business as an Educational Institution

If the executive is to discharge the three major responsibilities of top management that are required by society, and also to surmount the two most likely major barriers to the fulfillment of those responsibilities, he must view his business as an institution for problem-solving and learning. That is what it must be to survive. How can the educational aspects of its activities be self-consciously formulated so that they might be recognized and evaluated as formal processes of the business?

One important thesis serves as a guide in this task. *Whatever activities are suggested must meet the needs and expectations of people while simultaneously contributing to the vitality of the business, the economy, and society at large.* The activities proposed must enable people to make use of the organization in which they work to adequately channel their drives, meet the obligations of their consciences, provide experiences of mastery, and enhance both self-image and aspirations for partnership with power. They must facilitate the ability of people to act directly, both individually and in concert, on the personal and social problems which confront them. Formally defined educative processes carried on in the business organization will serve all these purposes.

Training

The concept of the business as an instrument for solving problems enables the leader to deal with pressing social issues far more effectively than has been done to date. Two major social devices have been evolved to deal with the problems of the displaced and the chronically unemployed. One of these is broad scale retraining and rehabilitation efforts, financed by the federal government and carried on at the local level. This program envisions a continuous effort to retrain and rehabilitate individuals. The second instrument is the negotiated pay arrangement by which the financial advantages which accrue to management as a result of labor saving efforts will be shared with those who are displaced by those efforts.[1]

Both of these devices have serious shortcomings. The first program assumes that people can and will be retrained and that when they are retrained, there will be jobs for them. The results of community training efforts have been mixed and often disappointing. In some cases it was said that the candidates were not sufficiently motivated for retraining, that they had insufficient education for higher-level jobs, or that they did not want to move. Modest success was reported when the retrainees could go directly to new jobs from their training; and better success was achieved with on-the-job training. When companies retrained their own employees and constructed new plants near the sites of the closed obsolete plants, the reported success was considerable.[2]

These results were predictable. Community retraining programs for individuals fail to take into account the relationship between a man and the organization in which he works, and the demoralization which occurs when a man is separated from his work organization.[3] Such disillusionment inhibits the development of motivation to be retrained and to establish new ties to another organization where the same process might occur again. "I like my job," Allen Dodd has his major character, an executive, say in *The Job Hunter,* after having found a new job, "but I have no faith in its permanence or the permanence of any relationship between a man and an organization."[4] A retiree describes the demoralization experience vividly: "you don't prepare for [the fact] that you are standing alone and unprotected against the world. This realization hits you about three weeks after you retire. The company is no longer standing there beside you, or behind you, to tell you what to do, when to come or when to go, to speak a word for you in court, to defend you against outsiders, to tell all and sundry that, since you are one of its very own, you are a good and honorable guy — and does anybody want to fight about it?"[5] In less dramatic medical terms, the late Dr. Harold G. Wolff summarizes: "In short, prolonged circumstances which are perceived as dangerous, as lonely, as hopeless, may drain a man of hope and of his health; but he is capable of enduring incredible burdens and taking cruel punishment when he has self-esteem, hope, purpose, and belief in his fellows."[6]

Little wonder that comparatively few displaced people took advantage of rehabilitation opportunities, particularly when those who were doing the retraining often had difficulty in finding new job possibilities for their proteges. Thus, well-intentioned programs may become only temporary devices to preoccupy people before they are once again left to their fate.

This is particularly true if individual people who are left to their own devices are not given support and incentive which will stimulate them to want to learn, to find new opportunities, and to use new skills.[7]

The second instrument, the negotiated pay arrangement, softens the shock of displacement and change by providing a financial cushion and even job security. In many instances negotiated pay is no more than a temporary expedient because the displaced people will have to find other jobs or work part-time in their own organizations. If they must find other jobs, they become part of the problem with which their company retraining programs are supposed to deal. If they work part-time, they may have financial security but lose some of the psychological value of working consistently. Barring some improbable miracle, these methods are not likely to make impressive dents in the ranks of the residual unemployed, to alleviate the problems of those who are being displaced, or to capitalize on the psychological values of work. If, however, the psychological meaning of the work organization to the individual who works in it, his expectations of his leadership stemming from his psychological needs, and his egalitarian tradition are all taken seriously, there are other alternatives.

Suppose a number of people are to be displaced from a plant because of increased efficiency. Rather than turn them loose individually and attempt to retrain them for jobs which are to be found, conditions might be created under which the company can more effectively help itself as well as its employees. When a plant must displace people from their jobs, both the company and the community incur major financial costs. The community must pay for individual rehabilitation, unemployment or welfare costs, and economic incentives to companies to set up a new plant. The company usually must pay separation bonuses and the costs of moving some people to other locations if it has them. Using the same amount of money which might be spent by community and company for these purposes, a corporation might establish a new kind of business in place of the one which is being automated or closed.

This would mean that the corporation uses some of its staff, plus the resources of local and state industrial development commissions, to create an initially subsidized new business under its own corporate name. Those who are to be displaced could be retrained as a unit and start functioning in the new business as a group, while retaining their ties to the original organization. If the new business were too far afield from the direction of the corporation, or if the corporation did not want to maintain it as part of the larger corporate structure, it could be sold or reconstituted as a complete, functioning unit. If the employees and the management together can make such a shift, the integrity of the work group in the organizational structure could be maintained.

The results of company retraining efforts as contrasted with community retraining efforts are evidence of the usefulness of this concept. At least one small company has implemented the concept by taking over not only the physical plant, but also all of the employees of another company which was vacating that site. The new management felt it would be considerably cheaper and more efficient to employ an already organized and cohesive work group than to hire new people individually.[8] Owens-Illinois entered the sugar business in the Bahamas when its timber operations there had to be suspended for twenty years.[9] Using this same principle, the United States Army reduced its psychological casualty rate and increased both efficiency and morale when it shifted from sending individual infantry replacements overseas to sending units.

Some will argue that such a concept imposes an undue burden for the host corporation, which already bears a tax burden, a bonus burden, and an increasingly heavy social burden, all posing problems for the economy and the society as well as the business. The concept is not new, however. Many companies did something similar during World War II. They developed and operated facilities for the federal government whose activities were far from the basic business of the contracting corporation. Even today Pan American Airways operates the Cape Kennedy establishment and many other companies operate large enterprises on a contractual basis for the government. Some have gone into the formal business of training school dropouts and the unemployed in community programs.

Another alternative which would make use of the psychological meaning of the organization is the in-company training program for displaced or unemployed individuals. Success has been reported in this sphere already, particularly with dropouts and young men who might become unemployed after high school graduation.[10] Detroit's Federal Department Stores report an unusual achievement: taking a group of dropouts, who lacked the minimal education and could not pass the elementary psychological tests to qualify for rehabilitation, they trained them to be successful department store salesmen.[11] Such efforts could include many of the young women receiving aid for themselves and their dependent children, if communities would establish complementary nursery facilities. In turn, the nurseries could serve the multiple purposes of caring for the children during the day, providing social and psychological stimulation for them, and ensuring that they are given adequate food and medical care. Such an effort would serve both to habilitate the adult and prevent the same social tragedy from handicapping the child. It would interrupt the vicious cycle of generations on welfare rolls.

John F. Merriam, Chairman of the Board of Northern Natural Gas Company, has called for a nationwide network of "learning pools" operated by business and industry. If business and industry had earlier assumed the responsibility for training the unemployed and the not-yet-employed, he said, they would create an image that is vital for survival. A presidential council, headed by Ben W. Heineman, Chairman of Chicago & North Western Railway, has called for businesses to take a hand in retraining. Senator Winston L. Prouty of Vermont has led a movement to provide employers with a tax credit to do what Merriam and Heineman propose. There are still other alternatives. Thomas J. Watson, Jr., calls attention to the National Labor Market Board in Sweden, which is composed of representatives of labor, management, and government. Its task is to anticipate and plan for the effects of technological change.[12]

Whatever the alternatives for dealing with the impact of technological change, most people favor increased technical efficiency in manufacturing and data processing. A positive public climate can be maintained if management demonstrates that it has carefully considered the impact of technological change on employees and that it wants to help solve the resulting problems with them.[13] Furthermore, the more management demonstrates its willingness to lend a hand with the social problems of unemployment, the more it will be respected for using its power constructively.

Apart from problems of poverty and rehabilitation, there is the general task of training young people in marketable skills and increasing the proficiency of craftsmen who already have basic skills. This is now done largely by vocational and technical schools. The conception of a vocational school to train young men and women so that they can be employed is good. Vocational schools, however, operate under severe handicaps. Their equipment tends to become obsolete because of inadequate budgets. Teaching, divorced from the realities of the working world, also tends to become obsolete. Without the concrete prospect of a job and a bond to an organization in which they will work, it is difficult for many students to invest themselves in training. Furthermore, they rarely have the discipline of working on products which must be sold, or of being responsible for rejects and errors.

Vocational training would be more effectively conducted in businesses. The same formal curricula could be followed, apprentice criteria could be maintained, and the training would be in a work context. Much of this was done after World War II as on-the-job training, with appropriate compensation for employers if established standards were maintained. It would be in the employer's self-interest, as well as that of young men and women, to have continuous skill-training programs in every business where specialized competence is important. In addition, many millions of dollars of school construction could be saved.

There is an additional reason for carrying on vocational training within the business and that is the needs of the business itself. Retraining of workers threatened with skill obsolescence has not been undertaken on a large scale by American business, although some companies have made significant efforts.[14] In 1964 the Ford Motor Company had about 23,000 men enrolled in various retraining programs.[15] The Douglas Aircraft Company and others have undertaken on-the-job apprenticeship programs to convert skilled workers into super-skilled aerospace electronics technicians. The Norma-Hoffman Bearings Company in Stamford, Connecticut, recognized that many of its employees could not take advantage of high level training opportunities because of gaps in their educational backgrounds. It worked out a program in cooperation with a local education authority to fill the gaps. In 1965, 191 New England manufacturers were training 18 percent more of their employees than in 1962. The National Screw & Manufacturing Company in Cleveland concentrates its recruiting on untrained men, offering two hours a day in the classroom and six on the job, with eight men in each class. Local 3 of the International Brotherhood of Electrical Workers has established a school at Southampton, New York, for rank and file employees to study "liberal arts," paid for by the union and electrical contractors.

These are straws in the wind. There is no question that the business organization is becoming increasingly an educational institution. The only question for the executive is whether he guides the process in his own and the organization's self-interest or whether it just happens.

In-Service Education

The problems of displacement and unemployment are not limited to blue-collar or hourly rated employees. Obsolescence of technicians and managers has also become a pressing issue for all businesses. An engineering student of a decade ago would barely understand today's courses. Schools of engineering are urging the conservation and development of engineering manpower. The dean of one school calls for a national attack on the problem of obsolescence by means of broad and versatile programs for continuing education as a long-term investment and responsibility.[16]

To counteract obsolescence among executives, American companies in 1965 put an estimated 500,000 executives through in-service education courses, management seminars, and formal academic programs — twice the number in such activities five years before.[17] IBM's expenditures for upgrading personnel nearly doubled between 1958 and 1963.

Various people have called attention to the fact that knowledge is the focus of contemporary culture. Everyone is now required to learn at an increasingly accelerated pace, and understanding becomes a requirement for a widening range of decisions about society and social problems. Inevitably, business must also be education-centered. Intellectual obsolescence is so much a threat to both man and organization that learning will become a formal part of work. Some companies already require every manager to be involved in at least one period of instruction each year; many more will soon be doing so. It has, as a result, become appropriate to suggest that businessmen take sabbaticals.[18]

The rapidity of change alone is not the problem, although that is severe enough. In addition, the composition of the work force is becoming sharply different. The increasing numbers of people entering technical and professional fields are not as startling as the fact that there are more professional physical scientists than general clerks, and more engineers than typists in the federal civil service. Like business, the federal government has had to provide for specialized training at full pay, plus tuition and subsistence costs. Furthermore, 80 percent of the graduates of Ivy League schools — and between 40 percent and 60 percent elsewhere — apply for advanced schooling. This means that such graduates who enter industry will both want and need to continue to learn at a high intellectual level.[19]

The implication of this discussion is that in addition to training the unemployed, training the already employed for skilled tasks, and similar self-interested social functions, every business organization must carry on a continuous process of advanced education. It is not enough to say that those who want to advance must be sufficiently interested to take the initiative in seeking out training. A business has too much at stake to leave the initiative for combating obsolescence to its individual employees. When a man is not able to keep up with his job, he is not the only one who suffers; the business suffers too. For its own survival, the company must use education as preventive maintenance against the social corrosion of occupational obsolescence. The Bechtel Corporation has made it possible for all of its employees who have bachelor's degrees to pursue an advanced program in business administration by taking courses at universities wherever they may be assigned in the United States, and getting credit for them through the University of California. Bell Laboratories also has a program leading to advanced degrees.[20]

Training people for basic wage-earning tasks is one thing; preventing obsolescence, another. Neither by itself provides for strengthening the leadership function. This is the goal of management development.

American business and industry has been heavily involved in management development since the end of World War II. Limited hiring during the depression days followed by the manpower demands of World War II, together with rapid expansion and the increasing complexity of the management task, created a plethora of executive positions and limited numbers of qualified and experienced candidates. As late as a generation ago, a reasonably intelligent and diligent man could succeed in becoming the head of a business. A man can no longer depend on those virtues alone for achievement. Today's business complexities call for that breadth of education and experience which enables an executive to lead professionals. Executive manpower shortages are still predicted.[21]

The evolution of the "paper curtain" and the often unrealistic academic requirements for many jobs have limited upward mobility. If, in addition, middle-management experiences will no longer adequately provide the apprenticeship training for rise to the higher levels, and if seniority has decreasing utility as a basis for advancement, then there will have to be a range of avenues through which men can become executives. Already many are drawn from engineering and scientific ranks. Of Stanford University's engineering graduates, more than half of the twenty-five-year alumni responding to a questionnaire are presidents or vice-presidents of their firms. Of the five-year alumni, nearly a quarter are not working in science or engineering; they already have more advanced degrees than their seniors.[22]

Ellison L. Hazard, president of Continental Can Company, points out that although more than 90 percent of contemporary business leaders have college degrees, only one out of five college students is majoring in business, and three out of five will be earning their livelihoods in the commercial world. This means that many come to commerce without preparation for business responsibilities. Mr. Hazard argues that business is better prepared than are undergraduate colleges in training men and in helping them learn the required skills. It is already spending half as much for training and development of management as it costs to run the nation's colleges. Sixty-nine percent of college graduates entering corporations undertake a three- to four-year training program, and 70 percent of those fail within the first three years.[24]

Therefore, management cannot rely on business schools or universities for more than generalized background training for business leadership. Even if all of those entering management ranks were to go to schools of business, such schools cannot mold a complete professional product any more than can any other professional school. One speaks of the practice of law and the practice of medicine not only because professional people have a body of professional knowledge, but also because they must continually refine and update it in practice. So it is with management.

Business schools are enmeshed in the same difficulties as the larger universities of which they are a part, and they are presently struggling to overcome the fractionation of diverse departments which prepare specialists.[25] In addition, they are caught up in "the mechanical system of lecture courses, departments and examinations." [26] Even as the business schools work toward establishing programs for generalists, there are limits to what they can do, despite the major contributions they have made. They continue to face certain inherent limitations of academic institutions: they are often divorced from the daily reality problems of the subject matter they teach. No business school operates a business as a medical school operates a hospital; it is nearly impossible for them to teach those subtle elements which translate the subject matter into finished skill — the feel or artistry of the leadership role. The acquisition of that skill requires interaction not only with problems, but more important, with leaders skilled in solving such problems.

There are two kinds of professional schools where one is not taught by those who are themselves expert practitioners in the field: teachers' colleges and schools of management. Apart from departments of education in teachers' colleges or schools of education in universities, there are few professional teachers in teachers' colleges. Similarly there are few expert managers in schools of business. Rather, there is a wide range of special-ists — in accounting, law, marketing, personnel, and behavioral science. A student in a business school may major in any one of these areas and get a smattering of the rest. He becomes a specialist. Only after he has risen in the hierarchy is he expected to assume responsibility for the func-tioning of other specialists. However, never does he view himself as a generalist, as an executive per se, with general knowledge of all areas which he must organize and combine for the purposes of a functioning organiza-tion.

Although some complain that management has been on an often mis-guided self-development binge, the various factors thus far reviewed make formal management development activities imperative.[27] All organizations must have systematic ways of replenishing, developing, and producing their own leadership if they are to be masters of their own fates. Many do. What, then, is the problem?

Currently, management development activities are largely left to training departments. The result is the same as would happen if a man left his son's upbringing to the public schools or tutors. Learning is relatively divorced from role and function. What is left out is the executive himself, as a paradigm, an identification figure.[28] The implication of the argument is that business leaders will themselves have to provide continuous intensive leadership training within the organization. To teach decision-making, for example, is not merely to instruct rational analytic process, but more im-portant from a leadership point of view, it is to teach the extended process of building the organizational context for decisions.[29]

This line of reasoning does not imply that the executive must abdicate his leadership role. Only if he continues to carry it out will he have a psy-chological basis for teaching.[30] If the business is a problem-solving insti-tution and if he is a problem solver within that framework, that activity is his subject matter. His role is his strength. An executive can teach in two ways. First, he can do what he ordinarily does, enabling others to learn from observing him. This is a hit-or-miss system which fails to take into account elementary psychological principles about how people learn best. Second, he can do what he ordinarily does, but at the same time build into his daily activities both formal teaching circumstances and conditions which facilitate learning. It is the latter that is asked of him.

Specifically, the executive must concern himself with developing the capacity for leadership of those who report to him. He does this not solely because the business needs continuing sources of leadership for its own survival, although that fact is significant. More important, a democratic society needs leaders and there is never enough of them. Relatively few prominent people assume a serious responsibility for societal leadership. There is even the complaint that a high proportion of gifted young people are shunted away from leadership roles because most of the intellectually gifted now go into graduate or professional schools. They are there indoctrinated in a set of attitudes appropriate to scholars, scientists, and professional men rather than leaders of society. So imperative is the need to develop leaders who can define and act on social problems according to democratic values that a number of programs have been created for that purpose in the last five years under major foundation grants.[31]

In the process of teaching others, the business leader will also be taking potentially effective steps to resolve a dilemma alluded to earlier: to mitigate the possible creation of a power elite drawn from a limited number of universities and business schools. Drawing on a conglomeration of people from a multitude of sources with a vast variety of skills, his teaching efforts can facilitate the development of extensive perspectives, capabilities and sources of leadership contribution.

Such possibilities make urgent a critical re-examination and reappraisal of developing trends which point toward a new conception of the organization. They also stimulate serious thinkers about business to evolve ways of effectively training leaders while simultaneously minimizing the threat to a democratic social structure and a competitive enterprise system. In the process of doing so, the executive has the best opportunity for accomplishing his three major tasks: managing the business for survival; acting as a social engineer, and maintaining democratic values — and in addition, preparing his subordinates for the more complex demands which will be made on them as leaders.

8 / The Role and the Learners

When the subject of teaching leadership is raised, the questions are asked: Leadership for what? What kinds of leadership will the organization need for regeneration? What immediate and specific activities and practices will confront the leader of tomorrow? How will these differ from today's practices? What can be anticipated? What knowledge is available to help in preparing leaders for their tasks? Who is the executive to teach?

What Is Leadership?

Contemporary leaders can provide a starting point for our discussion. Responding to a survey, a number of presidents of large American companies commented at length on the requisites of those who would succeed them.[1] An interpretive summary of their views would go something like this: He must be a person whose general knowledge and understanding of the whole organization is such that he can fit specialized contributions into profitable patterns. To be able to understand as a generalist, he needs a wide range of liberal arts knowledge together with fundamental knowledge of business. With that base, he is then able to view his business in global historical and technical perspective. Such a perspective, however, can only be the basis for the most critical requisite: "feel." "Feel" is a certain intuitive sensitivity for both the appropriate action and in relationships with people. The latter will continue to change drastically as social forces change.

The executive's perspective on his business must be visionary. It includes not only where it stands today, but, more important, where it should be twenty years hence. His is a future-oriented role both from the point of view of flexibility of concept, goal, and technique and because of the need to discharge his trusteeship function by providing for his own succession. The executive's task is one of continuous reappraisal, risk, and social responsibility, and of acting rapidly on the basis of quickly assembled facts to resolve complex problems.[2]

The writers and scholars of business agree. They, too, call for the generalist who is a specialist in managing people, in creating a climate in which people can do their best, and who will be judged by what his followers do. He will be distinguished from his followers by his capacity to sense and seize opportunity by continuously weighing alternatives, being oriented toward results and responsibility. He will be responsive to the question, "What is this business all about?" [3]

Bernard Muller-Thym summarizes these goals and sets them in historical perspective.[4] He points out that modern business is a post-World War II phenomenon. At that time, he says, business became the primary organ in our society for the creation and management of wealth. "Since wealth is generated not by production or any other functionally defined operation, but as the net effect of the total system, the task of the design and management of the total business now appeared with a specificity and separate identity which had not been recognized before." Thus top management work became useful, and not part of what a subordinate could do. According to Muller-Thym, the unique top management tasks include:

1. The design of the business and of all the separate businesses which may be included in its structure.

2. Optimization of corporate resources.

3. The management of perpetuity. Management education is part of this task since it looks to the creation of a managerial group, advanced in prudence as in managerial competences, flexible and ready for the needs of the enterprise at any point in the future.

4. The management of innovation.

5. Keeping the business relevant to the culture, society, and polity in which it functions.

6. Springing from the design and goal-setting activity, keeping the ends of the business and its conduct well related to those larger ends which lie outside itself.

Some would say that these judgments, observations, and predictions are little more than wishful thinking. From a survey of 903 top executives, Ithiel de Sola Pool concluded that the job of heading a small company is different from that of heading a large one.[5] The head of a small firm is a production manager and a salesman. Much of his work is inside management. He considers the efficiency of his subordinates and how they spend their time. He addresses himself to the methods they use to process the firm's work. On the outside he addresses his main efforts to selling. The head of the large company, in contrast, addresses himself to two quite different concerns: the firm's public and its investment and expansion policy. He looks broadly at the national scene and the market, considering how his organization can better place itself within both. Pool's dividing line between small and large companies is four hundred employees.

Pool adds that the president of a modern company often feels more vulnerable than many of his subordinates. He may have brought nothing with him into the firm but his own brains and experience. His free hand as boss may prevail only so long as the results are good. He may be fired at will by the directors and often is. He seldom envisions himself as a man of great power. He is proud that he has done something notable in rising to the top, but his reward at the top is not unlimited power; it is income, recognition, and status. He, too, is just an employee.

Many firms have a collective leadership with several autonomous leaders, Pool points out. In such situations communications are baronial — indirect, slow, and nonaggressive. Open votes and controversy are rare. This pattern of restrained aggression is universal when mistrust is low and strong independent men collaborate with each other. Pool found another style of leadership to be more frequent than this one. In this pattern the head of a firm was arrogant, self-confident, domineering, boorish, sometimes even a tyrannical egomaniac. Pool wonders how such people rise to the top in conforming organizations. He answers his own question enigmatically: They get there because they have a talent no one can define. If Pool's conclusion is valid, all the statements of leaders and observers alike about the requisites of leadership are but cotton candy.

With more data at hand, more pressure for performance, and more effective ways of measuring performance and increasing competition, Leavitt and Whisler have argued that the top management position will be increasingly tenuous and that company presidents are more likely to be moving from one organization to another in the future.[6] This may raise questions about whether there will be sufficient continuity of management in a business organization to foster and develop the kinds of psychological ties which meet people's needs and expectations. Leavitt and Whisler predict that there will not only be top executive team operations, which already exist in such larger organizations as General Motors, but that there will be more accurate evaluation by colleagues of top level performance. This is likely to produce greater emphasis on performance and less on pressure for conformity. In addition to these responsibilities, Leavitt and Whisler add that the top executive will also be forced to think — alone and together with researchers and creative people. In their view the higher turnover which is likely to occur at top management levels is advantageous because it is conducive to greater flexibility.

The ideal of the leader in this culture appears to be a masculine figure.[7] But Abraham Zaleznik argues from psychoanalytic theory that it is fallacious to describe the managerial role and interpersonal behavior underlying it in terms of one set of ideals. He conceptualizes three kinds of leadership: homeostatic, or maintaining internal balance among people and forces; mediative, or dealing with environmental pressure, which is more aggressive than the homeostatic; and proactive, which seeks out environmental possibilities and is innovative.[8] The innovative leader is the man pictured as the aggressive executive, the outside man or public relations man in Pool's sense. The mediative leader will tend more to be an "inside man."

There is repetitive vagueness in statements about the requirements for good executive performance. John F. Kennedy is reported to have told Arthur Schlesinger that he did not know what the duties of the President would be. According to Schlesinger, Kennedy wanted to keep things flexible. "How presidental decisions are made," Schlesinger says, "in particular remains a mystery to me." [9]

The same mystery exists with respect to other kinds of leadership roles. John Fischer concludes from some thirty years of editorial experience that most editors are utterly incapable of explaining what they do, or why. "This doesn't mean that they don't know; it is simply that they can't put it into words which will convey much to outsiders." The primary piece of equipment for a good editor, Fischer posits, probably is an instinct, or hunch, which tells him what people will want to read a month, a year or a decade from now. "Equally important, and often harder," says Fischer, "he has to keep out of print those things which in his judgment don't belong there. This knack for projecting into the future, for estimating what people will be eager to read at some remote date, seems to be associated with three characteristics:

> A certain ordinariness. A good editor reacts, in his bones and his belly, the same way as most of the people in his audience . . .
>
> In addition to curiosity and intellectual companionship with his constituents, a good editor usually has the enthusiasm of an adolescent in the spasms of first love . . .
>
> Simple ruthlessness. Happy is he who is born cruel, for if not he

will have to school himself in cruelty. Without it he is unfit for his job; because the kindly editor soon finds his columns filled with junk. But the indispensable ruthlessness must be combined with a genuine liking for writers and sympathy for their work.[10]

These same considerations seem to characterize Charles de Gaulle. Henry A. Kissinger writes of de Gaulle: "To de Gaulle, sound relationships depend less on a personal attitude than on a balance of pressures and an understanding of historical trends. A great leader is not so much clever as lucid and clear-sighted. Grandeur is not simply physical power but strength reinforced by moral purpose. Nor does competition inevitably involve physical conflict. On the contrary a wise assessment of mutual interests should produce harmony." [11]

Douglas McGregor pointed out that good leadership depends more than any single thing on the manager's conception of what his job is — of what management is. Second, it depends on his convictions and on his beliefs about people.[12] Except for the most general, and often the most peripheral tasks, the reality of the leadership role, that for which the executive is to prepare others, defies simple mechanical classifications. How then does the leader prepare others to assume his mantle? Flexibility, imagination, psychological strength, judgment — all these are to be cultivated. Such adaptive skills are subtle. Subtleties of adaptation arise largely out of identification — the unconscious assimilation of behaviors, values, and perceptions — with more capable people.[13] Once again the importance of continuing personal relationships between the leader and his subordinates as a major medium for growth is emphasized.

Who Are the Learners?

If what is to be taught cannot be explicitly defined, and if much of the learning is to arise subtly out of the relationship with the leader, then the leader requires a concise picture of the kind of men with whom he will be maintaining such relationships. The changing cultural circumstances of the followers has already been sketched. What kind of people are the followers?

Usually those whom the executive is to teach will be younger than he. Even if they are not younger, one condition always holds: at that particular point in their relationship, the executive has more power, as reflected in his more responsible position. That strength serves as an attractive force for most subordinates; they want to become as strong.[14] This fact alone means that he has something to teach others, providing the power itself can be used as a facilitating device. If it merely stimulates fear or exacerbates dependency, it cannot be used for teaching leadership skills.

Not only are the learners likely to be younger than the executive-teacher, but they are also likely to be increasingly more educated and sophisticated professionals in their fields. Half of the young men now reaching adulthood have education beyond high school. Consequently, most of them join the professional, technical and managerial class, expecting high opportunities for themselves and even greater ones for their children. They are a growing professional middle class of "knowledge workers" who already outnumber "labor." How to fit them into organizations and society as a resource is the real "social question" of an industrial society.[15]

In 1963, 45 percent of the men arriving in top management positions had master's degrees and 18 percent had Ph.D.'s. The Ph.D.'s were basically in science and engineering and 80 percent of the master's degrees were in business administration.[16] Projecting the data, by 1970, 70 percent of the presidents will have master's degrees and 30 percent will have Ph.D.'s.

How do these figures suggest a problem of fitting young people into organizations? Describing contemporary college graduates who are entering the corporation, Eugene Jennings notes that they recognize that authority is important and therefore relate to it properly. But by "properly" he means they have limited trust of authority figures; they detach themselves when they can no longer learn. The "brighter" ones who move along steadily and get to the top have what Jennings calls "maze brightness." Such a person is sensitive to the values of his organization, and to the differing values of various departments. He recognizes which have higher priority for the organization as a whole. He has, further, the capacity to understand the exercise of power, which means both the institutional right to act and the capacity to apply it. He also knows the boundaries and limitations of the possible, and the holes through which he can thrust his aggressive drives. He does his job and, in turn, becomes more powerful than the authority to whom he previously was subordinate.

The young men whom the executive will teach are not only highly intelligent but they also want to use themselves and their lives effectively. A man's work is a major way of justifying his existence. Today such men are not looking for jobs. Rather, as H. Marshall McLuhan comments, "The young today reject goals — they want roles — R-O-L-E-S — that is, involvement. They want total involvement. They don't want fragmented, specialized goals, or jobs." [17]

These are the young people who, wittingly or not, take John Gardner's concept of self-renewal seriously: "for the self-renewing man the development of his own potentialities and the process of self-discovery never end." [18] Such a young man, according to Edgar H. Schein, comes to the organization asking, "Will the job provide an opportunity to test myself, to find out whether I can really do a job?" "Will I be considered worthwhile?" In most cases, Schein adds, a college education gives the graduate a sense of being special, of having attained something not available to all members of society, and of having special skills which, he is told, will be considered valuable in any job situation. Therefore, he is particularly vulnerable to experiences of failure or rejection by the organization. As Schein observes, one inevitable outcome of prolonged education experience is the expectation that the person will continue to grow and develop. Implied are such questions as "Will I be able to maintain my integrity and my individuality? Will I be able to lead a balanced life, to have a family and to pursue private interests? Will I learn and grow? Will the organization in which I work meet my ideals of the rational business organization described in economics and business courses?" [19] These young people are more interested in the quality of life than in the division of the economic product.[20]

What happens when these expectations are not met? Lawrence Stessin asserts that the lack of challenge in business is reflected by the frequency with which recent college graduates change jobs. As evidence of the lack of challenge he points to a College Placement Council finding that three out of four companies cannot hold new employees for more than two or three years — despite the inducement of extra pay.[21]

Students today are more flexible and better prepared both academically and socially. Their attitudes toward industry have changed; they are determined not to become "organization" men and will not trade their integrity and individuality for security. Able and sensitive, intensely concerned, particularly where they have been influenced by academic values of questioning and learning, they rebel at the thought of the "stereotyped" life of the businessman. Their orientation is to trust fact not authority; they want to examine assumptions and remake society. They ask of a business how its goals fit their goals, especially their wish to make a social contribution. They do not believe that business has seriously come to terms with the major social problems of the world. If they want to do so, then they will be attracted only to those businesses which promise to do something toward alleviating hunger, disease, and poverty.[22]

More intellectual and socially minded, today's young man is more likely to have an intellectual stereotype of the business executive and to be subject to an equally strong stereotype himself. In a survey of 114 corporate executives and 132 intellectuals conducted by the Opinion Research Corporation, both the intellectuals and the businessmen saw the intellectual as a critic of the established order who is oriented primarily toward ideas.[23] According to the survey, the intellectual valued creativity more than technical skill, had difficulty dealing with practical problems, and was generally underpaid. He sought broad social changes and was somewhat alienated from the mainstream of society. The executive, as both groups saw him, was primarily interested in raising the nation's productivity and was wary of governmental solutions to national problems. He was respected in the community, preferred gradual social changes, relied on intuition and experience in decision-making, and put great emphasis on financial rewards. About half of the intellectuals said that the executives did not like them, and 50 percent of the executives felt intellectuals did not like them. Yet 63 percent of the intellectuals and 76 percent of the executives reported that they liked members of the opposite group. Although stereotypes inevitably distort the perceptions young people have of business and vice versa, it would be a mistake to dismiss their career aspirations and preferences merely as reflections of stereotypes. Young people already in business share some of the same views.

Daniel Yankelovich, a psychological consultant to industry, told the Institute of Life Insurance that a number of the nation's best-educated, most promising young adults have lost enthusiasm for their business careers.[24] He said that there was a "crisis of purpose" among the top 10 percent of those between eighteen and twenty-five years old whose family affluence has already assured them of economic achievement. "For many, the problem of finding meaning and purpose through the pursuit of traditional goals remains achingly unsolved," he reports. The reason is that society is depending more heavily upon technology and complexity of organization for the achievement of its goals. This headlong trend toward complexity — and its consequent "depersonalization" of the organizational structure — has made it more difficult for many young people to satisfy their individual goals by pursuing their careers.

It would be a mistake, too, to classify the "demanders" as disgruntled intellectuals who should not be in the business world anyway. In 1964, 100 out of 600 graduates of the Harvard Graduate School of Business belonged to the Student Small Business Placement Program of that school.[25] These men deliberately sought to avoid "the stultifying atmosphere of big business." Among the complaints of a sample of them, most of whom had had business experience, were: "There is an unbelievable waste of good men in big business . . . Large corporations make 'cabbages' out of many people who could be made into useful members of the business community." "There are a lot of us who just don't want to be tied down to one line, one product or one man. And we don't want to be constrained by the politics of a large corporation." "I think [competition] is humanly destructive in every sphere except sports and politics . . . If there is competition, it should be with the product, with the company's existing condition or with other companies . . . There you are at the top, standing on a pile of bloody bodies, all of them supposed to be 'your friends.' " "[A member of middle management] is confined by the position he occupies in the structure . . . He may never get a total view of what's going on. The person who wants to get the whole picture is not only resisted by top management. He's also a threat to those at his own level." "Later on in life I want to look back on what contribution I have made and see that it's a real living thing."

Roger Blough, chairman of U.S. Steel, argues that the business can satisfy the young intellectual.[26] In fact, Blough says, because of its complexity, twentieth-century business needs the young intellectual today more than it ever needed him before. He notes that business and industry already employ more Ph.D.'s than all of the liberal arts colleges in the country combined. He emphasizes the rapproachement between the intellectual and the business leader by noting that in the ten years between 1954 and 1964 among the two top executives (presidents and vice-presidents) in business corporations, the number of college graduates had risen 23 percent and the number holding advanced degrees had increased 53 percent. Further, he argues, transferability of intellectual interest from one type of work to another is usual in business, business provides both an opportunity for freedom of inquiry and the possibility of doing something about it, and conformity in business is disastrous folly.

Blough's response does not answer the whole question for the intellectual. John S. Fielden, dean of the School of Business of Boston University, says that there is a conflict between the demand for loyalty to an organization in the business world and the intellectual's loyalty to a discipline or an art.[27] For the intellectual, respect and obeisance are due only to those who earn them by scientific or artistic attainments. For the businessman, however, power stems to a great extent from seniority because he values, not quick flashes of brilliance, but stability and wisdom which come from experience. The businessman is uneasy with abstractions, but the concrete talk of profits seems inane to the intellectual who thinks the businessman sees these as an end in themselves. The intellectual tends to think of problems analytically and conceptually, digs to understand — something that there is not always time to do in business. The businessman perforce leans more heavily on intuition and judgment. "Today's young person, faced with the prospect of going into a large organization . . . looks up over incredible years of rank to the top of an organization and finds it a most unsatisfying view. It is small wonder then that he takes the non-organizational route — the one where intelligence breeds its own hierarchy, where a young scientist can catapult to the top of his discipline by virtue of his intellect and creativity. He thinks, '*Myself,* the doctor.' " Fielden argues that companies *must* remove the shackles of seniority and inane management training courses. "When we were young," he recalls, "we too felt we had infinite capabilities. Is it surprising that our young people feel that they are not likely to be used quickly enough in many of the jobs now offered by industry?"

For Drucker, the question is almost academic. He believes that the competitive position of business as a career will inevitably deteriorate further in the next few years — simply because there will be so many opportunities for young educated people in higher education and in state and local government. Furthermore, the brightest do go on to graduate schools and business neglects the graduate schools.[28]

While the discussion has thus far centered heavily on up-and-coming younger men, these are not the only ones whom the executive is to teach. Many will have been in the company for years, some will be older than their boss. Among them will be men who have long been shelved, some who have been passed by, and some who are highly successful in their own right. Failures or successes, they share two problems. First, they are bombarded by a literature which extols youth, creativity, and flexibility, and by inference they will too easily believe they are less useful than someone younger with more formal education. Second, the contemporary emphasis on change is bewildering to so many who loyally served in an organization structure which, only yesterday it seems, appeared to be so important. While their personal goals may be less obviously altruistic and self-fulfilling than those of their younger colleagues, nevertheless, they, too, live with many of the same enduring aspirations. Most are capable of increasing their competence. A major aspect of the executive's work with them will be a seasoning process, which will be discussed later.

The Composite

What seems like a plethora of paradoxes is really a clear definition of the leadership role. In fantasy the leader is omnipotent — at once a generalist and a specialist; simultaneously more mobile as an individual, yet more cooperative as a member of a team; more intellectual, but with an acute sense for the commonplace. He is supposed to be a man — aggressive, charismatic and stable — but also to exercise restraint and exert self-control. Confusing? Yes. Contradictory? No.

Leadership is an art to be cultivated and developed. Like any other form of art, if it becomes stereotyped, it is no longer art, merely replica. An artistic achievement is varied in texture, composition, symbolism, color. It is dynamic in the eyes of the viewer because it takes on new meaning with each perception. In short, it lives. So it is with the work of the good leader. In different circumstances, at different times, with different problems, he chooses different modes of action. It is this flexibility, together with a conception of and appreciation for his role, which makes him like a diamond — solid, strong, yet many-faceted and therefore sparkling. That is why the role cannot be learned by prescription or content; rather, it has to be learned out of identification and in a relationship.

The leader's teaching relationship will be, more often than not, with younger, professionalized men. The younger men will be to the experienced executive as a symphony is to music of the people. They are likely to have technical brilliance but to lack that wisdom which makes for humanness. They will have to learn that by working with the artist. They, too, want to become diamonds, in their own right — bigger, more brilliant than their predecessors — and they should. There is one qualification: they want not only to sparkle, but to be useful as well.

Part Three / Toward Action

To be a professional is to apply knowledge and skill. To be an executive is to act, to implement, to do. The professional executive combines both functions. This section elaborates the steps of executive professional action by delineating the psychological role of the executive, by specifying and elaborating the human needs to be met, and by integrating much of the literature on the psychology of management. It walks the executive through who he is psychologically, toward what psychological goals of others he directs himself, and by what specific activities he can make effective use of himself toward attaining those goals. By so doing, it counteracts some of the psychological clichés of the current management literature and executive confusion about what appear to be disparate points of view on motivation.

The core around which action, application, and theory are integrated is that uniquely human characteristic, conscience. This dominating force, growing more powerful with increasing education, personal freedom, and economic security, has gone largely unrecognized in contemporary managerial conceptions. Without our being aware of it, ours has become the "Age of Conscience." Less encumbered by social and economic obligation, stripped by psychological knowledge of so many rationalizations, man is left with the inescapable reality of having to please himself.

9 / The Executive as a Teacher

To say to the executive that the business organization must be viewed as an institution for problem-solving and learning and that he must be a teacher of leadership is to state a truism. Unless his leadership-teaching role can be formulated to simultaneously serve his multiple responsibilities the executive will only be left frustrated. There are no prescriptions or recipes for the leader's teaching role. There is, however, a wide range of data which can be marshaled as a guide for him. Before doing so, two parenthetical considerations should be emphasized:

1. As observed in Chapter 5, effective solutions for the problems of middle management would serve as models for dealing with problems of poverty and technological change. That is, modes of diminishing artificial barriers between levels of the same organization, of enhancing communication and creative problem-solving activity, of advancing skills, and of increasing group cohesion — all of which are demonstrably useful in the hard world of economic realities — can become models of methods for the solution of broader social problems. The reader may make his own extrapolations because the underlying psychological considerations are the same regardless of the kind of organization or the nature of its task.

2. Although the perspective throughout has been from the stance of top management, the development of leadership capability is the responsibility of everyone who supervises another person. Young men usually do not begin their careers under the tutelage of the company president (unless he is their father). The issues to be discussed in this and subsequent chapters therefore apply across organizational levels.

The Teaching Role

Just as there is no single way to lead, so there is no one way to teach. Every executive brings his unique talents, skills and personality to his executive task. These will be no less diverse in the teaching task. Joseph Adelson, a psychologist, points out that there are many styles of influence, many modes of connection which bind the student and teacher to each other. Building on the work of anthropologist Merrill Jackson, he proposes five types of teacher-leaders.[1]

The first of these types is the *shaman*. The shaman heals through the use of personal power. He focuses his audience on himself. When his skills are combined with unusual gifts he becomes charismatic. He has power, energy, and commitment, all of which organize people around him. Perhaps Churchill is the outstanding recent political example of such a leader.

The second type of leader is the *priest*, who claims power through his office. He is an agent of omnipotent authority and those who organize around him differentiate themselves from others. A priestly structure is characterized by continuity; it has a past and a program for the immediate and distant future. It has a hierarchy with roles and places in a hierarchial ladder.

The third type is the *elected leader*, one who endures trials and self-transformation, training, or some other form of rite to achieve his position. The *missionary* is the fourth type of leader. Usually mission involves a utopian view of the future and a program for achieving reforms. Much of contemporary business leadership incorporates the priestly, elected, missionary conception. Power is delegated by the most powerful. People in one company or unit are differentiated from others. There is continuity, hierarchy, and election. Most organizations have some kind of mission, however prosaic.

The fifth kind of leader is the *mystic healer*, an altruist who seeks to find the sources of illness in the patient's personality. Translated into teaching-leadership functions, this is the task of trying to discover the statue in the marble, a Michelangelo kind of leader who discerns what could be created from raw material. This style of leadership requires not only acumen but also that one make himself secondary to the task he is doing. It requires considerable sensitivity and flexibility to vary one's attack according to the phase of teaching or according to the student.

The shaman type of leadership, similar to what is frequently discussed in management literature as authoritarian, is most effective in crisis situations. At such times the organization needs a strong figure to follow. The danger is that the subordinates remain powerless and therefore never learn how to use power except as charismatic leaders. Having been rendered powerless, they are rarely able to become charismatic. The organization is threatened when the leader departs. It either declines in power and effectiveness, brings in an outside management, or becomes vulnerable to "pirates." Such leadership is characteristic of many first generation organizations, built by the leaders who run them. It is not conducive to personal growth of subordinates or to organizational survival.

The priestly type of leadership, incorporating the sense of "election" and the conviction of the "missionary," has all the advantages and disadvantages of structure. The subordinate can see himself as part of a tradition and can readily measure his progress. The danger lies in its pressure to conformity and its potential for molding men in the image of a system at the expense of their individuality and originality. It is not without reason that the phrase "military mind" is often heard. The function of the subordinate becomes imitative and always carefully correct. He establishes what Adelson calls an "*ersatz* identity." He plays the part, but he may often be lost as the price of "belonging."

The mystic healer type of leadership is the most demanding of all styles for it requires of the leader to renounce personal pursuit of power in favor of building strength into the subordinate and into the organization. If survival is the prime requisite of the organization, and if the successful leader is the one who can build survival potential into organizations by seeing the most in and getting the most out of people, the mystic healer model for leadership will increasingly be required.

The concept of the leader putting his men before himself is not new. The military teaches its officers that they must take care of the physical needs of their men before they attend to their own needs. Such a concept, however, is easily misconceived as implying weak, vacillating, overkind, irresponsible management or a be-kind-to-others "human relations" philosophy. As a matter of fact, it is the most difficult type of leadership philosophy because it is the most realistic. It comes to grips with psychological and social data about human motivation which are usually ignored at great cost to management, the organization, and the employees.

The mystic healer type of management philosophy is the most difficult of all because it calls for a sensitive and delicate molding activity. Many will recoil at the use of the word "molding," thinking that it implies manipulation, control, and direction by the executive of the life of his subordinate. That is not what it means here. Inevitably, a company's system of rewards and punishments, modes of guidance, varieties of opportunity, all contribute to eliciting or suppressing the potentialities of the executive-to-be. No one is really free to grow as he will without the influence of those who exercise power over him. Unless the leader faces that reality, he deceives himself with clichés: "all development is self-development"; "the right of every man to determine his own course"; and "the best will rise to the top." The leader does have influence on the subordinate. If he accepts that fact, and takes it consciously into account, then it will not influence his behavior without his awareness; it will not be necessary for him to feel guilty about his efforts. If he can accept the fact that he has such influence, then the question is only how can he use it most wisely. First, he must understand that he cannot really shape any other human being into a preconceived form. He cannot make something of another person other than what that person is. If he tries to change a man he will flounder on resistance, and may even cause the subordinate to fail out of conflict between the momentum of his own personality and what his boss wants him to be.

What then does shaping mean? It means to follow the grain of the person and help it achieve refinement in a form that it could not achieve by itself. Just as the sculptor follows the natural confluences of a piece of wood, as the photographer captures previously unperceived dimensions of beauty in an ordinary subject, so the leader must discern the most likely potentials of the subordinate and encourage their fruition. Instead of providing a range of experiences for all promising young men alike, what obscure talents does this man seem to have and what experiences will foster those specific ones? Where does he sparkle most in his relationships? What experiences give him his greatest gratification? With what kinds of bosses does he work best?

The leader will need to work more closely with some, more indirectly with others. He may have to choose specific colleagues to help with each individual. He certainly will have to consider how to bring together a range of such men whose talents complement each other and stimulate each to further growth. This is a different focus than the usual managerial maneuver of pitting a group of young men against each other, dissipating talent in rivalry and defensiveness. It fosters a need of one man for other men who work with him, not because a team is better for a company, but because working with others who bring out the best in him is good for him. A man in such a situation needs no urging to be loyal, to be on the team or to develop himself.

There is always a danger in such efforts — the tendency to try to shape a man in one's own image, or to drive him to become what one had himself wished to become but could not. That danger is best avoided by trying to discern and understand what the subordinate himself is and what he is striving to become. Then the leader must not help too much or he will only encourage the dependency of the subordinate at the cost of his autonomy. There are no prescriptions for judging how much stress and frustration a subordinate should be allowed to experience nor are there arbitrary junctures for the superior to offer his assistance. He should have enough to understand the complexity of human relationships, to learn that there is pain in leadership, to discover how easy it is to hate when one is frustrated, and to realize that the building of relationships of trust with others is a slow, arduous business.

The second danger is that the superior will try to be a psychotherapist for the subordinate. He must not. In an effort to be understanding, too many bosses either dig too deeply into a man's life or assume that they must solve all his personality and family problems. There are professionals far more capable than the executive whose work it is to do that. The executive must teach the subordinate about the job the subordinate must do. Certainly he should be helpful and compassionate. The less deeply involved he is in the subordinate's personal life, the better for both of them and their combined task. Personal pressures and problems can be reasons why performance and learning are temporarily impaired, but they cannot be excuses. Respect for human personality means to hold man as an agent responsible for his own actions. It also means that one demands of a man what he is capable of giving to his immediate task. If this is not demanded, the subordinate feels guilty and the superior feels cheated. The consequence is contempt, each for the other; such feelings impair the personal relationship which is critical to the teaching-molding task.

Has the leader a right to mold and shape? Of what use is aging, experience, and wisdom if not to be the leaven for those who are younger? Of what use is pain if not to teach others to avoid it? The leader not only has the right; if he is a leader, he has the obligation.

The Process of Identification

Identification is an important aspect of the teaching situation; a successful teacher must be a good identification figure and the learner must be able to learn from him by identification.

Identification, Freud observed, is the earliest expression of an emotional tie with another person. "A little boy will exhibit a special interest in his father; he would like to grow like him and be like him, to take his place everywhere. We may say simply that he takes his father as his ideal." [2] The child also identifies with his mother out of his emotional attachment to her and imitates her behavior. By identifying with the mother first and imitating what she does, the child acquires skills and develops his earliest competences. As he does so, he increasingly resents his mother's efforts to take care of and to help him; he interprets her aid as interference with what he wants to do. By every successful act of identification with the mother, the child makes the mother less necessary to him.

Identification of a boy with the father is an essential step toward becoming a man, but it necessarily means not only love for the father but also rivalry with him. The important point is that identification is not simple imitation. For identification to succeed, the child must first love, then imitate, then assert his relative independence to practice the behavior he has learned. Furthermore, every step of development is hard-won and bound to be aggressively defended. Such a situation occurs frequently when parents forbid or compel certain acts.

As he grows, the child differentiates himself from other people. Rivalry occurs when he observes that another person has greater strength or skill in some area than he, and he wants to obtain that particular personal asset. That rivalry, in turn, begets competitive struggles with those whom he admires. Instead of simply imitating all of the behavior of the loved rival, the child becomes more selective in his identifications. He takes in only those traits of the other person which fit his social context, his stage of development and the skills he already has. As he has successes and failures, pleasures and disappointments, and also experiences competition, he learns what he is not so good at, as well as what he can do well. These experiences contribute to his selectivity of identifications. For example, a child who finds that he does not have the language skills which other children his age have, may be reluctant to learn them if they are not evident at home and he has no social base for using what he is being taught in school. This is one of the problems of teaching disadvantaged children.

Increasingly the identification process centers about rival figures as the child wants to become as powerful as they. This process is a critical one for the child's identification with his father and particularly for the development of the superego. The experience of aggressive feelings, hostility, rivalry, competition, and differentiation is as important to the identification process as affection for the admired person. Inherent in identification, as understood here, is increasing independence and competence. Any kind of identification implies, "I don't need you; if you don't want to do it for me I can do it myself; and if you don't want to give it to me I can give it to myself." When the child makes selective identifications, he is saying, "In this respect I like you and want to be like you, but in other respects I don't like you and don't want to be like you; I want to be different, in fact myself." [3]

Identity, an enduring and consistent image of oneself, arises out of selective identifications which fit together with the child's constitutional and developed capacities. Identity is a continuous sense of intrapersonal harmony which makes the future a flowering of the past.

Identification serves many purposes for the child.[4] It is important in and promotes learning. Out of identification the child learns to speak. Subsequently he acquires other intellectual knowledge. He also learns by identification how to deal with the demands of his environment and of his innermost feelings. Identifications also form the base for the ego ideal. In normal development, the ego grows through the process of identification, a process of voluntary psychological acquisition which continues through a lifetime. However, if development is hampered, there is a tendency for the child to fall back to an earlier stage where he could exercise his capacities without interference.[5] In this sense, the forward motion of development is like that of an army; when attacked it falls back to a previously prepared solid position. When natural development requires further activity of the child and it is blocked, he falls back to a still earlier, more passive level. That is, he regresses.

The psychiatrist Joost Meerloo, taking a more global view, points out that all civilized action is learned from parents and former generations.[6] In the course of growing up, man absorbs and internalizes from his environment and its history and culture the multiplicity of meanings condensed in his verbal communications. He also learns to identify with many guiding personalities. He plagiarizes without knowing it. This remembrance of Eleanor Roosevelt from *The New Yorker* is an example.

> She resembled the one incomparable schoolteacher that every lucky student encountered and sat under for a year in elementary school, to his permanent benefit and delight. At first . . . there was something both forbidding and comic about her . . . Once in her class, though, we understood. Watching her and listening to her we began to see that she not only believed in but lived all the difficult optimistic blue-

stocking virtues. We came to know by heart her maxims, "You can do it," "Try, try, again," "We must remember those less fortunate than ourselves," "You must be important to yourself," . . . All her life she worked at an impossible profession — one in which disappointment and limited success were encountered every day — but she was incapable of discouragement. When we let her down she took our failure as her own and announced that ". . . today we must go back and see what went wrong." A little annoyed at her, a little ashamed at our own indolence we would try harder next time . . . Like all great teachers she made the classroom into the world. Although she could not permit herself even the smallest luxury of boredom or inattention, she did not begrudge us our other, softer, world of love, home, games, and long holidays. Thus was she saved from didacticism and shrillness . . . because she knew no division between life and principle, she expected the best from herself every day. Sensing the honor she paid us, we almost learned to expect no less from ourselves, and the unforgettable year with her went by far too quickly.[7]

© 1962 The New Yorker Magazine, Inc.

Out of infantile mutuality and dependency gradually grow the more mature form of identification, imitation, self-assertion, and independence in which process the variety of communication clues plays a tremendous role. Out of vicarious living grows competitive assertion and finally the uniqueness of originality. Evidence from the research laboratory in studies ranging from animals to adults, supports this psychological thesis.[8]

A generalized process of learning how to behave and what to become occurs through identification. This evolution continues on into adulthood. Identification occurs among adults because one has a strength that the other wishes to acquire. In organizations the leader, the power figure, has certain strengths and the subordinate wants to acquire those which fit his needs. Sometimes the leader's strength is more than he knows. Sociologists speak of such "added strength" as charisma.

Part of the reason the leader has strength, often unknown to him, is because of transference. People who are neither their peers nor their challengers have affection and respect for those who hold high formal positions. As long as those in high positions can retain this affection and respect, they are more likely to retain their positions in the structure of authority. This is one reason why political incumbents often have an advantage over their challengers. The institutional arrangements of an organization facilitate such transference feelings — by making some people more powerful than others — because organizations cannot be effective as decision-making agencies without authority.

To the extent that power is attributed to another because of transference, leadership exists as a consequence of the nature of the individual's early relationship with his father.[9] They look to the leader, as they looked to the father, as one who controls the means of satisfying or frustrating their needs. But if they cannot identify with the ego ideals or goals of the leader or if he cannot successfully help them reach those goals, they will no longer follow him.[10] This is a particularly important point in organizations, because people become affiliated with them to achieve certain goals. Nothing else holds them together, unless there is external compulsion. In work organizations, they have been brought together to achieve the purposes of the organization, but they also have their own purposes. In identification with the leader, in projecting transference feelings upon him, they see him as instrumental in obtaining both goals, or more accurately, the single goal which serves both organizational and individual purposes.

Here simplistic psychologizing and sociologizing must be avoided. It is not merely that the leader controls rewards and punishments, or offers routes to certain concrete satisfactions. Identifying with him enlarges people's capacities by helping them to meet the demands of their superegos and to develop their sense of identity. Gandhi, for example, served just such a purpose for his followers.[11] By identifying with such a leader, his followers were able to mobilize unsuspected inner resources. In effect they responded to moral or superego challenges with heightened self-urgency.

By acting as the focal point of unity — the ego ideal of the group or organization — the leader serves as a device for knitting people together into a social system.[12] With such a leader, said Freud, a group is capable of high achievement, abnegation, unselfishness, and devotion to an ideal. Without such a leader, the group falls apart because people then lose their medium for establishing ties through each other — identification with the leader. A group without a leader is a mob. Every group needs a leader and moves toward a leader. The leader must himself be held in fascination by a strong faith in an idea in order to awaken the group's faith. He must possess a strong and imposing will which the group, having no collective will of its own, can accept from him. When the leader, standing for an idea, is accepted by his followers, he acquires what Freud calls "fasci-

nation" or prestige, which in turn makes for his dominance. The maintenance of prestige depends on the continued success of the leader. Here we
see once again the impact of transference. Prestige, as Dr. Robert Waelder
puts it, is the reputation for victory. "Loss of prestige may therefore
embolden all enemies and dishearten and demoralize all friends and so
bring about a radical change in power relations." [13] In identifying with the
leader, the members are psychologically identifying with the father because the father represents what the child would like to be. In times of
stress — transition, conflict, pressure — the ego ideal of the leader becomes
an especially important social anchor and orienting point for the followers.[14]

Man, no matter how well educated, how sophisticated, how competent,
still needs the purpose which comes from pursuing ideals. Inspiration is
largely the transmission of ideals as bases for action; and while ideals
comprise an important stimulus to action, they are translated into behavior
through the medium of a role performance — something which a person
does as part of a position he holds in a social structure, whether a family,
a community or an organization. In identifying with the leader the subordinate establishes or expands a professional model for himself. This can
be seen in all occupations; it is an important part of all professional
training.

Although the major factor in career choice among professors is self-
generated and self-absorbing interest, their own university teachers, according to one study, exerted the greatest influence. The best-liked teacher is
a key person in the psychology of becoming a teacher. Not only does the
best-liked teacher influence the decision to teach, but also he serves as a
professional ideal for the young teacher to follow. Philip H. Abelson,
editor of *Science,* says that the professor's most important role is to motivate the student to pursue continuing scholarship throughout his life, and
to acquire a sound value system and the capacity for independent thought.[15]

Although the "father" in the group is first a transference figure, ideally
he increasingly becomes an example of how to look at the world in a
more rational way.[16] Rather than weakening his followers, he becomes an
ego-strengthening figure. As the followers become more mature, they come
closer to his level of competence in the skills they acquire from him by
identification.

Concern with the development of occupational or professional identity
is even more important for executives than for teachers and scientists because, in contrast to other groups, business executives as a whole make

their career choices and mature in their leadership roles relatively late.

In one study of executives, more than half did not decide to enter business until their formal education was completed and they were already employed.[17] As a group, vice-presidents in staff positions decided earlier than did line executives; more staff vice-presidents decided to enter business while they were yet in high school. The managerial vice-presidents committed themselves to business during late college years and immediately after entering the labor force, while technical vice-presidents decided on a business career after being a part of the labor force for one year or longer.

These findings indicate that the executive has an important role in helping younger men make their career decisions to become leaders in business. He has the opportunity for contact with them at the optimum time. Furthermore, the same study indicated that interpersonal influence exerted by individuals of importance in the life of the executive-to-be was a major factor in his choice of career, and those persons were also the most significant general source of knowledge about a career in business. The impact of such a person was particularly significant for men who became managerial executives.

The executive who would be instrumental in the development of career identity has another powerful force operating for him in addition to the identification of the younger men with him. Most of the 102 men in this study had fathers who were in the business and proprietor class of society. Over-all, it appears that business today recruits its top executive talent from a higher segment of society than a generation ago — from business and managerial classes and semi-professional ranks rather than from tradesmen and artisans.

Identification is not simple imitation but the adoption of spontaneously selected aspects of the model which "fit" the person who is identifying and which will further his maturation. This is not the same as making the subordinate just like the superior. In fact, the executive might say to his subordinates, as Emerson did in his essay, "Self Reliance," "Insist on yourself; never imitate. Your own gift can present every moment with the cumulative force of a whole life's cultivation, but of the adopted talent of another you have only an extemporaneous half possession."

Yet, under some circumstances, identification can be little more than imitation. This is what happens with "priestly" leaders who lean heavily on molding men to fit the system. What results is called in clinical jargon one form of "identification with the aggressor."[18] When superiors are threateningly aggressive to their subordinates, there is a tendency for subordinates to cope with the resulting anxiety by impersonating the aggressor, assuming or imitating his manner, and thus making himself not the frightened person but the one who frightens. It is this phenomenon which leads to the displacement of hostility downward in an organizational hierarchy, and to regression in the subordinates which inhibits or warps their subsequent growth.

This is quite the opposite of the more creative and constructive identification which has just been discussed. More positive identification leads the followers to absorb those aspects of the leader which stand for a helpful, understanding, strong figure who respects the efforts of his followers and who in addition, has shown his followers something of how to do the work they want to do.[19] By contrast, identification with the aggressor stimulates rivalry and competitiveness among the followers for the special attention and affection of the leader. There may be pseudo-democracy in the group, but underneath such a posture it is clear that the group goals come from the boss alone. That being the case, the leader is seen as a depriver, to be feared, and the goals, being his, are to be defeated.

While managers tend to score higher on conformity than does a normative sample of college students, higher management tends not to reward them for it.[20] Those who scored higher on conformity were independently rated as less effective by top management than those who scored lower.

Another problem with imitative identification is that it breeds frustration and anger when the follower fails at being merely the extension of the leader. Thus, as Selwyn Becker points out, where an individual anticipates a mutually beneficial outcome, he would rather share it with someone like himself.[21] When he expects to cause discomfort to someone or to suffer discomfort as a result of another's actions, he would rather that the other person were dissimilar to himself. In imitative identification there is a tendency for the senior executive to avoid those situations where he must be realistic with the subordinate, to try to persuade him to a different way of doing things rather than to point out his failure. This in turn means that "feedback" is disguised and the underlying message therefore unclear. If the subordinate fails to succeed in his imitative role, Becker notes, the superior takes it as his own failure, a personal insult and a reflection on his capacity as a manager. Obviously, imitative identification limits the range of solutions a group will examine.

Under ideal circumstances, leadership climate is not simple imitation of one hierarchical level by the level below it.[22] Rather it is a process of interaction in which the values and role model offered by higher levels are transformed in keeping with the needs of the followers and the requirements of the organization.

Identification as Need Fulfillment

If man learns most of what he knows from others, and fundamental to being able to learn from others is being able to identify with them, then one of the leader's basic tasks is to create the conditions for identification with him. Parenthetically, by doing so, he also creates conditions conducive to identification with others to whom he delegates authority.

The task of creating conditions conducive to identification is largely one of establishing modes of fulfilling the needs detailed in Chapters 2 and 3. If those needs are now viewed in the more abstract form conceptualized by Edith Jacobson, the continuity between the most elementary needs for identification and their counterparts in adult life is readily apparent.[23]

The foundation of all identification is the infant's wishful fantasy of merging with or being one with the mother. Most people as adults seek closeness to other people, not only for the exchange of affection and support, but in addition to attain a sense of completeness or of being related to someone outside themselves. Something of this is seen in the wish to give and receive affection, part of the constructive drive. It is seen also in the wish for closeness to power, close social relationships in organizations, and the experience of identification with the leader as consent for him to lead. The need for "oneness" with the environment contributes to the need for using the work organization as a psychological anchor point and for using the relationship with the work organization to help maintain the feeling of psychological continuity.

This is not to imply that every person seeks closeness with every other person, or that all need closeness to others and to organizations in the same degree. Karl Menninger indicates that people need a range of contacts of different degrees of intensity and intermittency: very intimate (as in the family); moderately intimate (as with friends); less intimate (as with acquaintances of different groupings).[24] There is also a need to have some privacy to retreat from all of these.

Once there is sufficient closeness, a basis for even the most primitive of human ties, the relationship can be sustained only if it is gratifying or pleasurable. This means that the relationship must have more in it than expressions of affection. Adults expect the leader to recognize worth, work, and achievement. They expect any leader to be responsive to their needs. They also want rewarding social ties in their work. Above all, they want to respect themselves as competent adults.

A gratifying relationship for the child is one which provides support, protection, and guidance. Even in adult situations, persons with lesser power require the same of those who wield power over them. In an organizational society people require steps to be taken by their governments and organizational leaders to support and maintain their psychological well-being. They have long since come to anticipate that among the results of their delegation of political and economic power should be social and economic well-being. Such needs arise when the forces which impinge upon them are too great or complex for them to cope with alone or unaided. In varying degrees, they require the boss at work to help them grow on the job, to represent their feelings to higher management, to show them how to do better, and not to exploit their dependency on him. From the organization, among other things, they seek support, security and the gratification of legitimate dependency needs. Here the operation of transference to the organization is evident.

With gradual physiological maturation, the child wants to use his new-found body skills and to control himself. He demands freedom from the adult, and he regresses if that need is not met. Therefore, one of the consequent psychological needs is for growing independence. Out of his work, the adult seeks increasing mastery of himself and uses his work as one way of controlling his fantasies. The work organization provides avenues for mastery through the use of skills and competences. It reinforces psychological defenses and self-control. In social relationships the egalitarian tradition militates against submissiveness and encourages individual self-determination and democratic responsibility. With higher levels of education and greater pressure for controlled behavior, there are more refined avenues for the constructive expression of aggression. The need for meeting the demands of the superego is both a continuing and a pressing one for adults.

Identification is fostered for the child when he can test reality — make mistakes and learn from them, and observe the consequences of his behavior. An outcome of this experience is the later requirement of the individual that he have the freedom to try himself out, to make his own mistakes; he needs his work to enable him to contribute to solving problems and to his mastery of his world. This experience, too, fosters the concept of expertise as a condition of leadership and the recognition that the competence of a leader will vary with the situations in which he is expected to lead. It sets the stage for the expectation that a fundamental function of the leader is to manage the organization for survival.

Once the child feels supported in his quest for independence and is confident in his testing of reality, he begins to strive ambitiously and to work toward realistic achievements. In a democratic society he is urged to aspire to leadership, to envision himself as a potentially free adult. He is stimulated to initiative and responsibility. As an adult, he demands that the leader maintain democratic values. In his work he finds the opportunity to provide money, status, power for himself. He also seeks to reinforce his position in society, his role as head of the family, and his sense of worthiness. In part this comes from the work itself; in part from his role in the organization. In his ambitious strivings he fuses and channels his drives in keeping with the demands of the superego and reality, as well as expanding his ego.

A continuing part of the whole identification process is the need for expression of aggression through rivalry with favored models, from whom one then "takes" aspects of behavior which contribute to his growth.

The child must consolidate his views of the "good mother" and the frustrating or "bad mother" into a single view of the adult as both good and bad, not either alone. By learning to accept others as imperfect, he learns to accept himself as imperfect, to establish multiple identifications and to consolidate them into an identity. Adults do much the same. They turn to different people — in both social and organizational relationships — to learn different skills and to help them foster their diverse talents. They take traditions from society, aspirations from leaders, values from religion, purpose from institutions, and ideals from parents, welding them into a more or less compatible composite to maintain psychological equilibrium.

Mutual Means

These are the continuing needs to be fulfilled by the process of identification. Their fulfillment simultaneously fosters identification. When people seek to fulfill these needs in an organizational setting, out of their relationships to each other and to their leaders, the efforts by which they do so in turn become what Irving Knickerbocker has called *mutual means.*[25]

When the executive views his role as leadership-teaching, the essence of his task is to enhance the capacities of each of his subordinates and to enable them to strengthen each other toward accomplishing their mutual goals and fulfilling their joint needs. The leader's work is largely to create these common means by his own efforts and the activities of those whom he would lead. To the degree to which he is successful in creating such means, the leader will not need to persuade or propagandize his followers to follow for they will discover by their own experience their common objectives and their needs for each other and the organization. The leader will then have identification by consent.

How will the leader know when he has won such identification? One of the most striking illustrations is this description by a spokesman for a company of infantry trainees of their drillmaster: "He has instilled in us a pride in the army that I'm ashamed to say we didn't have when we first entered. He first taught each of us to be men. Next, he taught us to accept responsibilities. Then he gave us a gift of priceless value, to be 'men among men.' " [26]

The concept of mutual means becomes more imperative when it is recalled that traditional organizational structure is yielding to new forms of organization. These are likely to have one generic feature: temporary, expedient work groups.[27] They may be called task forces, project groups, or something else, but they will be concerned with accomplishing a given task. The new organizational forms will also be likely to have one central dynamic: instability. Groups will be formed, finish their task, and new units will be formed from previous groups for new tasks. The varied groups will share one property — whatever their task or composition, they will all be part of the same organization. They will be the woof interwoven with the warp which is the organization.

Another military example will clarify the issue. A World War I infantry division was organized along traditional chain of command lines. Some men gave the orders and others followed them. Masses of men and armament were mobilized to bring overwhelming force to bear on a given point or line. They were in relatively stationary positions for long periods of time. A contemporary bomber crew or mobile combat unit, however, is a highly trained group of specialists who work in intimate proximity with each other and who must function as a team. Often such a unit is far from its base and command. Decisions must frequently be made at the combat site. Such groups cannot be commanded as an infantry division of a bygone era. A commander has many such teams at his disposal, each often physically distant from the others, each with its own mission, and each always on the alert. He is first a trainer of his units, then a strategist; his units become their own tacticians.

The business executive is increasingly likely to find himself with units of organization which have the same qualities: teams of skilled personnel, charged with functional responsibility, oriented toward results, subject to rapid mobility requiring flexible adaptation, while simultaneously seeking to meet their own needs. The word "mutual" assumes greater meaning as the traditional concept of authority expressed in hierarchy diminishes in importance. People have to do for each other what in a more paternalistic and authoritarian structure superiors alone did for them.

Mutual means is not an idealistic conception of means-end relationships. The reader will find no clichés about "being nice to people" because "in the long-run it is good for business." Rather, this discussion is about psychological realities which result from the nature of the task to be performed, the organization required to accomplish it, and the people who are doing it.

Having reconceptualized psychological needs in this chapter, that framework can also serve to explicate mutual means. Recapitulating the psychological needs of people as a referent for the discussion makes it possible to more systematically organize a diverse range of activities or means which meet those needs. By juxtaposing both the needs and the activities which meet them, a psychologically sound rationale is provided for the activities. In addition, their direct relationship to the goal of organizational survival becomes clearer.

This frame of reference offers another advantage. There is an unremitting flow of psychological concepts, activities, and slogans in the management literature. The executive often gropes to evaluate them. Using this statement of needs, the reader has a stance from which he can do so. He may now ask how prospective and projected activities meet the organized structure of needs whose fulfillment facilitates identification. This is in contrast to judging such activities in terms of isolated "needs" which have little or no defined relationship to each other and less to organizational survival.

For example, a case is frequently made in the human relations literature for "giving people status." Doing so has often resulted in providing status symbols for people. These symbols may temporarily relieve underlying anxiety, or conceal or disguise it, or appease it. However, unless status is understood as a derivative of more basic needs and treated as such, efforts to meet these status needs are no more than gimmicks which serve to stimulate more feelings of anger, resentment and apathy. The title on the door and the rug on the floor only emphasize the hollowness of many "executive" positions, whose incumbents have no real function or power.

To facilitate discussion, the psychological needs as enumerated in this chapter will be grouped under the three headings specified in Chapter 2: ministration needs, maturation needs, and mastery needs. These will be considered as the separate but interrelated contexts of mutual means.

10 / Ministration Needs

Ministration needs, as defined earlier, are those which require someone else to do something to or for the person who has the need. These are needs which cannot be met by the person himself. Like an inaccessible itch, they must be restlessly endured. Sometimes, if endured long enough, some disappear. Those which are not fulfilled are usually psychologically veiled, leaving a residue like scar tissue on an unattended wound. Unsatisfied, they remain as a point of vulnerability for the person.

These needs are often inadequately encompassed under the rubric of "dependency needs" or the need for "inclusion." [1] Actually they extend beyond that category, which sometimes implies passive leaning on another. They are frequently the core of an interdependent relationship with the organization which meets them.[2] They might be called "guest needs" because they stem from the fact that the person who has the needs approaches the organization in which he seeks work to actively place himself with it for their fulfillment. That he may not recognize clearly the presence of such needs, and that seeking a job in a given organization is one way of fulfilling them, is irrelevant for present purposes.

In this sense the person is a "guest" and the organization, the "host." It is with respect to these needs, to recall an earlier metaphor, that the organization is the warp and the individual one fiber of the woof of the relationship. Ministration needs include the need for closeness, for gratification, and for support, protection, and guidance.

The Need for Closeness

Although always imperative, the need for closeness is most crucial at the beginning of a relationship with the organization. It is at this point that people become "attached," and the attaching process must take place at a time when they are most confused about the new job and the strange organization. They are more heavily dependent then than at any other time in their organizational careers. Unless someone takes them in hand, they literally cannot begin their work, let alone become part of the organization.

An adequate orientation reduces anxiety. Much of the turnover among newly employed people is due to their concern that they might fail, their feeling of desertion about being left to "muddle through," and their impression that no one really cares about them. When careful support is given to new people, turnover is reduced and productivity is increased.[3] Effective support includes those factors which usually are left out of introduction to an organization: orientation to the idiosyncrasies of those with whom they are to work, encouragement to seek out answers to their questions, and recognition of the inevitability of their anxiety.

One useful way of doing this is to have someone in authority talk informally with the new person or incoming group. In speaking with them, the "orienter" should not only tell them how to get around the organization physically but also psychologically. He should point out the various barriers to actions and how these are dealt with in the organization, how to address and inquire of various superior figures, and those kinds of questions and behavior which may threaten one or another person or department. The orienter should meet regularly with the new person or group during the first several weeks of employment to allow opportunity for expressing concerns about relationships with others, particularly supervisors, and to reinforce the guidance given earlier when the new people did not yet have an image of the organization clearly in mind.

The same process should be followed with people who are new to a given department even though they may be veterans in an organization. There is little recognition in management of the high cost in anxiety and dollars of the initial confusing adaptive experience. One vice-president of a major corporation reported that it took him a year to learn his way around the executive suite after his appointment. All the time he was inhibited lest he take one false step which would indicate to his superiors that he was incompetent.

For the young man coming into the business world, the process of introduction into the organization is a particularly critical one. The introduction must undo some of the distorted expectations and stereotypes which will interfere with his "attachment" and subsequent success. Simultaneously, it must take account of the fact that he comes with needs and expectations more refined and intense than those of a skilled blue-collar worker. As Edgar H. Schein has pointed out, if a new man is to become effective, he must have or acquire these characteristics: competence to get a job done; ability to accept organizational "realities"; ability to generate and sell new ideas; loyalty and commitment; high personal integrity and strength; capacity to grow.[4]

When the young man enters an organization, he customarily encounters two barriers, both of which can be lowered. Too often these serve only to reaffirm his stereotyped anticipations and to deny his needs. The two barriers are the organization's perceptions of him and its conceptions of how he is to be prepared for competence.

In addition to the traditional stereotypes which the executive has of the intellectual, Schein observes that there are specific biases about the new recruit to managerial ranks: He is overambitious and unrealistic in his expectations regarding the possibilities of advancement and increased responsibility. He is too theoretical, idealistic, and naive to be given an important initial assignment. He lacks the maturity and experience to be given executive responsibility. He is unduly security-conscious and disinclined to take risks. He is reluctant to recognize the difference between having a good idea and getting it implemented. He is potentially a highly useful resource for innovative ideas, new approaches, and better management, but he must be broken in before this resource becomes available to the organization.

Traditionally, the process of introduction and orientation is based on a tacit assumption that the incoming man must learn to delay his ambitions, suppress his fantasies of achievement and become "tamed." Most orientation programs assume that these controls are to be established by confrontation with harsh reality or by some degree of "caging." A wide variety of orientation strategies follow from this assumption, most of which work against the need for closeness.

In some organizations a man is left to his own devices to sink or swim. In others, he is confronted with an initial task which is intended to set him straight, the "upending" experience. Some rotate him through jobs, presumably to learn while he is working but often he does little genuine work. Some concentrate heavily on training, using work stints as incidental to and reinforcers of training. Schein advocates an integrative approach: after an initial period of work at a task for which he has immediate responsibility, the individual would undertake full-time training.

Immediate responsibility in keeping with his capacities makes a man an integral part of an organization. He is therefore "close" to it and to others in it. Subsequent training communicates that he is held "close," that is, in esteem, and is being strengthened for further maturation and more effective mastery. This opportunity to confront problems responsibly and to look at experiences conceptually also provides a sense of increasing mastery and stimulates the drive to become even more capable. It is basic to the identification process.

The necessity for something more than "sink or swim" is reinforced by Duncan Norton-Taylor's observation that companies frequently give incoming college men jobs that high school graduates could handle.[5] "American business needs to make the entrance job exciting, challenging and rewarding and to make it as big as possible rather than as small as possible," Drucker comments. "It needs to stop looking on men in their twenties as trainees, and to accept them instead as what they are — adults with more years of schooling under their belts than any earlier generation of men."[6]

A number of organizations are already doing so.[7] They put young men into positions where they simultaneously have important responsibilities and can get an overview of the whole operation before taking on specialized functions. Such an effort bespeaks organizational commitment to strive toward a management-employee relationship based on mutual respect and understanding rather than one which places major reliance upon such notions as "loyalty," "contentment," and "togetherness."[8] More than that, the first-year job challenge correlates strongly with later performance and success.[9]

To give a new man important responsibilities and to insure that he has a reasonable opportunity to fulfill them adequately requires placing him with a supervisor who is sensitive to his needs and capacities. This personifies the issue of "closeness." Schein advocates an apprenticeship under a particularly supportive kind of coach, or a part-time work, part-time training setting which gently nudges the new man into increasingly difficult tasks. To avoid or alleviate unrealistic expectations, he urges that the work of recruiters be coordinated with that of the first supervisors.

The issue of dependency immediately comes to the fore in the orientation relationship. In McGregor's words, "Psychologically, the dependence of the subordinate on his superiors is a fact of extraordinary significance."[10] The adult subordinate's dependence on his superiors reawakens emotions and attitudes which were part of his childhood relationships with his parents, and which apparently have long since been outgrown. However, young men coming into an organization are still struggling with their conflicts about becoming independent, even though they may be unaware of that struggle; the struggle is often reflected in problems with and about authority.[11] Ideally, the supervisors themselves should have long since resolved their dependency conflicts. Inasmuch as most adults continue to have such conflicts to varying degrees, supervisors will have to be prepared to contend with both their own and the younger men's efforts to manage these feelings.

Schein suggests training to heighten the supervisor's awareness of the difficult problems both supervisor and supervisee will face about this issue. He proposes that opportunities be provided for supervisors to communicate and consult with each other about supervisory problems. On the basis of earlier discussion in this book, it would be even more valuable for the superiors of supervisors to consider these issues so that they are recognized and accepted throughout the organizational hierarchy as an open problem in all authority relationships.

"Closeness" is often a feeling. Physical closeness is frequently, but not always, related to psychological closeness. People can live or work next to each other yet not feel close. The concern of this discussion is primarily with psychological closeness and secondarily with whatever physical or social circumstances foster it.

The issue of closeness does not diminish in importance with the termination of the introduction and orientation program. Psychological needs are neither present nor absent, nor do they occur as single forces. They always exist, in greater or lesser strength, as part of a configuration of needs. They should be conceived of like the facets of a prism, as planes of a whole personality. Observed closely, they will be seen to fuse into the core need — survival. Other needs — dependency, support, activity, achievement — appeared in this brief discussion of closeness. When other need-meeting activities come to the fore, closeness, too, will recur as a theme.

The varied ways in which closeness is related to other aspects of work are illustrated by several research findings. People in certain kinds of jobs, like service occupations, are more likely to have close friends doing the same or related work than are business people.[12] People who are less competitive with each other can be closer to each other spontaneously. In turn, this further emphasizes the need for more competitive people to be able to identify with the leader in order to be able to be closer to each other. Another way in which closeness arises is out of division of labor.[13] People tend to identify with those with whom their own acts are coordinated: the "we" of a team, a company, a military unit. People of similar personality types, closer to each other because they think the same way, are superior in decision-making when the issue calls for a thorough examination and choice among similar obvious alternatives.[14] People who are not so close, who come from different departments and levels, do better in exploring extreme solutions. The greater the number of followers whose values are similar to the leader's, the greater his authority will be.

The concern with one's ability to control his own psychological distance from others is an important component of the psychological contract a man has with the organization in which he works.[15] One major, often unconscious, basis for choosing a job or profession is how close a person has to be to others in the course of carrying it out. Another version of the same issue is whether a superior should visit his subordinates in their homes or let them call him by his first name.

Closeness is affected by the kind of work process an organization undertakes. People are further from each other in an assembly line operation than in a group task, in scattered selling assignments than in a chorus. Closeness is also governed by the size and degree of formality of an organization. There is merit to the conception that no organization which exists as a separate identifiable entity should be larger than four hundred people. Ideally, too, it should have no more than five hierarchical levels. No person should have more than six others reporting to him so that he can both support them adequately and be their contact for interrelationships with other work groups. The larger the organization, and therefore the greater the distance of people from each other and from the leader, the more tension there is between superiors and subordinates and the more alienated they are from each other.[16]

This discussion has several implications for the leader-teacher. He must recognize the basic importance of the attaching process. He would do well to define for himself and his colleagues some of their conceptions about incoming young men and how they learn best. He can examine their validity and consciously rectify misconceptions. Once he has clarified his perceptions of new men, he can design a strategy to foster closeness tailored to his organization. The specific orientation program he evolves will be supportive and also will encourage responsible action. It will automatically take account of the dependency needs of the new men if such needs have been openly discussed throughout the managerial hierarchy. Once he examines the organization's work processes to see which aspects militate against closeness, he can then evolve methods for ameliorating the increased distance.

This process usually facilitates identification and alleviates early turn-over. It will not do so for all people, nor should it. Many young people need to experiment with several different kinds of jobs in as many organizations to be able to discern which meet their needs best. In fact, it probably would be a good idea to have young men leave the organization after a few years. If they return after trying others, both they and the executive can be more certain of the man-organization fit. The more effective the orientation program, the more clearly the younger man can visualize the organization and make a judgment about his future with it. Young men's choices can then be made positively on the basis of satisfaction and need-fulfillment, rather than negatively because of frictions and difficulties.

The Need for Gratification

The need for gratification in one's work is self-evident. Part of the gratification, John Gardner comments, comes from doing something about which he cares deeply. "And if he is to escape the prison of the self," he adds, "it must be something not essentially egocentric in nature." [17] This means that some aspect of one's work should be in the service of an ideal or other people. In most elementary terms such a part of one's work is a way of giving.

Much of the gratification from and in work results from the fulfillment of other needs. Gratification is a sense of feeling good about and within oneself. It is not necessarily to be equated with pleasure; to attain the summit of Mt. Everest is gratifying but the experience is hardly pleasure-able. Gratification may result from enjoyment, relief, discharge of tension, relaxation, reduction of fear, rescue, and many other experiences.

One form of gratification is described in the contemporary research of Herzberg and his colleagues.[18] Herzberg differentiates between those aspects of work which he calls "satisfiers" and those which he describes as "dissatisfiers." Those job factors which provide the most permanent gratification, the "satisfiers," are achievement, recognition, pleasure in the work itself, responsibility (stature more than status), and advancement. Traditionally, management has tried to make work more gratifying by offering good working conditions, job security, salary, and similar attractions.

These fringe or "hygienic" factors are important because they are "dissatisfiers" if inadequate, but they do not produce the same long lasting motivation and dedication as the "satisfiers" which Herzberg has enumerated.

The Herzberg "satisfiers" are not unitary; they are not satisfying just because they are called that. What makes them gratifying is that they serve a variety of the facets of personality differentiated here. Gratification is like that; it derives from many dimensions of experience and personality. The problem in trying to understand and meet the need for gratification is that executives equate gratification with pleasure and look upon it as being a single, pleasant experience. They then fall too easily into the trap of trying to please people by being "nice" to them, and finally become disillusioned when that effort fails, as it must. Motivation is more complicated than that. Gratification is an epiphenomenon — something which appears concomitant with and as the result of something else. It has no specific referent and therefore cannot be satisfied directly.

The Need for Support, Protection, and Guidance

Support is one of the basic dimensions of good leadership.[19] It is also a *sine qua non* of organizational life. Despite its importance, the most glaring deficiency in contemporary organizational functioning is the almost universal inadequacy of support. This is evident in the repetitive response to a simple question. If one asks people in almost any organization, "How do you know how well you are doing?" 90 percent of them are likely to respond, "If I do something wrong, I'll hear about it." Too often this topic is discussed as if praise were the answer; it is not. What people are saying in such a response is that they do not feel sufficient support from their superiors. Praise without support is an empty gesture.

As in the family, the most critical support comes from superiors who have greater power. It includes not just approval and praise, but many other actions as well. Support is reflected in positive answers to questions which Likert and his colleagues frequently use in survey research, such as: "To what extent does your supervisor try to understand your problems and do something about them?" "How much help do you get from your superior in doing your work?" "To what extent is he interested in helping you get the training which will assist you in being promoted?" "How fully does he share with you information about the company, its financial conditions, earnings?" "How much confidence and trust does he have in you and you in him?" [20]

Support produces more effective solutions. A foreman who uses a problem-solving approach with his people, supporting them in their search for effective solutions, is more likely to obtain solutions of high quality and acceptance than one who applies extrinsic incentives.[21] Support is essential to learning.

Support is more than just something a man needs for self-serving reasons. It is related directly to the productivity of the organization, and to cascading morale. According to the study by David G. Bowers, there is a high positive relationship, for example, between a supervisor's supportiveness and the self-esteem of his foremen. There is also a high positive relationship between the foreman's self-esteem and his estimate of what his subordinates think of him. According to the research findings, his estimate bears little relationship to the actual attitude of his subordinates. As his self-esteem diminishes and as his estimate of their attitude becomes poorer, he alienates himself from his subordinates; he assembles them as a group more often, but to exercise his authority rather than to seek their advice. As this occurs, his behavior toward his subordinates becomes less supportive.[22]

The destructive effects of pressure without support have long been known. Over the years a series of studies by members of the Institute for Social Research of the University of Michigan and researchers in other universities have shown repeatedly that low production groups are characterized by supervisors who exert pressure for production but do not support their people. High production units are characterized by supervision which is experienced as less threatening and more supportive. High production supervisors tend to be more employee-centered; low production supervisors more work-centered. High production heads are more democratic, invite suggestions and participation of their subordinates; they delegate more and spend less time in actual production work. Low production supervisors, in contrast, are more authoritarian, dictatorial, and dogmatic.

Subsequent studies have indicated that support does not mean being preoccupied with "human relations" considerations at the expense of the task. Rather, the supervisor who is most competent, has three kinds of skills.[23] To coordinate the activities of one organizational family with another, the supervisor must have administrative competence. To integrate organizational objectives with individual member needs, he must have human relations competence. To accomplish his other assigned tasks, including the performance of technical operations, he must have technical competence.

Likert advances the principle of supportive relationships as a guide for evolving the operating procedures most suitable for a particular company in the light of its history and current situation.[24] Under such a principle, the leadership and other processes of the organization must insure that each member will view the interactions and relationships which occur in the course of his work experience as supportive. The corollary of this principle is that an organization effectively utilizes its human potential only when each person belongs to a work group which has a high degree of group loyalty, effective skills of interaction, and high performance goals which it has helped set itself.

One condition for supportive relationships, according to Likert, is that the form of the organization should be one of multiple, overlapping groups in which each supervisor is a "linking pin" — a leader of the group below and also a member in the group above. In addition, persons at all levels are members of other groups (committees, representational groups, and the like) which help link the organization laterally. In such a structure, traditional methods of job organization and work facilitation, "scientific management," should be used as means to an end rather than an end in themselves. Traditional measurements of performance should be supplemented with periodic appraisals of human organization variables. All of these data should be used to appraise the health of the organization, and to bring about an awareness of where weaknesses exist and where improvements are needed.

There will be a certain level of conflict, pressure, and tension in an organization when such a principle is used. Likert argues, however, that if this principle is implemented, all levels of the organization have more influence and the social system thus constructed is tighter than it would be otherwise. If the principle is applied correctly, the manager does not lose influence because others become influential; instead, he gains influence. In terms of the central theme of this book, there is greater identification with him and less resistant defensiveness.

The research of Eric Trist and his colleagues at London's Tavistock Institute further illustrates the point. Trist contends that there is an optimum level of grouping which can be determined only by an analysis of the requirements of the technical system with which people are working. The most effective group does not occur on the basis of people's friendship on the job, but rather on the basis of task orientation. Trist reports that grouping produces its main psychological effects when it leads to a system of work roles such that the workers are primarily related to each other by way of the requirements of task performance and task interdependence. When this task orientation is established the worker has a range of mutually supportive roles (mutually supportive with respect to performance and to carrying stress that arises from the task). As the role system becomes more mature and integrated, it becomes easier for a worker to understand and appreciate his relation to the group. The critical prerequisites for a composite system are an adequate supply of the required special skills among members of the group and conditions for developing an appropriate system of roles.[25]

The effects of being able to evolve a composite system are demonstrated in the Tavistock research. From their studies of mining groups, Trist and his colleagues report that work groups as large as fifty in number can be capable, under certain conditions, of self-sustained regulation. When a composite group was formed of men with many skills, and the group was made jointly responsible for all its tasks, the men rotated tasks, shifts, and activity subgroups among themselves. Comparing the composite group with miners working under traditional organization, the Tavistock researchers found that nonproduction work took up 32 percent of the time in conventional groups but only one half of 1 percent in the composite group. The absence rate was 20 percent of the possible shifts in the conventional groups, 8.2 percent in the composite groups. The conventional groups were never ahead of their cycle timetable; in fact, they were behind in 69 percent of their cycles. The composite group was ahead in 95 percent of its cycles. Productivity was 3.5 tons per man-shift in the conventional group versus 5.3 tons for the composite group.

Some would argue that support from peers also means control by them and therefore group participation constricts the individual. Nowhere is the evidence about group support more impressive than from the studies in group risk-taking.[26] The evidence indicates that groups of people are more willing to take risks and make better decisions than the same people would as individuals. Apparently, group risk-taking provides for greater diffusion of responsibility and the likelihood of fewer feelings of guilt if there is failure. Some individuals are always better than the average of the group, but on the whole, group decision-making has much to commend it.

The importance of yet another form of peer support is reflected in military experience. S. L. A. Marshall, the military reporter and historian, points out that during World War II, the army acted toward speech as if it were afraid of it. "In training, men are told to think," he says, "yet they are never told that if they remain dumb in combat, they will commit slow suicide." Comparing World War I with World War II, he reports that there was more "talking it up" among infantrymen in the first war, more shouting of directions to fellows, and more discussion of the situation with anyone else close to the soldier than in World War II. Marshall complains that the army of World War II was "about the mutest army we ever sent to war." No one ever said to them, "When you prepare to fight, you must prepare to talk. You must learn that speech will help you save your situation. You must be alert at all times to let others know what is happening to you. It is when you talk to others and they join with you that your action becomes important." In many situations, he reports, when the soldiers engaged, though the men fought willingly, they fought to no avail because the words which might have held them together were left unsaid.[27]

To point out the support function of the work group and the advantages of group participation in decision-making and productivity is not to offer that practice as a panacea.[28] The mutual means for meeting any or several needs are necessary but not by themselves sufficient conditions for organizational survival. All supervisory practices and motivational efforts are affected by various forms of environmental and operational constraint. Therefore they must be viewed as a configuration. The question for the executive must be not is this or that technique good, but rather, "What is the impact of the total effort?"

Robert Dubin has noted some of the constraints on participation. Reevaluating the evidence, he points out that worker autonomy is only one factor contributing to differences in productivity. He reports: "When worker autonomy . . . is combined with two other dimensions of supervisory behavior found significant in combination in English factories, the combination still accounts for less than one-fifth of the variance in productivity. Furthermore, there is reason to believe that worker autonomy may be relevant to batch- or unit-production technologies, but probably not to mass production technologies, and almost certainly not to continuous process technologies." [29]

In other words, where there is no possibility of forming a group around the task, then there can be no group participation in decision-making. Whether certain technologies actually do make it impossible to form groups is another question.[30] Men who operate as isolated technicians can still be brought together to talk about the problems of the plant as a whole. Management does not often conceive of such individuals as being capable of discussion and decision-making at the plant level.

The importance and limitations of peer or group support is reflected in other ways. Problems requiring reaction to environmental changes are more quickly solved under shared responsibility.[31] Problems involving co-ordination of action among operators are more efficiently solved with a competent centralized authority. If the leader has little leadership ability, groups produce inferior performance on both types of problems.

Support, then, is a multifaceted phenomenon. It is a basic psychological platform made up of style of leadership, method of operation or pro-duction, interlocking of roles, participation in decision-making, and, some-times, simple human contact which makes help possible. A group of sub-ordinates will more likely become supportive to each other and thereby, cohesive, when their respective skills contribute directly to their joint and collective mastery of the work. No amount of friendly congeniality will supplant this requirement. Given joint and collective task mastery, close-ness will arise from the mutual support. The members of the group will be able to meet many of their own ministration needs. They will care for and about each other.

The lessons for the executive-teacher hardly need elaboration. Support is definable, palpable and manageable. It is attainable by managerial in-vention. Specifically, the executive can weigh the kind of supervisors to whom the younger men are assigned to ascertain their effectiveness as agents of growth. If he cannot tell in other ways, he can learn by attitude studies of subordinates which supervisors are too angry or too dependent to be trusted to support new men (or the older ones, for that matter). Job descriptions and definitions of responsibility can contribute to defining complementary task roles. However, often the work group itself can report what types of additional skills are needed to accomplish its job.

If the task itself is defined clearly enough, the executive has to create mutually supportive groups whenever possible, even when the work of the individuals might seem to be readily accomplished by themselves. If they do not need each other for task accomplishment, they will not use each other. If they do need one another, the channels for cooperation and communication are open. Such group organization also diminishes rivalry for the attention and favor of the superior and fosters interdependence.

Whether the group can work together depends on how well the leader facilitates the ability of the individuals to speak candidly about problems with him and with each other. It is the leader's focus on facilitating work performance which makes support an instrument for individual and group achievement.

Protection is the second dimension of good leadership, but is rarely discussed in the management literature, and then only in terms of "safety" needs.[32] Yet it is expected that those who have leadership power will be protective in varying ways. Such a tacit assumption occurs in many different contexts ranging from prayer to the petitioning of public officials. A man who loses his job because of changes in technology usually feels his company has not adequately protected him. Protection is a major ministration function of a union.

There is evidence to indicate that when a supervisor encourages efficiency at the same time he is "going to bat" for his subordinates, his work group reacts with high standards of performance.[33] When he does not "go to bat" for them, they respond to his efforts toward efficiency with low standards of performance. The same study suggests that when reward for efficiency is accompanied by close supervision, the work group attains its highest cohesion. The supervisor in such instances protects each individual member and the work group as a whole by "holding them together."

Another form of protection is protection against the jealousies and personal maneuvers of senior competitors.[34] Still another, particularly for younger and more creative people, is protection from their friends. "The first restraining force for one who steps off the path of custom . . . is the clutching hands of intimates and colleagues," observes John Gardner.[35] Often supervisors have the same effect: "You don't get paid to think."

With so much pressure for action in the business world, the irreplaceable asset of the executive is the one most flagrantly dissipated: time. Superiors rarely recognize their responsibility to protect the thinking of their subordinates, thereby exacerbating the impulse to act at the expense of thought. Young executives particularly are entangled in the conflict between reflection and production.[36] The superior must protect the subordinate by requiring thinking time and by refusing to let the subordinate equate busy work with deliberation.

A more common form of protection is that provided by having some systematic program for being aware of individual skill, experience, talent, and achievement. Ralph Cordiner calls for a practice of company-wide opportunities and movement of people to avoid the tendency of managers to choose their successors from among those few people who report to them. A paper program is never enough. "The chief executive," Cordiner asserts, "should make it a point to know, personally, the most promising men in the organization who might someday qualify for the highest positions of responsibility. He should see that these men receive challenging and educational assignments that will help them stretch their capacities." [37]

Job definition and description, continuing education, adequate communication, and participation in decision-making are all forms of protection. An open, supportive relationship with one's superior and with the organization at large, where the subordinate can actively look out for his own interests, offers the most effective possibilities for protection.

Guidance, the third dimension of good leadership, includes both the step-by-step learning, the building blocks of ego development, as well as the opening of vistas and the encouragement to pursue them. This might be called the facilitation of the learning process. In business and industry, guidance usually appears under the heading of management or executive development and the opening of vistas, under the rubric of coaching and counseling.

There are two schools of thought about executive development.[38] The life process theory says that executives are products of years of systematic guidance. Executive development is therefore a form of character building; brief courses and programs are useless. The other school says that executive development is chiefly a result of being exposed to the use of the right skills at the right time. These skills are to be subsequently reinforced by an understanding of their psychological, sociological, and economic underpinnings. There is no clear evidence for either position and no necessary conflict between the two. As everyone knows from his own experience, personality is an unfolding process; however, single events or brief experiences have important impacts. Most of those who have devoted considered effort to executive development agree that the organizational climate of the firm — rules, procedures, methods, and skills that the leading executives in that firm adopt — determine what the potential executive believes and does. Identification once again becomes a critical issue.

Management development programs have been subject to diverse and often severe criticism. George Odiorne lists six fallacies in such programs.[39]

First, self-development in a full-length mirror. Odiorne complains about those courses which require the participant to take an intensive psychological look at his feelings. He contends that one cannot observe the system at a distance and that a person's behavior does not always resemble the inner experiences which accompany it. A man may feel one way and act another; in an out-of-company course, it is hard to tell which he does in his real life circumstances. Second, imitating the presently successful. What is expedient today may not work tomorrow; such teaching should not be focused on the methods and experiences of today's leaders. Third, the myth of the executive personality. Odiorne holds that there are no definable personalities of people who have become successful executives. People who develop in themselves the readiness and ability to take appropriate actions which suit the situation of the moment become successful executives. Fourth, the Horatio Alger Illusion. Not everyone can become an executive, even by dint of hard work and development programs. Fifth, the false line of the secret weapon. There is no single special kind of knowledge which will make one a successful executive. Sixth, training which breeds self-awareness. He questions whether becoming more aware of oneself and his impact on others is necessarily management improvement.

These criticisms argue against a magical conception of management development. In their specifics they are less powerful. The more aware a person is of his own behavior and its impact on others, the more opportunity he has to control it voluntarily. Too much behavior "happens" involuntarily and often at considerable cost to the person and the organization. Ignorance of oneself may serve to preclude painful questions about oneself but it does not contribute to resolving problems that he causes. As long as a man's personality is his most important instrument for occupational success, he pays a price for remaining ignorant of it. He is doomed to repeat the same mistakes. The modern business world has increasingly less room for incompetence, whether it be the inefficiency of a machine or the ignorance of a man. The conception of automated processes, cybernation, hinges on direct feedback of performance to both machine and man.

Odiorne is on stronger ground with respect to executive personality and undue attention to pragmatic methods which enjoy contemporary success. However, it is better to use what is effective as a point of departure rather than to ignore what can be learned from it. By studying the relationship of given personalities to specific executive roles and by distilling wisdom from successful effort, a body of knowledge can be developed and transmitted. Though learning such knowledge will not by itself make anyone a successful executive, it can become an important ingredient in the preparation of would-be executives. While only one of a score of equally capable executives may become the principal one of a company, the rest also will have improved their skills by learning.

The criticisms of Raymond Katzell are more useful. Katzell describes three possible weaknesses in educational programs for executives.[40] He says that they apparently are not sufficiently integrated into a total program. Katzell contends that there is too little attention to the emotional barriers to effective action, and that there may be danger in overemphasizing administrative techniques at the cost of knowledge. Thus, he argues against isolated gimmick-type technique programs and for a continuous process of learning. As would most psychologists, Katzell indicates that understanding one's own feelings is basic to self-controlled action. He refers to less generalized weaknesses such as the lack of correspondence between development programs and individual needs or organizational climate. Sometimes such programs are directed to problems over which the participants have no control; or they may be inadequate to the issues to which they address themselves.

Douglas McGregor points out that contemporary elaborate programs for management development provide few opportunities for career development of professional specialists.[41] He delineates the difference this way: For the professional person, promotion or advancement means receiving rewards and recognition for becoming more proficient at his professional work. Whether in private practice or in academic institutions, he is accustomed to choosing among alternative opportunities in terms of whether they will facilitate his proficiency. Thus, the ideal of many lawyers is to be a lawyer's lawyer. Management, on the other hand, is accustomed to exercising a substantial amount of "career authority" over its managerial employees at all levels. The individual is evaluated, promoted, rotated, and transferred in terms of the needs of the organization, almost irrespective of his personal career motivations. These incompatible points of view, McGregor says, are certain to come into conflict as professional employees become more numerous and indispensable to industry. Taken a step further, the conflict already exists not solely because professional employees are becoming more numerous, but because executives are becoming increasingly professional and will therefore have more of the values of professionals.

Criticisms of middle-management development are more narrow and specific. Among them, these are typical: (1) there is a lack of acceptance of development among middle management personnel; (2) there is lack of time among such personnel to attend programs; (3) it is difficult to determine the training needs of middle managers; and (4) there is inadequate time to present such programs. Typically such criticisms arise when executive development is delegated to training personnel who have little power to influence the organizational climate, who are asked to create "package programs," and who have little thoughtful support from top management.

Furthermore, when a self-improvement program is simply imposed on those lower in the hierarchy, they will view it with fear and suspicion. Some, bitter about being "sent to school," have little wish to learn.[42] They perceive such programs as criticism of them, often do not understand what is expected of them, and look upon the program as a waste of time. Their anger becomes especially acute if they are evaluated on their performance in training when they believe they should be judged only on their managerial accomplishments.

These criticisms argue for the planned, continuous involvement of the executive in the definition and refinement of the career goals of the subordinate. His teaching should be formally conceived and integrated with his ongoing executive work. If the prime task of the executive is to coordinate and lead the efforts of others toward organizational goals, he must give careful attention to helping his subordinates understand and take into consideration people's feelings. Teaching content and function in the context of feelings, he makes it more possible for subordinates to use their combined learning for solving organizational problems and accomplishing organizational goals. The contemporary practice of teaching management content and human relations as if they were independent of each other, and of assigning the teaching to training directors or extramural programs, vitiates much of the teaching effort.

Narrowing the executive's teaching activities to specifics, he can ask these questions as a basis for his efforts: What does the subordinate want to learn in the next year? How will that propel him toward more distant goals? How much of that can he learn in this position? What does he need to know of which he may as yet be unaware? What does the executive or the organization require him to know and how much of it is to be learned in the present experience? Combining the answers to these questions into a general statement, how can that generalization be subdivided into monthly, even weekly, units of experience and teaching?

Often the most important things a man has to teach are precisely those which cannot be so easily specified. The executive should ask himself what are the most important lessons he has learned, what were the most difficult obstacles to surmount, what events caused him the most pain? Although his subordinate can only experience vicariously what the executive did, he can learn from that experience if it is introduced as a consideration toward better problem-solving.

Suggesting that the executive ask questions and make plans implies that teaching by experience alone is uneconomic. A planned effort gives the teaching its proper perspective, takes into account the range of content, and insures that both subordinate and organization will receive their just due. This is not an argument for rigidity, for the lesson plan of the elementary school teacher. The executive's "plan" should be his road map, and not be mistaken for the road itself. Like all maps, it enables him to choose alternative routes with varying circumstances.

There is much argument about teaching methods: lecture versus group discussion; teacher-centered versus student-centered. At one extreme is the free-floating method of group dynamics; at the other, the typical university lecture course. The particular method an executive uses obviously will have to be related to the subject matter or experiences to be learned, his own relative proficiency with different skills, and the context in which the learning takes place. Sometimes he will teach by assigning tasks, at other times by communicating specific knowledge or by asking judicious questions. The ideal method for more formal teaching, if there is one, seems to combine both the leader-centered and the student-centered methods.[43] This combination means that the teacher presents the main points, followed by a discussion for purposes of clarification and elaboration. Whatever the varied methods, organized effort will assure sequential learning, integrated experience, and discernible achievement. Its results will be evident to both the learner and the teacher.

In the process of organizing for teaching, the executive will find himself changing with each experience. The fact of his teaching will compel him to reflect upon what he is doing, as well as upon the nature and problems of the business. Stimulated by the need to convey his thoughts, he will think more. Required by the subordinate's questions to justify his actions or decisions, he will examine his rationale. He himself will continue to grow, as all good teachers do.

To teach effectively, to guide well, the leader-teacher might take advantage of the work of those who have studied the learning process intensively. Jerome Bruner points out that the single most characteristic thing about human beings is that they learn. The will to learn, called curiosity, is inherent and needs only to be stimulated. The teacher is basically a stimulator. The reward of curiosity, Bruner goes on to say, is its own gratification. "We would think it preposterous if somebody sought to reward us with praise or profit for having satisfied our curiosity," he remarks. In his words, curiosity feeds "on a rich diet of impressions" implemented by concrete acts.[44]

If curiosity provides the internal incentive to learning, uncertainty is the external counterpart. Faced by that which is vague, inchoate, or diffuse, a person tries to make it less so in order to master and control it. Every scientific advance, as well as every step in intellectual growth, follows the same pattern. Each moves from the passivity of curiosity to the activity of satisfying it and mastering the unknown. As Bruner describes it, the wish to master becomes interwoven with the drive to achieve competence. Both are further stimulated by attainment; the more one becomes skilled, the greater his incentive to learn. Several forces contribute to attainment or achievement. The task to be learned has to be delimited: it must have a beginning and an end. It must have built-in measures of accomplishment. Achievement must bring approval from respected figures.

Bruner's discussion of the learning process is essentially a recapitulation of the identification process. When a person has learned, he has become a judge of his own efforts, incorporating within himself the judgments of those he esteems as well as those resulting from his own experience. He has then become independent.

The last motive for learning Bruner calls reciprocity — a deep human need to respond to others and to operate jointly with them toward an objective. This was called "closeness" earlier in this chapter. The learning problem, says Bruner, is often the failure to enlist the natural energies that sustain spontaneous learning-curiosity, a desire for competence, aspiration to emulate a model, and a deep-sensed commitment to the web of social reciprocity.[45]

But, he points out, learning is not just a matter of feelings. In order to use knowledge outside the teaching situation, the student must have an understanding of the fundamental structure of whatever subjects are taught. Basic ideas and themes must be learned in progressively more complex forms, against their broader context. Furthermore, spontaneity — the shrewd guess, the fertile hypothesis, the courageous leap to a tentative conclusion — is to be encouraged by a teacher who feels free to be intuitive. "If the teacher will not risk a shaky hypothesis," asks Bruner, "why should the student?"

Bruner's discussion of the cognitive and emotional aspects of learning recalls the previous discussion about the most effective modes of supervision — those which concentrate on both the task and people's feelings about their work. The maturation of the ego, the growth of the individual, requires both. Perhaps it is no longer so strange to think of the business as an institution of learning.

Nathaniel Cantor puts it in a somewhat different way.[46] In his view, learning which makes a difference in one's behavior is not additive but integrative. A fact attains meaning for the individual only as it is assimilated and integrated into his continuing experience. For Cantor, the essence of learning is to see interrelationships and to readjust and modify behavior. To learn is to reshape, reform, and remake one's experiences. Cantor gives recognition to the emotional side of learning. There is always a struggle, he says, between the ties of the old knowledge and the challenges of the new; and the executive-teacher runs the danger of defeating his own efforts by pointing out what is "wrong" with the learner. A person must have some certainty about himself and what he thinks he knows in order to feel that he has some mastery over himself and his fate. This need for certainty militates against learning too much too fast. By definition, to learn is to be self-critical, to doubt what one knows. Doubt is tolerable in small doses.

Devoting so much attention to the process of learning might seem to imply that what is learned is unimportant. Not so. The assumption here is that the role of the executive has its own content and demands expert knowledge of many kinds. Since the content will vary from one position to another, and among companies, there is no need for elaborate discussion of content here. In that area the executive is likely to be his own best expert. However, there are various ways of conceiving the content to be learned. David Ewing offers one way which transcends traditional functional lines like marketing, finance, and production.[47] He describes three layers of managerial knowledge: (1) methods and techniques for solving already defined problems; (2) realities inside and outside the organization that affect management decisions; (3) information affecting the choice of desirable goals, policies and standards. Although these layers are not neatly separated, they differ markedly in emphasis, and there are significant qualitative differences between them.

There is an infinite number of ways to organize content. The executive himself is the best judge of what he can teach. Anyone else's prescriptions for organizing content become "canned" modes of presentation. They vitiate the power of the teacher's spontaneity. But if the content is to reach the student-subordinate, in keeping with the conceptions elucidated by Bruner and Cantor, it must do three things. First, it must touch the learner where he "hurts." It must relate to what he wants and needs to know, what concerns him. Second, it must put a name on or organize what he has not known so that it can become real for him, and therefore, capable of being mastered. Finally, what he is taught must open avenues for action commensurate with his position, skills, and knowledge.

In addition to intellectual content, the senior executive must teach skills. The most important of these is skill in human relations. The executive's own behavior is the model he will communicate to his subordinates. What he does will have to be the basis for what he would teach. There is little point in trying to teach what he himself does not strive to practice.

Second to his own practices, the most useful device for teaching human relations skills is coaching. "To be a coach," says Mortimer Feinberg, an industrial psychologist, "is to be both informational and inspirational. The coach integrates the unique capacities of the members of his team. He also lifts people up and out of themselves." [48]

The executive may feel inadequate to such a task. However, there is no reason why he cannot improve his coaching skills. Coaching skills of managers can be improved, provided that a sound series of actions is carried out with persistence. Walter Mahler suggests a plan for acquiring coaching skills that would include periodic instruction on coaching techniques built around both day-to-day coaching and more formal coaching as in performance reviews, with "bench marks" for improvement.[49] Inasmuch as the executive will be coaching in one form or another, it should not seem frightening to suggest skill practice and training in that technique while he is doing it.

The third device in teaching human relations skills is through the review of the subordinate's experiences with other people. Some of this will be integrated in coaching; some, in more structured learning experiences. It will not be surprising if the executive feels himself to be insecure in teaching human relations skills. Few executives are as formally knowledgeable about this aspect of their work as they are about their more traditional management skills like finance or marketing, or even engineering. Professional knowledge about human relations rests largely in behavioral scientists. Unless the executive is himself a behavioral scientist, his reluctance is understandable. Yet, such skills can be taught by the executive, with the help of various kinds of training experiences conducted by professionals.

Robert Katz has proposed a four-phase program for developing such skills, which is adapted here.[50] Once the subordinate has reasonable confidence in the superior and is comfortable in his new relationships, Phase I can be undertaken. In this stage the goal is to help the subordinate increase his awareness of the adequacies and inadequacies of his observations and actions involving others, and his reasons for acting as he did. This can be done by asking him to report on and discuss some of his interactions. The superior should raise questions with him about how he thinks this or that person felt, and how he felt in those circumstances. The focus is not on determining right or wrong, but on bringing psychological considerations into continuing view.

Once the subordinate understands that psychological considerations are part of his business with the superior and spontaneously brings them into their discussions, the stage is set for Phase II. In this phase, continued emphasis is given to developing self-awareness and sensitivity by carrying on the same kinds of discussions. An additional focus is introduced: the development of knowledge, attitudes, and skills which will enable the subordinate to gather facts and data and put them together more understandably and effectively. The subordinate has to learn what to look for, to do so objectively, and to gather and organize the data necessary for understanding. A good medium for doing this is the written case study. The subordinate now can be asked to look more comprehensively into human relations problems in the organization and to write up his findings for discussion. Summarizing a case demonstrates how difficult it is to get an accurate view of the situation. It helps the subordinate to experience a new way of thinking about human relations problems. Among the questions he can ask to help him are these:

Who or what is the problem? Who is "hurting"?

What does the problem mean psychologically to the people involved?

What are their respective feelings as they express them? What feelings which cannot be openly expressed, does the case writer infer from what is said?

Is the problem a chronic one, or is it acute? What does that imply for possible solution? What are possible alternatives and their psychological as well as economic costs?

Not all problems are solvable; is this one?

Having alerted himself to interpersonal relationships and particularly to his own impact on others, and having evolved a way of organizing and studying human relations problems, the subordinate is ready for Phase III. Now he returns to a more intensive look at his own experiences. In this phase, he continues his discussions with his superior, but a new dimension is added, a process record. The process record is a written report of what went on in an interaction between himself and another person. It is a moment by moment description of what went on between them, what was said and what was done. This can then be reviewed in discussion about what each person's respective statements and actions communicated to the other person. Every word and action communicates feelings which can be understood if they are given attention. A process record and subsequent discussion heightens the subordinate's recognition of that fact. Such books as Ruesch and Kees' *Nonverbal Communication* and Berne's *Games People Play* can help the subordinate become alert to these communications.[51] Another helpful technique is to have the subordinate tape record his interactions for later discussion. In Phase III, the subordinate learns to understand in greater depth the communications of others and to express himself more clearly.

In Phase IV, these experiences are consolidated. One way of doing so is by role-playing exercises. Norman R. F. Maier has refined role-playing to a highly successful device for teaching human relations skills.[52] He describes this tecnique and cases for carrying it out in several books. Other consolidation experiences are group dynamics laboratories, managerial grid exercises, and seminars conducted by psychiatrists and psychologists. Consolidation experiences are more valuable when both superior and subordinate have had the same ones and thereby have a common communications language.

Throughout this discussion of ministration needs there has been a repetitive pattern of sequential experiences for the subordinate or learner. The pattern is the same whether the focus is orientation, support, or guidance. In the beginning of a relationship, the new person is anxious and threatened. These feelings inhibit learning and adaptation. The first step in his new experience, which will determine the success of the rest, is to learn that the superior understands and accepts his feelings of inadequacy and insecurity. This step is completed when he recognizes that the superior wants to help him become more adequate and secure with respect to his job. At this time, the subordinate is most dependent on the superior for detailed guidance in those areas in which he is ignorant. The subordinate is also dependent on the superior to open the discussion of his natural anxieties so that they may be dispelled. Few subordinates can spontaneously initiate discussion of their anxieties.

In the second step, the subordinate moves toward greater initiative. He may check first with the superior, particularly if he is doubtful about a potential action. Here, the superior intervenes only if asked for help. If he intervenes too soon, the subordinate justifiably feels hostile; if he does so too late, the subordinate feels temporarily helpless. Both feelings interfere with the superior-subordinate relationship. Usually, superior and subordinate become accommodated to each other.

This accommodation is reflected in the third step. The subordinate acts without checking. Only when he specifically needs help does he turn to the superior. As the superior responds to these requests, the two men develop a complementary role relationship. They need each other to accomplish their joint responsibilities. This needed relationship fosters mutual understanding and trust.

In the fourth step, the superior's role is one of watchful waiting. The subordinate acts independently, but with the knowledge that he can always call upon the interested superior when the complexity of the task exceeds his experience. In the fifth step, the superior may intervene to correct occasional errors. His task is now largely to help the subordinate polish, expand, and become more sophisticated in what he has learned.

These stages are more apparent than real. They should be accomplished in approximately eighteen months with a superior; the process will take longer in highly complex tasks. The stages fuse with each other. Having attained a higher level, the subordinate may regress in the face of unusual anxiety or a task which exceeds his capacities. Often the subordinate can retrospectively recall a turning point, a threshold of confidence, in his experience with a given job or superior. After that he no longer feels uncertain, afraid, and strange. His image of himself in that role shifts from negative to positive. He is "in." The identification process for that stage of development is complete.[53]

The term "coaching" has been used to refer to the communication of the teaching of skills in the context of a personal relationship with the learner. Counseling refers more specifically to help with personal problems which interfere with the learning experience. Although it was said earlier that the roles of teacher and therapist differ, there is common ground between them. The executive inevitably will find himself treading on that common ground when he tries to help alter some aspect of the junior man's behavior which inhibits his growth.[54]

There are specific indications of such inhibitions. For example, the subordinate may resist needed and appropriate changes in his behavior. He may preoccupy himself with trivia at the expense of the larger task. He may not be able to organize himself to accomplish his work. He may resent supervision, be unduly critical of others, or otherwise unnecessarily irritating to others. Conversely, he may be too sensitive to the aggression of others.

These are "pathologies" which interfere with growth, the negative side of the personality about which the superior may have to counsel the subordinate. The specifics for doing so are to be found in many books on employee counseling.[55] Counseling may also facilitate "blossoming." The counseling process, ideally, is a mode by which the subordinate continually evaluates his own performance, looks at and seeks to modify his own behavior.[56] In the counseling relationship he can hear himself talking about his own behavior, concerns, and problems related to the job. When he does so, the respect of the superior for the junior man's struggle conveys and reinforces trust and confidence.

The executive who would counsel his subordinate for these purposes automatically has to face certain expectations which the person to be helped has of him.[57] Consciously or unconsciously, the person being helped will expect the other person to treat his problem as important. Such an attitude makes him worthy of consideration. He will expect that the other will also maintain the communication between them, not leave it all to him. He will anticipate further that such assistance will open aspects of the problem which he has difficulty expressing himself. The superior is expected to be sensitive to the subordinate's tension in the counseling situation, and to help ease it by becoming the ally of the subordinate as he tries to organize his thoughts and feelings. How much the subordinate will welcome the interest and help of the superior depends on how helpful he thinks the superior intends to be.

When the subordinate is discouraged, confused, and his morale is low, he usually has a hopeless feeling. The tendency of the superior is to reassure him. The superior's quiet trust that the subordinate will surmount his problems is more helpful to the subordinate than reassurance. The superior personifies reality, the job to be done, competence and strength. Identifying with the superior, the subordinate acquires some of the superior's confidence in him and greater capacity to tolerate his own struggles. If he understands that the joint task of superior and subordinate is to help the latter become more capable, he will want to continue that process. Thus a spiraling process is set in motion leading to greater mastery, enhanced self-image, and willingness to face more challenging problems.

Everyone has a period or periods in his career when, as a result of some synthesis, his potential effectiveness increases enormously.[58] There are no instruments to help predict when the "blossoming" is apt to occur in individual cases. Psychologists who are studying learning processes, and many experienced executives, know that when the unfolding begins to occur under favorable circumstances, an individual can make phenomenal contributions. Counseling, in effect, is the temporary "hothouse" which creates those circumstances. In microcosm, the counseling process is the model for the fulfillment of ministration needs.

11 / Maturation Needs

Maturation needs imply that a person has the potential for development and expansion; if circumstances are conducive, the process will unfold naturally. The needed circumstances include congenial climate, adequate psychological nourishment, and protection against inhibiting or destructive external forces. In addition, special provisions are required for individual uniqueness.

In many respects, maturation needs are silent. They do not cry out to be met as do ministration and mastery needs. If they are met, the person unfolds; if they are not, he vegetates. Occasionally someone may ask, for example, why an obviously intelligent man is in a lowly position. Apart from that kind of observation, it may never be apparent to the man himself or to others that he might have been able to do better, that he has not grown as he might have, or even that he is stunted. Maturation needs could even be viewed as anti-stunting needs. They are needs that prevent intellectual and competitive scrawniness. Fulfilled, they increase the potential of both the person and the organization. Unfulfilled, they deprive both the person and the organization of capacity. There are two major components in this conception of maturation needs: the need for activity and self-control; and the need to test reality.

The Need for Activity and Self-Control

The natural tendency of the human organism is toward growth, learning, and problem-solving. To speak of stimulating the person to those activities is to discuss the conditions for creativity. Creativity is another name for fruitful spontaneity in the service of personal, technical, organizational, or social problem-solving.

At a professional meeting some years ago, a panel of psychologists and a playwright discussed the process of creativity. The gap between the statistics-laden sterility of the psychologists' comments and the rich imagery of the experience which the playwright reported was testimony to how little is yet known about creativity. When Alexander the Great visited Diogenes and asked whether he could do anything for the famed teacher,

Diogenes replied, "Only stand out of my light." Perhaps, John Gardner notes, the best stimulant to creativity is to leave people free to do their work.[1] Yet some things are known about the conditions for creativity. It would be cavalier not to consider their implications.

What is meant by the term creative? In the conception of Abraham Maslow, to be creative is to be able to confront novelty and to improvise while enjoying change.[2] These are also the essential characteristics for flexibility in rapidly changing organizations. Creativity, therefore, is not limited to artists. The survival of individuals and organizations hinges on their capacities to be inventive, to find ways of flowering despite seemingly adverse circumstances.

Arguing that the past has become useless in many professions, Maslow calls for developing a race of improvisors. These are people who can divorce themselves from their past sufficiently to handle problems by improvisation if necessary. To do so, such people must feel strong, courageous, and confident enough to trust themselves in their contemporary situations. One thesis of this book is that an important way of developing "a race of improvisors" is to create organizational conditions which will foster that kind of behavior. In the previous chapter, it was apparent that adequate support in the form of complementary roles and group decision-making under favorable leadership conditions increased the capacity for improvisation and self-trust. What are some of the other factors which increase the improvisation potential?

One inhibiting factor is knowledge. While creativity is essentially a combination of previously unconnected ideas, that definition presupposes prior knowledge in the form of ideas derived from education and experience.[3] If the knowledge is solid in the sense that the possessor is certain of its validity, and if it is upheld tenaciously, there is no internal need for something new. Much of what is learned is taught as truth or dogma, whether it be arithmetic or sales technique. Systematic learning often inhibits truly original creations.[4] One reason for such creativity-inducing efforts as "brainstorming" is an attempt to surmount the barriers of traditional knowledge and customary ways of thinking.[5]

A second factor which inhibits creativity is that the object or idea being created is necessarily exposed to the harshness of a hostile environment. A new idea may threaten the possessors of the now-obsolete one. It may mean that the idea-generator gains new power, or that he stimulates feelings of inadequacy in those who did not think of it. Whatever the case, a new idea more often generates hostility, attack, and rejection than enthusiastic acceptance. Protection therefore is a sine qua non for fostering creativity.

John Gardner addresses himself in detail to this significant issue, pointing out that the need for protection is why a vigorous tradition of freedom of thought and enquiry is essential to the continuous renewal of both individuals and organizations. Gardner observes that the innovator has always been a threat to the status quo; even in an era in which innovation is highly valued, he still tends to be viewed as a disruptive force ("If you don't like it here, why don't you go somewhere else?"). But, Gardner says, that image of the innovator is no longer appropriate for the contemporary world, which both requires and thrives on innovation. To protect the innovator and simultaneously to stimulate the innovative process, he advances what he calls, "A set of attitudes and specific social arrangements designed to ensure that points of view at odds with prevailing doctrine will not be rejected out of hand." [6]

Gardner advocates "a department of continuous renewal" that would view the whole organization as a system in need of constant innovation. This segment of organizational structure and the implied attitude behind it set the stage for what then seems to be natural activities: infusion of new blood and well-designed personnel rotation; far reaching organizational restructuring; reduction of excessive demands for coordination, administrative review, and endorsement; less reliance on the processing of data and increased examination of unprocessed reality — the feelings and attitudes of people experienced in personal contacts; and an accent on flexibility rather than on massive strength. Two of his suggestions are devoted to new people and different experiences for them. The others are concerned with alleviating the encapsulating pressures of the organization.

Stimulation is a third factor necessary for encouraging improvisation. To stimulate people requires more than protection against encapsulation by the organization. In order to focus on stimulation, one must study first the psychology of the creative individual. All men are creative to some degree because a modicum of innovation is required for survival. If the creative person is not different from other people, then his processes of creativity are an enlarged, more successful version of the same processes which occur in others. Methods of stimulating creativity in those who are less highly creative may be inferred from observations of highly creative people.

"Creativity," says Donald W. MacKinnon, "is a process extended in time and characterized by originality, adaptiveness and realization. The more creative a person is, the more he reveals an openness to his own feelings and emotions, a sensitive intellect and understanding self-awareness, and wide-ranging interests, including many which in the American culture are thought of as feminine." [7]

According to MacKinnon's studies of creativity in architects, persons who are highly creative are inclined to have positive opinions of themselves. Their self-images include being inventive, determined, independent, individualistic, enthusiastic, and industrious. The less creative architects revealed themselves to be more concerned with being virtuous, of good character, rational, and sympathetic to others. In the terms of reference of this book, the less creative people were more superego-oriented and more self-controlling, and therefore psychologically more "on guard."

The traditional organizational hierarchy and its demands foster the personality traits which characterize the less creative people. Even the most benevolent organizations reward virtuous behavior, not originality. Thus they militate against their own survival. This is not to carp pejoratively against organizations as oppressors of men. Every organization has to maintain its internal stability and can tolerate only a limited amount of internal dissension and turbulence. By definition, innovation is conducive to dissension and turbulence. The problem in industry is no different from what it is in the public schools or other organizations.

Paul Torrance, who has given much attention to creativity in the classroom, reports that creative students are estranged from their teachers and are not very well liked by them.[8] Torrance points out that it is difficult to like people who cannot accept the status quo. When teachers and parents were asked which of sixty-two personality characteristics should be most encouraged in children, they ranked "being most considerate of others" highest of all. Highly creative students often get so involved in the problems on which they are working that they give little time to social amenities. The teachers and parents ranked independence of thinking second, but independence of thinking requires independence of judgment and courage. The teachers ranked independence of judgment nineteenth and courage twenty-ninth. The teachers would prefer courtesy to courage. For them, it was more important that the student be on time, energetic, industrious, obedient, and popular or well-liked among his peers. The teachers wanted the student to be receptive to the ideas of others, versatile, and willing to accept the judgments of authorities. While they rated determination as the third most desirable quality, it is apparent that a student resolved to do what he wants would not please them. For them, day-dreaming or fantasy which might be productive of ideas was not to be equated with industriousness or busyness. Curiosity which might lead the student to the threshold of learning was not as highly valued as being studious. Sincerity might not be acceptable if it were candidly honest.

The same kind of phenomenon is reported in the relationship of university administrators to their faculties. Administrators tend to revere status, prestige, and power, and to value the authority of rank above the authority of knowledge. When administrators prefer and reward charming, sensitive, dependent, loyal professors, and when these criteria compete with professional knowledge, demoralization and disenchantment set in to impair academic creativity. The argument can be documented by computing the dollar cost of faculty turnover in addition to the experiences of distrust and alienation.[9]

Promptness is hard for the creative student because he is more likely to regard his own thoughts as more important than an arbitrary deadline. The creative student is likely to be a self-starter, but teachers are more apt to want him to follow their instructions. Highly creative students are likely to regress occasionally, to be more childlike. Such regression is necessary if they are to draw creative fantasy from the preconscious and unconscious levels of thought, but it is also irritating to teachers. The determination of the creative student to follow his own thoughts may make him seem emotional or even irrational to the teacher, particularly if the student is bold in his ideas but shy in social relations. His determination may also make him seem negativistic, especially if he is unwilling to accept the teacher's answers or "no" for an answer. Such students, Torrance notes, have an unusual talent for disturbing existing organizations and appear to be domineering when they are creating.

Obviously, no organization can exist if each person strikes off in his own determined direction, however individually creative that may be. Understanding what creativity is psychologically and what the conditions for its unfolding are, can contribute to organizational survival. From the MacKinnon studies it is apparent that the less people are defensive, the more they can be receptive to new ideas, experiences and feelings, and the more creative they can be. They are able to tolerate more complexity, diffuseness of feelings, and the disorder of different thoughts and ideas in their confused, embryonic state. They are not impelled to have answers immediately. But why are they less "on guard" psychologically?

MacKinnon reports that the parents of the creative architects were characterized by an extraordinary respect for the child and confidence in his ability to do what was appropriate. They granted him unusual freedom to explore where his interests took him and to make decisions for himself. They expected him to act independently but reasonably and responsibly. This expectation apparently was vital for the child's sense of personal autonomy which, in turn, became the hallmark of his creativity. However, personal autonomy, by definition, did not allow for intensive closeness with the parents.

Despite the freedom granted the child, he had a clear conception of right and wrong and standards of conduct. Both of these, it was expected, would be internalized by the child. Discipline was usually consistent and predictable, but rarely harsh or cruel. In half of the families there was no corporal punishment. The families of the creative architects moved more frequently, thus providing greater opportunity for roaming, exploration, and varied experiences. As students, their grades tended to be mediocre unless the subject or the teacher caught their imagination. They were profound skeptics, accepting nothing on faith or authority. Containing so many varied and often conflicting ideas, they were not always pleasant people, and they frequently experienced much psychic turbulence.

Gardner Murphy summarizes four stages in the creative process. First, is immersion "in some specific medium which gives delight and fulfillment." Second, is the acquisition of experiences which are then consolidated into an ordered pattern. The third phase is the sudden inspiration or illumination, and the fourth is the "hammering out" and perfecting of the creative work.[10] In the studies reported by Jacob W. Getzels and Mihaly Csikszentmihalyi, the most original and artistically valuable drawings were produced by students who had handled the most objects, scrutinized the objects they handled, and selected the most unusual ones to work with during the pre-drawing period. They describe this as "discovery oriented" behavior. "This concern with discovery," they report, "set apart those who were interested in formulating and solving new artistic problems from those who were content merely to apply their technical skill to familiar problems capable of more or less pat solutions."[11]

Inferring from these and other corroborating studies, there are certain generalizations which might be constructed for leadership-teaching behavior that will promote creativity. With Diogenes, the leader would do well to present the task or challenge, indicate his support in accomplishing it, and his confidence that the subordinate will succeed with it. He would expect relationships with the subordinate to be oriented around their joint task, and not be disappointed that the subordinate "didn't like him." He would establish and communicate the criteria for performance; penalties for failure would be self-evident. Varied experiences would provide the context for the subordinate's explorations. A permissive atmosphere for "crazy" ideas to be expounded and examined would give rise to more of them. Opportunity to choose among challenges and problems, when that was possible, would permit people to seize and develop those which most excited their curiosity. Sometimes that opportunity can be provided by allowing the subordinate a portion of his working time to follow some problem which has aroused his interest. Although that interest may not at the moment be of major concern to the organization or the superior, the freedom to follow one's interest stimulates a flow of ideas. One consequence is that the superior would have to contend with the questioning, doubting, and restlessness which followed. Such an atmosphere can become the setting for what Murphy calls the "habit of creation." Creative insights come more frequently to those who work at them. "In every mind there are widening regions of creativity if once the spark has been allowed to generate the fire." [12]

This does not mean that the leader-teacher simply lets go of the managerial task or dismisses people's unadaptive behavior because "creative people are that way." For example, according to studies reported by Rensis Likert, a scientist in industry performs more effectively if there is frequent communication within the research organization than if he is isolated.[13] The number of patent applications and scientists' evaluations of each other's work are higher in laboratories where there is such communication, particularly if colleagues think differently from one another. With respect to their relationships with their superiors, scientists and engineers who see their administrative chief often perform better than those who do not. Their performance is still better when they can also set their own technical goals, or at least have some influence on their chief in setting those goals. Likert reports that the best performance is attained when the scientist has considerable self-determination about his work and when this is combined with free access to someone in authority.

Generalizing from these studies, Likert suggests that the potentialities of younger subordinates are best developed by the superior who can maintain close interest in the young man's work without dominating it. He suggests further that if the technical man's personal motivation is low, if he is not deeply involved in his work, it is not advisable to allow more than moderate self-determination. If his motivation is high, then full self-determination leads to best results. The same considerations would apply to executives.

Donald Pelz adds another dimension to the same findings.[14] For him, the increased communications means that the scientists allow their goals to be influenced by their colleagues. Thus, the most productive man is the one who himself allows his goals to be modified by others whose consideration he seeks. Pelz notes that the scientists with the high autonomy do not necessarily have higher average performance than those with low autonomy, perhaps because in a research laboratory it is a rare scientist who can be creative mainly from his own resources. Talented persons prefer reliable situations when their talent is relevant to the situation.[15] Too much freedom, then, may hamper creativity.

Once more the structure of the organization becomes a critical element, this time in the climate of stimulation. Gardner's suggestions for making organizations self-renewing and thereby hospitable for individual innovativeness are an important entree for thinking about the relationship of organizational structure to creativity. He calls particular attention to the need for organizations to combat their blindness to their own defects and their capacity for rationalizing their faults as necessities. Modes of internal self-criticism, infusion and rotation of new personnel, and the use of outside consultants were among his suggested devices. More important, however, he raises an issue for organizations similar to a factor which appeared in the descriptions of the parents of creative children. The parents of creative children encouraged high standards and aspirations. To be self-renewing, Gardner says, an organization must be interested in what it is going to become, not what it has been. Like a person, an organization runs on motivation, morale, and conviction.

If an organizational ego ideal is necessary for a climate of innovation, development of the "organizational ego" is no less necessary to pursue the aspiration. The discussion of management development, executive education, and identification was largely focused on increasing the capacities of subordinates, with the assumption that strengthening them for their tasks would strengthen the organization.

Developing the "organizational ego" is a Herculean task. Raymond Miles correlates the success of such an effort directly to the importance of the tasks the organization uncovers for itself.[16] The "organizational ego" is enhanced to the degree to which the organization discovers and uses the talents of its people to accomplish those tasks. Miles complains that the typical company wastes its human resources, sometimes because management does not know the resources exist and sometimes because it does not know how to create an environment in which they could be more fully utilized. These two reasons mask a third, less palatable reason: the process of unleashing talent is both challenging and threatening. Top management, Miles contends, is not at all certain how this talent could be guided or when, where, and if it should stop. "There appear to be real constraints on the amount of creativity, concern, and enthusiasm which the typical organization is equipped to handle," he says.

Perhaps so. Perhaps executives who have to contend with renewing organizations by stimulating creativity are like parents who are simultaneously gratified and appalled by what their children are learning in school. Not only are the parents unfamiliar with new math, but in addition, they are concerned with maintaining their own self-esteem in the face of the never-ending onslaught of precocious knowledge. Despite his own education, the contemporary middle-class parent is often as alien to the intellectual world of his children as were the immigrant parents of two generations ago to that of their children. No less is the older executive.

There are many reasons for the caution of the older executive. The depression of the 1930's still affects American business leadership.[17] First, there are more leaders from privileged families because there were fewer opportunities for poor boys to get ahead during the depression. Second, those who weathered the depression successfully solved problems of economic stagnation. They became highly competent at conserving and preserving their organizations in the face of declining markets. Theirs was a psychology of self-protection by constriction. Contemporary older executives (fifty-five to seventy years old) are therefore more likely to be more cautious and less imaginative than contemporary young men. The latter now face opposite problems: expansion rather than contraction; fruitful investment rather than conservation of costs. Perhaps the most conspicuous recent example was the contrast between Sewell Avery's protective management of Montgomery Ward versus the expansionist philosophy of Sears, Roebuck.

Little wonder that many executives are inhibited by their own fears about generating organizational environments conducive to creativity. Yet many organizations are actively trying to produce such an environment. The Aerojet-General Corporation has devised one way of stimulating creativity. The company has established a "New Concept Fund" to support the development of promising and unusual ideas which cannot be anticipated in ordinary budget projections.[18] Each plant manager is allocated a sum to support personnel with concepts which warrant further investigation. Under the plan, the plant manager decides which ideas merit support. Allocations are renewed or continued if, after initial investigation, the ideas appear to be worthwhile.

Although not everyone is or can be highly creative in the imaginative sense most people are more potentially creative than is recognized. Furthermore, the conditions for creativity are also the conditions for personal flexibility and growth. They constitute the climate for effective supervision and facilitate the identification process. A manager's effectiveness is reflected in the performance level of his subordinates.[19] Achieving effectiveness, however, is not just a matter of applying techniques, although they are an important component. It is not a matter of gimmicks or styles; rather it largely devolves on the atmosphere of the work place. How does it feel to be here, to work here?

Crawford Greenewalt succinctly describes the importance of this climate when he says: "Differences in managerial competence are not due to one person, nor to the few geniuses that cross the stage from time to time, but arise out of the creation of an atmosphere which induces every man or woman connected with the enterprise, no matter what their position, to perform his or her task with a degree of competence and enthusiasm measurably greater than what could be called their normal expectations . . . Business success, then, can be measured by summing up the small increments of extra effort on the part of all the people who are joined together in a given enterprise."[20]

One way of introducing the issue of climate is to examine how subordinates view themselves and their superiors. From the many attitude and morale studies, it is evident that people can explicitly state their expectations of their leaders. These expectations are consistent both within groups and across varied organizations. They are stated in common sense terms: justice, courtesy, consideration; job competence; knowledge of subordinates' performance; control of the work group; straightforwardness and decisiveness; appropriate psychological distance; reasonable assistance.[21] Such expectations are far from being universally met. For example, a survey of 420 middle and junior executives discloses that a majority of them feels severely handicapped by a lack of guidance from above: 58 percent said their superiors had not told them — even in general terms — what was expected of them to qualify for promotion.[22] A majority stated or implied that their work suffered because of lack of communications. Almost half said that their superiors seldom or never commended them or otherwise rewarded them for outstanding work; 22 percent said that the companies did not reflect their true worth and another 40 percent said they did not know whether their worth to the company was recognized or not. They held these opinions despite the fact that 82 percent said the companies gave promotions regularly. Almost all said their companies consider efforts at self-development in selecting men for promotion, and more than 80 percent felt that their best chances for success lay in their present firms. Although they rated their bosses high on knowledge of and skill in traditional business principles, more than half rated their bosses as only fair or poor in the ability to motivate people.

Lyman W. Porter and Edwin E. Ghiselli contrasted the differences in self-perceptions between a group of middle managers and a group of top managers. Top management perceived themselves as capable, determined, industrious, resourceful, sharpwitted, enterprising, sincere, sociable, pleasant, dignified, sympathetic. Middle managers discerned themselves as discreet, courageous, practical, planful, deliberate, intelligent, calm, steady, modest, civilized, patient. Porter and Ghiselli observe: "Top managers see themselves as the 'dynamic brains' of the organization. Their role is one of thinking up new things to do, new areas to enter, new ways of doing things. They are action-oriented idea men. Middle management people, on the other hand, seem to see themselves as filling a role that could be called the 'backbone' of the organization. Their chief forte is that they provide the careful, thorough investigation of ideas and plans that is necessary before these can be put into extensive use. They lend the stability to the organization that is necessary for it to function over an extended period of time." [23] Such perceptions are typical of many young and middle managers.

According to another study, when senior executives rated themselves high in authority — that is, had a self-image of being powerful bosses — their juniors tended to characterize themselves as low or uncertain in responsibility.[24] When seniors rated themselves high in responsibility, their juniors tended to describe themselves as high in authority and also, except for small organizations, in responsibility. In other words, when the boss swings his weight, his subordinates run scared; when his concern with the work problems of the organization begins with consideration of the impact of his own behavior, subordinates feel more capable. When seniors rated themselves high in both responsibility and authority, juniors tended to delegate less to their subordinates. That is, when seniors tightened control, the juniors did also. In large organizations, when seniors delegated more, juniors also delegated more. In small organizations, this appeared to be less true because the senior was more likely to oscillate between delegating authority and revoking it. The leadership process, the researchers say, may be more smoothly maintained in a stratified organization where interactions are more formalized and less personal than in smaller organizations.

The less the subordinates trust their superior, the more they will evaluate him on the basis of his technical, administrative, or structuring ability.[25] The obverse of this is the more they will expect the leader to make the decisions and tell them what to do. Thus the leader loses the initiative potential of his subordinates.

The issue of self-perception is made even more poignant when an executive begins to generalize on the basis of his current experience and defines his future in terms of the present. If the present is unfulfilling, the future, in his eyes, holds limited promise. In this situation, the "reservoir of talent" becomes endangered. Aspiration wanes. Managers, in a study by Hjalmar Rosen reported earlier, not only saw the future as "more of the same" but also did not tend to predict change in their situations.[26] Rather, they felt they must accept the status quo or find new jobs elsewhere. No sense of mastery, of reciprocation, of affecting the organization here. The inert hand of the present lies oppressively on the buds of creativity.

These perceptions are particularly important for several other reasons. Dero Saunders reported in *Fortune* that, "The younger men swear it won't happen to them . . . and have concluded that the concentration on work and achievement shown by today's senior executives is downright maladjustment." Saunders says further that they have deliberately tempered their business ambitions in order to more fully enjoy their families, their community life, and their recreation. In addition, they hope to modify the business environment. He quotes William E. Henry to the effect that change occurs in something as basic as the attitude toward the outside world: "Whereas the young (say 30 to 35) executive looks upon the external environment as a thing to be manipulated or adjusted to, for the middle-aged executive the outer world begins to take on a kind of life of its own and to be seen as greatly more complex and full of unknowns — at times even *malign in influence.*" [27] Saunders goes on to say that since the nature of the outer world itself presumably does not change as a man grows older, the executive's changed attitude toward it must reflect a slow inner erosion of vigor, self-confidence, and decisiveness.

The *Fortune* article also reports the impressions of the faculty of the MIT Sloan School of Management about two groups of executives with whom they work regularly. The senior executive group, men from forty to fifty-five years approximately, take a ten-week program at MIT. The Sloan Fellows are young executives between thirty and thirty-eight who return to MIT for a year of study after ten years in industry. According to faculty observations, the senior executives wonder whether their efforts are worthwhile. Their questions are less likely to be about the system in which they find themselves, and more about moral, ethical, and philosophical issues — how things fit together. The younger men more often ask, "Why?"

To counteract these negative forces, Saunders recommends letting middle management know where they stand through some regular, impersonal assessment procedure. Such a process, to be discussed further in this chapter, discourages the building of unfounded hopes for the future. In the terms of this book, it becomes a statement about reality. He also advocates setting low compulsory retirement age to allow earlier promotions; decentralization of the company into the largest possible number of autonomous divisions to provide more top management jobs; finding ways to bolster the egos of middle-rank executives whose upward movement is blocked; and capitalizing on what might appear to be personality defects on executives by building jobs around these qualities.

These are largely ego-supporting devices. Only one — creating more divisions — relates to stimulating activity. However, the task for the senior executive is to change the "dampening down" process which limits horizons to a stimulating process which expands them. To do this he must remove artificial barriers and alter the perspectives of those who seem themselves circumscribed. No doubt there are as many ways to do this as there are executives. These recommendations comprise a foundation upon which the executive may build his unique structure.

First, the executive must establish trust. This is done largely by meeting those ministration needs which are appropriately fulfilled in the business situation. Trust will be further facilitated if the executive looks to himself and his behavior first when problems occur, rather than seeking to blame others. This does not imply that trust is to be purchased by self-blame or that the executive should maintain a constant attitude of *mea culpa*. Rather, the executive who continues to ask himself about the influence of his behavior on that of his subordinates will be able to single out many such influences. Concomitantly, he will be viewed by his subordinates as a person who assumes responsibility for his behavior. If he can initiate the pattern of being responsible for his own behavior, then his subordinates will be more likely to assume responsibility for theirs. If he cannot be self-responsible, then his subordinates will more likely scapegoat their juniors or cast about for objects of blame.

The executive-teacher can also increase capacity by increasing responsibility. Too often this is interpreted as meaning promotion to higher jobs. There are limited numbers of top echelon jobs, which is why Drucker feels that there are not enough places in businesses for all of the bright available young men. However, there is no limitation on the possibility of people thinking together about their joint tasks and problems, and about the innovations which can be evolved from such thinking. If the executive-teacher can create the circumstances in which his subordinates can change their self-images, then many — but not all — can be more responsible in their relationships with the organization. They can shift their perceptions from being "backbones" of the organization to being part of its "dynamic brains" by their confrontation with the basic problems of the business. Conceivably, alternative modes of organizing the business can be created out of such thinking which would make it possible for both organization and individual to advance to higher levels of functional responsibility.

Unless he can raise three questions about himself, the executive-teacher will have difficulty trying to ascertain the influence of his own behavior on that of his subordinates, and increasing their responsibility potential. These questions are: "Why do I need to be powerful?" "Why do I need to patronize others?" "Why do I need to doubt the capacity of others?"

Although these questions are not readily answerable, the executive can ask them from time to time. If he does so, particularly when he finds himself reluctant to trust his subordinates or to increase their responsibility in the sense described above, he may be able to observe the self-defensive aspects of his reaction. To the extent that he must protect himself or promote himself at the expense of others, he will be unable to build trust and to create the conditions for innovation.

Limited aspiration and pessimism about the future are fashioned out of defeat, however subtle that process has been. Higher levels of aspiration and optimism are the product of demonstrated success. In this context, success means what Robert W. White calls "the feeling of efficacy." He defines this as emotions "which accompany the whole process of producing effects." [28] The sense of competence arises out of cumulated feelings of efficacy. The importance of such feelings of competence — feelings that one is able to have some effect on other people and the environment — is that they are foundations of self-respect and security. For the executive-teacher this means that the tasks and activities of his subordinates must be structured in such a way that they can see the steps of success.

There can be success in failure, so this is not a fantasy. A department may fail to successfully market one product, but learn from that failure new ways of marketing which are then applied to the next effort. A successful research result may be economically useless, but the researcher has taken another step in his own development and that of his organization. Part of the responsibility of the superior is to point out the pattern of success when it is obscure. Another part is to engage the subordinates on problems to which they find they can make a contribution when neither they nor their boss realized previously that they might. The enhanced self-respect opens the sluices of aspiration and optimism.

Taken together, these actions are likely to contribute significantly to changing the perspective which subordinates have about themselves and the organization. They transform a prosaic process into one of verve and imagination.

The other side of activity, the first component of maturation, is control. Without control, activity is merely random behavior. To create conditions for the flowering of ideas and innovations is a noble aspiration — but an aimless one unless the ideas and innovations are channeled in the common interest.

The cornerstone of Douglas McGregor's contributions to the psychology of leadership lay in one sentence: "In the recognition of the capacity of human beings to exercise self-control lies the only fruitful opportunity for industrial management to realize the full potential represented by professional resources." [29] This statement, and the principles derived from it, which McGregor labeled "Theory Y," were powerful forces toward democratizing management. As with most innovations, the excitement of newer conceptions often overshadowed the lessons which had been learned from the old. In the eyes of some, all control other than self-control came to be viewed as bad by definition. Guilt was induced in managers who could not or would not be so democratic as to permit complete self-control by subordinates. Considerable confusion was created in managerial ranks when attempts to be more democratic sometimes led to conflict, open hostility, panic, and failure.

While to some degree ideas and innovations are self-controlled in group supportive efforts, even this kind of self-control cannot occur unless the group and its individuals are faced with responsibility and required to meet it. Therefore, the leader himself must exercise controls.

To speak of authority and control today seems contrary to contemporary concepts of democratic management and some of the practices previously advocated in these pages. However, the issue of control in management has been largely misconceived, partially as a result of not taking into account the meaning of power, transference, and father-figure conceptions of leadership. All systems and organizations need some form of direction. One of the major functions of leadership is to control the system.

"Regulation," says John Gardner, "need not involve the dead hand of conformity, the iron hand of authority, or the glad hand of conviviality . . . Only when responsibility is neglected does enforcement in a punitive sense become necessary." [30] Gardner points out that rigidity is not necessarily a quality limited to the leader; when people in even a democratic organization develop sacrosanct rights, the organization itself rigidifies. The more democratic an organization is, the more vividly the vested interests of its members will be reflected in its policies. Thus a stagnant democratic organization may be particularly resistant to change. Examples are to be found in many communities and churches.

Robert Dubin has expressed it differently: "We do not assume that men are exploited when led, or manipulated as puppets when supervised." [31] Leadership, teaching and supervision are active roles. There is no necessary conflict between being active and supportive. In fact, to be inactive is often to be unsupportive. Parenthetically, the opposite extreme is equally unsupportive. As Likert has pointed out, supervisory behavior in excess of normal expectations will not be favorably accepted by subordinates.[32]

In the terms of this book, the psychological distance is too close. The analogy is that children do not want their father to be a pal. They want him to be a father and to act as someone who is more mature, more experienced than they, and who can exercise *controls* to the extent that they themselves are not yet ready to do so.

There need not be conflict between support and control. Donald Pelz and his colleague, Frank M. Andrews, report that a scientist feels that he is autonomous when he works in a setting which is *neither* tightly nor loosely coordinated. In a relatively uncoordinated situation, one in which the members already enjoy considerable freedom, the most autonomous scientists were only average, or below in performance. Pelz and Andrews offer this explanation: "In loose or extremely loose settings, the most autonomous scientists tended to withdraw from outer stimulation (or to reduce inner motivation) which might have enhanced their performance. In very tightly coordinated situations, at the other extreme, autonomous individuals were motivated and stimulated; but the rigidities of the setting apparently prevented these factors from enhancing creativity. Thus, only in the middle range situations were two essential conditions present: a) high autonomy was accompanied by a number of strong motivations and stimulations, and b) the setting was flexible enough to allow these factors to improve performance . . . The wholly self-determining individual, who excludes even his colleagues from a voice in his goal-setting, may isolate himself from stimulation. Complete autonomy may encourage complacency rather than zest, narrow specialization rather than breadth." [33]

The difference between supportive and oppressive control is demonstrated in a study of 656 salesmen in 36 branch offices of a national firm.[34] When the salesmen felt they exercised some control over their manager, and when his control over them was a contribution to their efforts, high satisfaction and performance resulted. His supervision supported them when it rested heavily on his skill, expertise, and personal attractiveness. This is what sociologists call "functional control." [35] When the manager attempted to exercise formal control over the salesmen, by authority of his position, satisfaction and performance were low.

The issue of control is a delicate one. Too many people will jump to the conclusion that the position taken here is an authoritarian one. It is not. Neither is it a position which ignores, denies, or avoids the realities of power.

Another facet of the same problem is reflected in the observations of

Louis E. Allen, a management consultant.[36] Allen calls attention to the fact that organizations evolve through stages of maturity as do individuals. At each stage, a different style of leadership is required. During the first evolutionary stage of any organized undertaking, organizational requirements are not sharply defined or understood. Therefore people tend to put their own objectives ahead of those of the organization. A leader who can exercise positive, consistent authority is necessary in this stage. The natural or entrepreneurial leader exercises positive and consistent authority by building a personalized organization. But, Allen goes on to say, when enterprises outgrow their early leaders, then bureaucracy sets in. By following the early leader, the organization has established a stable pattern, policies have been evolved and accepted, and standard practices have become the organization's business. There are well-defined roles and practices. Centralized control is supported by sublayers of authority. If the strong leader does not "let go," the more capable people leave.

If the organization can move from an immature position in which it is largely dependent upon the leader to a more mature level of functioning, organized groups evolve. "In a mature group the individuals have mastered the skills required to work effectively with minimum supervision. They understand the nature of their own problems well enough to be able to make most of their own decisions," Allen observes. With such understanding, the members then put group objectives and requirements ahead of personal ones. Such a group is then ready for mature leadership, which Allen defines as concentrating on those efforts which get the most effective results through others. Specifically, "The mature leader knows how to lead so that people will understand and accept the limits of freedom within which they must work if they are to remain a cohesive undertaking." Allen's observations complement the experimental results of Likert and Trist, with the added component of the "limits of freedom" concept. The leader helps bring the followers face to face with their common reality.

Another aspect of the same phenomenon is the disorganization which ensues when the leader fails to exercise adequate controls. That complementary work roles are not by themselves enough to produce effective coordination is vividly illustrated by Moss Hart's description of what happens on the stage, the model situation from which the idea of complementary roles is drawn. "If (actors) cannot trust, or have lost faith in, the man who is to guide them and see them through that moment, they strike out in fear and hide their panic in bursts of temper and impossible behavior . . . the first necessity a director faces is the creation of a climate of security and peace, in which actors can do their best work. And he creates this most surely by assuming and maintaining an ironclad control of the proceedings from the moment the actors pass through the stage door on the first day of rehearsals until the curtain rises on opening night in New York." [37]

The organizational equivalent of Hart's experience is found in two studies of group processes. In one, it was found that "antagonism, tension, and absenteeism were determined in part by the failure of a group member to act as a 'leader' by providing orientations toward, evaluations of, and suggestions about the situation when these were demanded by other group members" if the group members expect that person to be the leader.[38] The more nondirective the group leadership, the more such disruptive behavior was likely to occur. According to the second study, when a group had a person in it who was uncontested as a self-confident decision maker, the better the group performed at later stages in learning.[39]

Abraham Zaleznik raises another problem about the issue of control.[40] If the senior executive is in conflict between the requirement that he exercise his power and his wish to be liked by his subordinates, he can easily get into difficulty. If he tries to deny his power by acting the role of the "nice guy," then, in Zaleznik's terms, he strips himself of status. Depreciating his power, he soon finds that the subordinates join him in that activity. Then decision-making becomes one continuous argument. In such a case, the subordinates soon become contemptuous of the superior. If that is the model offered them, then there is no point in the subordinates wanting to achieve the boss' position which promises nothing but futile argument.

Once more a caution must be raised. The reader who misconceives Hart's statement and these studies to be a case for authoritarianism should reread the statement and review the studies to discern what the director controls: the proceedings. He creates and maintains an organized, supportive context in which people can work creatively. He is not the star, but the facilitator.

A second caution must also be emphasized. The question is not group control versus that by the leader. Control might be viewed as a dimension on a continuum from complete group autonomy at one extreme to unquestioned dominance by the leader at the other. Optimum control on this axis will vary with the task, and with the sophistication, competence, and maturity of the group, as well as the situation in which the group finds itself. Control of some kind is necessary. When the group has an adequate perspective on the task to be accomplished, and has the requisite skills for doing so, then it may have correspondingly more control over itself and will need less from the leader. When the leader has a perspective which others do not or cannot have, then the leader will have to exert correspondingly more control.[41] In the latter case, the group will then have to identify with the ego ideal and strength of the leader.

A simple case in point may be drawn from the Trist study of the coal miners.[42] The miners knew their work and could spontaneously organize the most effective ways to accomplish it. However, they were unlikely to appreciate the complexities of marketing coal. They would have to depend on a leader who either did or could call upon someone who was knowledgeable. The miner would also have to trust that his management of over-all production would provide maximum income for them.

The opposite extreme is offered in an example from *The Battle of Dienbienphu* by the French journalist, Jules Roy. Roy contends that the French lost because their commander was inexperienced in the kind of battle he was waging. Roy suggests that the general might have done better to gather his principal officers, admit his limitations in that kind of operation, and ask them to agree among themselves on a strategy which he would then carry out.

Is conformity, overcontrol, authoritarianism not an issue? Is all that has been said on these issues merely a contrivance? Does the argument veer from one position to the other? Not at all. As John Gardner has pointed out, the complex interrelationships of people and functions in an industrialized society require a high degree of predictability of individual behavior.[43] One has to be able to count on others whom he may not even see, let alone know. For his part, the individual must perform predictably because others are depending on it. Without predictable behavior, organizations cannot function.

There is no need, therefore, to make a shibboleth out of democratic management. No democracy ever achieved anything without leadership. The leader has the task of welding together past ideals and present goals.[44] This is a point which is often neglected by those adherents of group dynamics to whom a leader with strength is anathema. Often such attacks on leadership are a function of people who, rebelling against their own strong needs to be dependent and against authority, adopt permanently dependent positions in university structures from which they then attack the very people who support them. Shades of conservative farmers taking New Deal crop subsidies and then voting Republican against the spendthrift New Dealers!

No organization can endure without leadership and none can endure for long without an ego ideal to hold it together. The leader must still lead. If he is to foster identification and growth, he must also control. Leadership control and self-control need not be contradictory. Freedom never exists in a vacuum, but always within a framework of responsibility. Freedom within a context of responsibility means mutual control of leader and followers of which self-control is but one integral part.

The Need to Test Reality

Stimulated activity under conditions which support its flowering into creativity and innovation creates, as Robert W. White puts it, a "constant connection between knowledge and action. We learn about the environment because we go out to it, seek response from it and find out what kind of response it can give," he explains.[45] By continuous testing of reality, a person learns what he can and cannot do, what the environment will and will not do under various circumstances, and the costs of alternative behaviors. He provides for himself continuous feedback on his own behavior.

There are two kinds of feedback: one's observations of the effects of his behavior and reports from others. It is an axiom that one learns best when he obtains direct feedback from the task itself, when he sees the effects of what he has learned on his method of solving problems. If a man does piecework, his feedback about quantity and quality is reasonably direct. Issues of direct feedback will be considered in greater detail in the next chapter.

Indirect feedback, or reports from others, requires examination first because in most organizations, anything more than the most simple kind of direct feedback about a man's behavior is almost impossible to come by. If a man's work is interrelated with that of others, it is more difficult for him to weigh his own efforts. Most men in managerial ranks must depend on the judgment of superiors as an indication of the effectiveness of their performance.

When the leader has already established and maintains controls, the subordinate's need for the superior's judgment poses two problems. One has already been discussed: the need to avoid such authoritarian management that is conducive to identification with the aggressor. That kind of leadership behavior leads to simple imitation and to the downward displacement of hostility. It is the antithesis of closeness, support, protection, guidance, and spontaneous activity. It is also self-perpetuating. Rigid control begets the need for more of the same. The second problem is to develop and reinforce self-control in McGregor's terms.

Performance appraisal is one important way of dealing with both problems simultaneously. Next to direct feedback from the task itself, the most useful kind of feedback is that which comes from someone whom the subordinate respects and with whom he shares a mutual interest in the same problems.

A variety of appraisal systems were formulated to provide feedback. Most have failed dismally. In a typical appraisal program, the superior analyzes the position description and the assigned duties of each of his subordinates, and judges how well the subordinate has fulfilled his assigned tasks.[46] While undertaking such an analysis seems relatively simple, forcing the superior to judge performance makes the process a psychologically complex and painful one.

In many companies, the formal performance appraisal is an annual event. It becomes a theatrical confrontation between individuals and organizations. In such periodic appraisals, according to studies in General Electric, there is a tendency to store criticisms and complaints, and then to fire both barrels — the items of criticism and the resulting anger — at the subordinate.[47] Praise on such occasions seems ineffective because the subordinate sees it as a wedge for censure. Criticism inevitably brings defensive denials of responsibility for poor performance.

Such mechanistic efforts are further impaired by the feelings which superiors have about appraising others. Anticipating the subordinate's denials and resistances, and afraid of his own aggression which is inevitably a part of criticism, the superior becomes confused by his own guilt feelings. Too often he feels he is destroying the other person if he is critical. He therefore glosses over criticism or goes to great length to deny his hostility. This, in turn, leads to "management by guilt."[48] Dishonest appraisal is destructive to both individual and organization; it undermines responsible leadership control.

The problems are not reason enough for abandoning the appraisal system, as Peter Drucker has suggested.[49] An appraisal system can provide a useful record of performance and a basis for individual development. It is necessary as part of the reality orientation that gives the ego data for making judgments and changing its efforts. Besides, superiors will be making appraisals and judgments anyway. The more candid the appraisals are, the more they can serve as a basis for communication and trust.

There are three conditions for the constructive use of appraisal systems. First, appraisal must be continuous. The General Electric studies show that performances should be conducted not annually, but on a day-to-day basis. Following an old education maxim, the more immediate the feedback on a given performance, the more useful and important it is. Furthermore, according to this research, when suggestions for improved performance are given in less concentrated form, subordinates appear to accept them more readily, providing the criticisms do not overwhelm the person. Besides, what other basis for a relationship of trust is there than continuous honest interaction?

Second, superiors must have training for appraisal. Before undertaking assessment, superiors must have an opportunity to discuss their feelings about judging others. They must be helped to learn to convey their feelings to their subordinates without concomitant guilt about being destructive. They need to learn, too, that people are not destroyed by having a realistic picture of reality to face, even if it means they must give up their jobs. The followings abstract from a letter is a case in point:

> Several years ago, during one of our austerity programs, we were required to cut our research staff by 10%. This was greeted, of course, by anguished cries from supervisors. When it got down to cases, however, it turned out that we could let about 6% go with no loss of any significance. Clearly we had been carrying a number of employees with no real justification for them. A fair share of those involved were employees within a few years of retirement whom no one had the courage to let go. By forcing some early retirements, we cleaned our house a bit at the expense of bitter hostility on the part of those who were retired. I was somewhat amazed that a little later, two of the younger men we got rid of came and thanked us! They said that they had realized for some time that they were not really doing a job but that since there was no pressure to get out, they just stayed on. When they were let go, they got new jobs for which they felt more qualified and seemed happier.

This is not an argument for firing people indiscriminately. It is a plea for giving people the facts and letting them make their own decisions based on them, rather than deceiving them into thinking they are doing well when they are not. In turn, it is a case for teaching the executive to effectuate his part of the appraisal process honestly, without being devastating.

The third condition for constructive use of appraisal is that it must be a mutual evaluation process. There are two bases for this condition. Young people are appraising their elders — if not formally, then by behavior. Abandonment of the values of elders, protests on college campuses, and the growing distance between generations are examples of appraisal by behavior. A more formal example is the contemporary effort to gauge the merit of college faculties.[50] Public criticism of professional performance in the classroom is spreading, along with student activism in general. There is organized public grading of teachers in more than a score of schools already; others are likely to follow. The Oregon legislature appropriated $500,000 for merit bonuses to deserving teachers at state colleges, and explicitly provided that students must have a say in deciding who gets them. Younger people entering business organizations come from a climate where they will expect to judge the superior's performance. They always have done so; now it is a more acceptable part of the ethos.

Another basis for making appraisal a mutual evaluation process is the fact that when two people work together, the most important common bond is their relationship. It must, therefore, be continually examined. In a superior-subordinate relationship, both parties influence each other and both have a responsibility for the task. This is what is meant by the phrase "reporting to." In order to discharge responsibility, each man must affect the other. Each has a different responsibility, but both share a joint task. If they are to carry out the joint responsibility in the most effective way, they must be able to talk freely with each other. The dialogue cannot be limited to what the subordinate alone is doing. Each party must have the sense of modifying the other. The talks must also include a joint setting of goals and the opportunity for each to express how he feels about the working relationship. The issue here is not of the compliant adjustment of one to the other, but of the interaction between them. Such adjustment leads to passivity and conformity; interaction is a precondition for identification and growth. Specifically, the subordinate must be permitted to express his feelings about what the superior is doing in the relationship and what the subordinate would like him to do to further the accomplishment of the task. Anger can then be expressed, not in hostile personal argument, but in constructive problem-solving efforts. Such a relationship facilitates task accomplishment.

That mutual appraisal is no quixotic fantasy is reflected in the General Electric research cited earlier. Superior results were obtained when the appraisal process became one of mutual goal setting for both superior and subordinate.

As is already apparent, performance appraisal is closely intertwined with coaching and counseling. Yet there are differences among problems and issues to be dealt with. Appraisal, by definition, is primarily evaluative rather than instructional. While the two are interrelated, their foci are different. Performance appraisal is therefore considered separately here to emphasize its function. The General Electric researchers also found that when separate meetings were held for different purposes, judging and counseling did not become confused. Pay and promotion discussions can be kept separate from the more frequent task-focused mutual appraisal and coaching efforts.

Lest the point be obliterated in this discussion of feedback, it should be evident that money, too, is an important source of feedback on performance.[51] It serves as a gross index of effectiveness and relative contribution to the organization. Salary discussions are not media for step-by-step improvement. Salary also serves as an index of comparative value: the higher the level in the hierarchy and the greater a man's education, the more likely he is to compare his pay with that of people outside the company. A man may have a good relative pay position within an organization, but that will not compensate for what seems to be an inadequate pay level when taken in a broader context. The higher he rises, the more he values merit versus seniority, pay versus benefits. Furthermore, the stronger and less defensive the subordinate, the more he will approve of a performance appraisal system.[52]

Performance appraisal as a method of testing reality has one other major advantage to commend it. The larger the number of his followers who find rewarding the same results as the leader, the greater is the leader's authority by their consent.[53] Mutual consideration of both the results and the modes for achieving them, the joint confrontation of realities, strengthen the leader's position — and simultaneously that of the followers.

12 / Mastery Needs

Ministration needs require supportive and facilitative efforts that come from outside the person; maturation needs require conditions for the natural unfolding within the person. When both needs have been sufficiently met at each step of the person's development, the conditions are then created for the next stage.

Once a child begins to differentiate himself from the context of the world around him and to identify with figures more competent than he, these identifications become the bases for new ties to the world.[1] With every step in his own competence, he not only becomes more independent but also masters more of his world and integrates that mastery into an ever widening interrelationship with his environment. The more psychosocial problems he resolves early in life, the more stimulating his environment is, and the more effectively the resolutions and stimulations are integrated, the wider will be his sense of mastery.

This is H. Marshall McLuhan's thesis, incidentally, that by having an ever widening range of communications media, increasing the input of stimuli, one is able to perceive the world differently and to be more confident of mastering it.[2] From their covered wagons, pioneers saw mountains as barriers. Distance was a great separator. Enclaves of difference arose — North, East, South, West; urban, rural. With airplanes, television, computers, and even more visionary technical devices, children of today are literally on top of the world. They can look down on mountains, they can see news on television as it is being made — even to the point of observing a man being murdered. They experience the world as being more amenable to fulfilling their own needs and aspirations; this is different from the way their parents experience it.

Every new maturational experience becomes integrated with others as the basis for further development. Each experience expands the ego and increases autonomy. Interference with this natural evolution brakes the development of the ego and impairs its integration.

Imagine a child who is developing naturally. His arms and legs grow at comparable rates so that they can function together in running or playing ball. He develops smooth coordination; the more effective the integration, the better he is as an athlete. Imagine the same child whose left leg grows more slowly than his right, or even fails to grow beyond a certain point. Coordination is more difficult, if not impossible to achieve. He limps. He cannot be an athlete.

It is easy to understand what crippling or maldevelopment means in physiological terms because the impairment can be readily observed. It is more difficult to do so in psychological terms. If a study showed that a high proportion of a sample of middle managers were physically handicapped, that would be an astonishing piece of information. When studies, as indicated in the preceding chapter, demonstrate that significant proportions of middle managers have limited perceptions of themselves and their roles, there is no response of astonishment. No one is aroused by the fact that a large number of college-trained men with years of experience in organizations view themselves as drudges and have little faith in their capacity to improve their own lots and the effectiveness of their companies.

The failure of the ego to continue its natural development is costly to both the individual and the organization. The individual is not only limited in one way or another, but self-perception also is distorted to the detriment of the person. When a person increases his competence and his power over his environment, he also increases his sense of self-confidence and self-respect. The more he is self-confident and the more he respects himself, the less he need fear change, fate, or innovation. As the psychoanalyst Dr. H. G. van der Waals has put it, "When a new step in the development of a more adequate conception of external reality threatens the self-regard of the child, as it often does, the child can take this step only when he has achieved at least some degree of stability of self-feeling and is lured by greater gain. Satisfaction derived from an adequately functioning ego is of greatest importance for psychic development, for it counteracts the paralyzing effects of too great an object-dependence and encourages the ego to bolder dealings with reality." [3] The same is true of adults.

If development does not occur naturally, if there are psychological impairments, then compensatory mechanisms must develop. Everyone knows people who are self-inflated, overweening or exploitative. The problems of executives who attack their subordinates, undermine their superiors or are in continuous conflict with their peers are commonplace. Organizations pay an astronomical price for such behaviors, which are efforts to prove to oneself and the environment that he is more adequate than he actually feels. Nor are these people able to change their behavior readily because they are too absorbed with their own impairments to fully grasp the realities of the outside world. Normal behavior requires consideration of oneself, of the other person and of the interest of society as a whole, as van der Waals has said. The impaired person becomes more concerned with himself than with the other two factors, and it is this relative lack of concern for the other two which keeps him in continuous tension with his environment. Such preoccupation makes it difficult for him to understand the past correctly and to anticipate the future accurately. His orientation to the world is distorted.

Thus, the issue of development and mastery is of primary concern to organizations which seek to insure their own survival. The greater the sense of mastery a person has in the organization, the more flexible, the more uninhibited and innovative he is likely to be, and, concomitantly, the less threatened by change. The less the sense of mastery, the more likely is there to be organizational passivity.

Leo Cherne captures the sense of concern executives should have about this problem. In his view, most organizational structures will be composed of second best people and will experience a constant downward pull to mediocrity if counteracting actions are not taken. As a prescription, he advises, "When you get a case of excellence, hang onto it, water and feed it with the best you have, protect it and don't let it die." He feels that the formula is to give it the one thing that it really demands — the chance to be itself.[4] Cherne's view differs somewhat from that offered here. He would concentrate on single individuals. The thesis of this book is that an environment which is facilitative for all permits individuals who can blossom more rapidly or abundantly than others to do so.

John Gardner's perspective on this issue incorporates both the concern voiced by Cherne and some of the issues already outlined in this chapter. Gardner says that one of the dangers of modern society is that men and women will lose the experience of participating in meaningful decisions concerning their own life and work, that they will become cogs in the machine because they feel like cogs in the machine.[5] He contends that all too often people are inert components of groups, not participating in any significant way, but being carried along like grains of sand in a bucket.

The fact that people are frequently cogs in a hierarchical machine, and more often feel like it, has led some to condemn industrial society and its organizations severely. It is true that organizations constrain individuals; it is equally true that organizations also contribute to their growth. A company may exercise controls over its employees; it may simultaneously increase their freedom by raising their standard of living, their level of skill and their occupational importance. The problem, therefore, is not organizations per se, but rather how they are managed. A chain can be used to shackle a man or to extricate him from the mud.

The question is how to further the experience of mastery, how to convert organizational shackles into links of strength. According to the conceptual model followed so far, there are three components to mastery needs: the need for ambitious striving and realistic achievement; the need for rivalry with affection; and the need for consolidation. The steps which the executive takes to further the fulfillment of these respective needs become the ego-expanding links of strength.

The Need for Ambitious Striving and Realistic Achievement

If ambitious striving emanates from the sense of competence, supported and encouraged by authority figures, and if the sense of competence arises out of mastering reality in step-by-step fashion, then the most important condition for fostering ambitious striving is the opportunity for people to face reality straightforwardly. Only then can they contribute directly to problem-solving and have a sense of mastery over reality problems. This condition is valid to the extent to which people have the capacity to deal with the given reality problem. For example, a passenger in an airplane may be happier not knowing what struggles the pilot is having with the weather because he cannot do anything about that problem. A passenger on a ship, however, should know if the weather threatens the vessel because there are some efforts he can make toward his own survival. Much of the time, however, management makes the assumption that the former condition is true: There is no point sharing decision-making with employees, they do not know and would not care. Although the employees cannot know everything and cannot contribute with equal competence to all decisions, when they are not aware of reality directly, they will construct their own to fit the facts as they see them.

To illustrate, an officer of a company encountered one of its employees and the employee's wife at a shopping center. During the casual conversation which followed, the employee was temporarily diverted by a passing friend. The officer and the man's wife continued their conversation, but there was an immediate shift in subject matter. The wife asked the officer if there was going to be a lay-off at the plant. Astounded that there should be such a rumor when the company had orders for two years' work, the officer wanted to know why she asked. As both she and the officer knew, there had been a change from a hard-driving plant manager to an almost nondirective one. The employees were waiting for the new plant manager to demand work from them as the old one had. When he did not do so, to them that meant that management was trying to stretch the work. There were obviously limits to how far a small company could spread its work, the men knew. Ergo, a lay-off would follow soon!

With the best of intentions, management had not kept the employees in continuous touch with reality. The executives would absorb some of the problems, the extent of which the employees would never know. From the management point of view, the employees did not have to worry about such issues. They had only to do their work and draw their pay. The management did the employees no favor, as the anxiety and the rumors testified. The employees could only feel helpless, victimized by forces beyond their control. Furthermore, the employees could learn nothing about solving some of the problems with which the whole company was confronted, and to whose solution they might have contributed.

Again, it must be emphasized that this is not a case for abandoning management to the group process, or for yielding the authority and responsibility of the executive. What is called for is an adaptation of the best qualities of the monarchical or priestly leader. The most important aspect of this conception is that the leader must always hold out reality as the focus of group efforts — the current and long-range problems which the organization faces. This reality must always include the psychology of people as well as social and economic forces and trends. The leader who would help people face reality communicates respect for and confidence in his followers. He does not limit himself to cajolery with respect to part of reality, e.g., "our market next year," or "We must do a better job of supervisory training." Nor does he make a black-and-white situation of good human relations versus productivity.

Douglas McGregor offered a four-point program for implementing such a conception:

1. An open presentation and discussion of management's view of the requirements for successful competition at any given point in time. This would include an analysis of the external forces and the internal problems reflected in the information on past performance and an examination of

possible "restraining" forces preventing a realization of the organization's capability.

2. An analysis of changes in performance of the organization that would be required to meet the demands of external reality.

3. An analysis by each subunit at every level of the contribution it can make to the total organizational effort.

4. A statement from each unit of the goals and standards to which the unit could commit itself relative to the first two points, including what help the unit would need in accomplishing these goals.[6]

Shared concern for organizational problems must evolve from the same kind of concern with the immediate tasks to be accomplished. If the shared concern is with either level alone, no precise relationship is established between the two. Therefore, people may have a sense of mastery over the task, but still be uneasy because whatever effectiveness they achieve related to their job brings them no closer to control over their fate. Or, they may have some way of exercising control over organizational decisions but have no way to act on intermediate steps to achieve their purposes.

A focus on the reality of task problems is an important first step. Virgil B. Day, vice-president of General Electric, reports that in his company's experience, the more the approach to employees can be problem-oriented and work-oriented the more likely it is to prove effective.[7] Local management and union officials, as well as employees, seem to be responsive to such an effort.

The concept of reality-testing can be applied to the individual as well as to the group. This means assigning a man to a problem which is sufficient to challenge him but not so massive as to overwhelm him. Most men want and seek such problems. Some companies are already providing them with the challenge they seek.[8] At W. R. Grace and Co., young men understudy top executives.[9] By doing so they establish both identification and a top management view of the enterprise. They also obtain experience in analyzing "whole organization" problems. This prepares them to move into top management roles early. As a result, many of Grace's executives are in their twenties and thirties. Thiokol uses a project approach to manufacturing rocket motors. In 1964 there were thirty-five project teams within the company. Each had its own manager who was responsible for the delivery of the product and, in that respect, was comparable to the president of a small company. No doubt many other examples could be found.

Lieutenant Colonel Lyndall F. Urwick, the British authority on management, argues that business deprives itself of the opportunity to prepare young men for managerial positions because it does not yet have an adequate conception of the role of the "assistant to." [10] Urwick notes that in the military, the commanding officer has a general staff: officers who assist him in carrying out his functions of command. "They help him think about the fighting and the main functions that contribute to fighting efficiency such as personnel, training, intelligence, tactics and logistics. They relieve him of much of the detail of coordinating these functions." In business, however, the "assistant to" position has not been effective because business has not yet defined "status, as distinguished from function, by the device of rank." Thus the "assistant to" is either an errand boy or becomes a rival of those who have greater seniority. Without such a structure, business lacks the machinery to train men practically for the transition from specialist to generalist. Urwick describes the military provision for doing this: "After three or four years as a General Staff Officer, he is moved back into 'the line,' with a higher rank but in a lower echelon. It is a salutary experience because of the tendency of bureaucracies to become remote from reality. The former General Staff Officer finds himself at the receiving end of the damn-fool letters he has been writing for the previous three or four years."

Giving a man a challenging problem to solve is only half of the reality-testing technique. The other half is made up of the conditions under which he is expected to solve the problem. Supportive conditions include giving him room to maneuver, freedom to make mistakes, setting limits, and defining expectations.[11] These conditions become both guidance and protective devices and, as such, establish the basis for the man to develop his own guiding mechanisms. Also, respectful treatment of a man's ideas gives him the opportunity to learn to treat others respectfully. Thus, extending the influence of support simultaneously strengthens mastery.

A conception that task accomplishment and organizational survival is the core of the man-organization relationship obviates arguments about productivity versus human relations.[12] In addition, it combines thinking and doing. That combination is now compelled by two circumstances: the competence and expectations of younger people, and the need for organizational flexibility. Muller-Thym advances the thesis that new forms of organizational structure require such synthesis at every center organized for the performance of an integrated task. This integration could not so easily be achieved in the older, more stratified organizational structure where so often thinking is separated from doing.

Apropos the implication of this for reality-testing and mastery, he quotes E. P. Brooks, former dean of the Sloan School of Management at MIT. Brooks' survey of executive development showed consistently that those managers who had functioned as members of a project team, or who had the opportunity to run even a small but integrated operation, or who, in their managerial careers, had moved from one functional area to another had developed more rapidly than their associates who had progressed through the standard organizational structure.

He adds that in productive research organizations, researchers disregarded organizational lines as required by the problems at hand; that they were establishing most of their own design criteria for the work as well as their intended patterns of association; that individually or collectively they arranged to tap directly into more senior sources of competence; and that the patterns of their group association at work followed the way they were able to use each other's specialized skill.

He summarizes the findings of those organizations which analyzed their own experiences with respect to the development of successful managerial personnel. These showed (1) that managers are shaped in a context of work and experience. Such experience is most effective when it requires the developing manager to cross functional lines, to be the center of mobilization for diverse competences and to make optimizing design and operational decisions. (2) The factors which make for the release of human energies and development of people are the same as make for operating efficiency. (3) The organization or work structure is one of these basic factors.[13]

Another mode of fostering reality-testing is by creating conflict, not by playing people off against each other or inducing anxiety, but by posing the unresolved problems. Essentially, this is to challenge people with reality. This was one facet of McGregor's proposals. Arthur Schlesinger, Jr. describes John F. Kennedy as doing just this: "He had the effect on people, in short, of forcing them to fresh approaches — exciting them because of his great interest and his own brilliance, and forcing them to a higher, more imaginative performance than the bureaucracy would ordinarily produce or tolerate." [14] Edwin G. Boring calls for creating "cognitive dissonance," by bringing into awareness simultaneous incompatible beliefs.[15]

He views such dissonance as useful when people are examining immediate problems where conflicting assumptions impede solution.

Parenthetically, it is important to recognize a crucial aspect of reality. Not everything can be made challenging or creative. Much of the world's work is routine. Harold Leavitt's suggestion is apropos: routinize what can be routinized, control what can be controlled, and then unbind and make challenging what cannot.[16]

The achievement motive, David McClelland notes, is stimulated by the mystic healer type of leader.[17] This motive, McClelland holds, is at the heart of a forward moving society. He distinguishes the achievement-oriented person from those who are affiliation-oriented and power-oriented by a simple example. Given the task of building a boat, the achievement-oriented person would obtain his gratification from making the boat. The affiliation-oriented person would have fun in playing with others with the boat but would be little concerned about the seaworthiness of the craft. The power-oriented person would be concerned with how to organize to produce the boat. Preoccupation with power or with affiliation is at the expense of getting the basic task done although both of the other motives are related to achievement.

Men who have the motive to achieve set moderately difficult but potentially surmountable goals for themselves. They are always challenging themselves to stretch their capacities. "But," writes McClelland, "they behave like this only if they can influence the outcome by performing the work themselves. They prefer not to gamble at all . . . They prefer to work at a problem rather than leaving the outcome to chance or to others." [18] They are concerned with personal achievement rather than with the rewards of success. Such men prefer situations where they can obtain tangible information about their performance. They also habitually think about how to do things better. From twenty years of study of this topic, McClelland concludes that those who have a high achievement motive are not born with it. It evolves from a particular kind of family matrix. Their parents set moderately high achievement goals and were warm, encouraging and non-authoritarian in helping their children attain these goals. The parallel between McClelland's findings about conditions conducive to the development of the motive to achieve and the previous discussion about family conditions which contribute to creativity is striking.

Just as there appears to be an enduring disposition in some people to achieve, there also appears to be in others an enduring "fear of failure." [19] This cautious behavior, too, seems to arise out of early relationships. The specific constellation in the relationship of the child to his mother seems to be as follows: the mother expects the child to become independent early and to achieve; unlike the mother of an achieving child, this kind of mother does not give much approval and recognition for independent behavior. However, she does punish him if his behavior is unsatisfactory. Her neutrality toward satisfactory behavior and punishment for unsatisfactory behavior develops a negative attitude toward achievement and fear of the consequences of failure. If she reverses her behavior and rewards satisfactory behavior while maintaining neutrality about unsatisfactory behavior, the child is motivated by the positive consequences of success.

There is a salient parallel between this kind of experience and typical reactions of subordinates to supervision. The phrases, "You're allowed only one mistake here," and "If you do something wrong, they'll tell you about it," reflect the tenor of typical managerial communication.

McClelland reports that men with stronger need to achieve, in his sense, as differentiated from the need to acquire power over others, earn more raises and are promoted more rapidly than others.[20] They work more readily with people whose expertise helps them solve the problems they face, rather than with people who are their friends. Companies with many such men grow faster. Countries with such a dominant motive have higher rates of economic growth than others.

The achievement motive can be taught, according to McClelland, although with less success if the environment does not support a man's desire to achieve. Training programs which have helped to increase such motivation are based on four concepts: identification, expectation, the individual's assessment of the situation he is in and practice techniques. Specifically, in McClelland's courses, participants were taught to think and talk like people who were achievers. They were encouraged to set realistic work goals for themselves over the next two years, and these were reviewed every six months. In playing various "experimental games," individuals could see the differences between their performance and that of others. They could examine some of the reasons why they differed and calculate what they meant in terms of their life goals. Finally, they had the opportunity to discuss their experiences with others undertaking the same training and obtaining similar support.

Behind such a program are several psychological propositions.[21] The more pretraining reasons an individual has that help him believe that he can, will, or should develop a motive, the more the educational attempts designed to develop that motive are likely to succeed. The more consistent the development of such a motivation is with the demands of reality, the more an individual can establish a "set" or attitude about the motive and relate it to actions; the more he experiences the new motive as an improvement in self-image and the more he sees it as an advancement on prevailing cultural values, the more likely he is to accept it and act on it. Thus, the more an individual commits himself to achieving tangible goals, keeps a record of his progress, is supported by others, and achieves membership in that supportive group, the more likely he is to continue with it. The relationship between the achievement motive and performance appraisal is apparent. Both relate to changes in ego structure and to the more effective mastery of reality.

From McClelland's various studies, the conditions for the achievement motive might be summarized as "expect, support, respect, leave them alone." The leader should make demands on people, expect them to achieve reasonable goals, and even some that border on the unreasonable. He should respect their capacity to chart their own course toward those goals if they are adequately protected and supported, acknowledge what they have to contribute toward reaching collective goals and, following Diogenes' dictum, "stand out of their light."

The same four activities of leadership are reflected in studies reported by Bowers and Seashore.[22] From a study of forty agencies of a life insurance company they defined four basic dimensions of leadership: support, interaction facilitation, goal emphasis, and work facilitation.

Liberating people from menial and detailed work gives them the scope to contribute to decision-making. However, if the leader does not understand what has happened, increasing controls, ranging from industrial engineering to automation, pose the danger of limiting that scope once again. Increasing attention to those things which are statistically measurable — at the expense of other potentials which are less measurable — can only serve to stifle and constrict. A major task of the executive is to evolve effective ways of maintaining individual and organizational as well as societal motivation toward achievement, while simultaneously diminishing the pressure toward power which can only result in sterile autocracy.

The Need for Rivalry with Affection

Demand is a necessary part of achievement. McClelland reports that the person with high achievement motive likes a situation in which he can take personal responsibility for finding solutions to problems.[23] In this fashion, the reality situation makes demands on him. Gardner holds that the educational system provides the young man with a sense of what society expects of him in the way of performance.[24] If it is lax in its demands, he will believe that such are the expectations of society. If much is expected of him, he will probably require much of himself. The need for the realities of a situation to pull a man out of himself has long been the theme of poets. In "Considerations by the Way," Emerson wrote: "Our chief want in life is somebody who shall make us do what we can." Goethe expressed the same thought somewhat differently in *Poetry and Truth from My Own Life*: "If you treat a man as he is, he will stay as he is, but if you treat him as if he *were* what he *ought* to be, and *could* be, he will become that *bigger* and *better* man." Hudson Hoagland, the noted biologist, states it in terms of social obligation: "In all human relations, accountability is a necessity . . . I cannot see how a modern society . . . can function unless the individuals believe they are free and responsible for their actions, and unless society can hold them responsible." [25]

Demand for high level of performance is an important part of challenge and dissonance, particularly when it occurs in the context of recognizing the realities of performance. A study of the experience of teachers shows that not only does the best-liked professor influence the decision to teach and serve as a professional ideal for the young teacher to follow, but also that the demands she makes have an effect on the kind of person the teachers become.[26] Women educated in a teachers' college showed less disillusionment with teaching than those educated in a liberal arts college. They see themselves in their professional roles more realistically. After a year of teaching, the latter view themselves not only as less inspiring but also as meaner and more demanding than they initially thought they would become.

The effect of demand is shown in other situations. For example, people learn faster when they understand the broader context of the system and how their training is a part of it. People do not learn skills or knowledge in isolation; there is always a network of prior knowledge into which the new fits. Thus, the better perspective a person has about his work, particularly the demands on his organization, the more likely he is to want to improve his performance.[27] A welder, for example, may demonstrate little concern for quality control or the number of pieces he produces until he learns that the pieces he is welding are vital components of an airplane and that people may die if his work is shoddy.

A study of managerial success leads the researchers to conclude that when a company demands high standards of performance from its management trainees in their first year with the organization, the trainees develop positive attitudes toward their work and internalize the high standards.[28] Once that happens the prospective managers turn in strong performances. They then experience success, which in turn leads them to promotion to a more demanding job. Thus these men rise in competence in keeping with the company's expectations of them. Of course, this makes for some friction with those who do not aspire, but that friction is one of the costs of survival.[29]

Demand in this sense is that specific expectation which arises from identification with the ego ideal of the leader — his aspirations, his goals, his values. The highest of these become the shared goals of the organization. They serve to lift people above their limited horizons toward the broader aim of the common good. This is the kind of demand which people, particularly the contemporary generation of young adults, want when they ask that the business have goals beyond the immediate one of profit. It is such expectations that the leader has to satisfy. At the same time, the presence of such demands and ideals with which others can identify leads to organizational cohesion, commitment, and greater survival potential. This is a particularly important issue in business because the social purposes of the corporation, unlike some other kinds of institutions, are not self-evident. They have to be more clearly and publicly stated to be instruments for identification.[30]

When confronted with a model who holds high expectations and makes important demands, the subordinate both aspires to emulate and succeed him. A college student should be motivated to pursue continuing scholarship throughout his life, based on a sound value system and independent thought. The role of the professor is therefore more than the transmission of information. The issues for teaching in the academic world are psychologically relevant for the leader in the business world; the fact of aspiration and its meaning is the same.

The emphasis on the ego ideal of the leader brings the question of values sharply into focus. This is an issue which has been largely ignored in the world of commerce except for discussions of right and wrong in business practice.[31] The value issue is much deeper than that. William D. Guth and Renato Tagiuri illuminate this issue by considering the relationship of value to corporate strategy.[32] Both executives and employees, they hold, are often unaware of their value and tend to misjudge those of others. As they define it, a value is an explicit or implicit conception of what an individual or a group regards as desirable. People select alternative courses of action on the basis of these stable personality characteristics. The key point Guth and Taguiri make is that the individual is uncommitted until he applies his code of beliefs to judgments and choices of alternative strategies. If he is not clearly aware of his values, an executive will make his choices according to them but without being aware that he is doing so. This may lead to unexpected consequences. These authors argue that the executive should examine his behavior from time to time to clarify what he stands for. He should take time to analyze what has gone on when he finds himself excusing behavior "because our values differ." By clarifying his own values, the executive opens the avenues to understanding those of others and makes commitment possible. Without commitment, corporate strategy will not be implemented. A tacit assumption is that the goals of the business fit the values of those who are involved in it or there can be no commitment at all.

At this point, an apparent contradiction must be resolved. In an earlier discussion in Chapter 6, it was reported that cultures in which there was a strong drive toward material achievement were marked by shallowness of thinking and psychosomatic symptoms. Studies of animals show that when individual males of the same species fight with each other, there is subsequently a high death rate among the losers, despite the fact that the injuries of the losers are insufficient to cause death.[33] These facts suggest that direct competition between individuals where one clearly is the victor and the other is the vanquished is literally destructive of life. In this chapter, the emphasis has been on striving and achievement as ego-strengthening activities. In the last few pages, "demand" or superego requirement has been emphasized. How can that which is good for people also be bad for them and vice versa? It might also seem that a case is being made against a competitive system when the costs of such competition are emphasized. Not so.

To clarify this issue, the content and nature of destructive competition must be defined. Obviously, not all competition is detrimental; not all people in all circumstances of defeat die. What kind of competition is it, then, that destroys?

From his psychoanalytic perspective, Robert Waelder observes that "historical experience as well as psychological considerations suggest that there are crucial issues which have a particularly high potential of violence. These are the issues which defy calculations of risks and costs, issues which by their very nature tend to be *non-negotiable,* goods which escape the calculation of costs because they are considered to be *priceless.* They are the issues involving *self-preservation, narcissism,* and *moral principles* . . . The most critical issues seem to be those which imply threats of death, of castration, or of moral death — or their latter day modifications and symbolic representations." [34]

Competition which is destructive has two conditions: first, as far as the research evidence demonstrates, it must be between *competing individual males* in which one wins a dominant position over the other as a result of which the second is thereafter submissive. A pecking order is established. There is something biologically accurate in the trite saying that the Devil will take the hindmost. Second, the competition must be that kind of rivalry in which the meaning of defeat, psychologically speaking, is that a person is destroyed. The defeat may be a devastating blow to his self-image. It may consign him to the economic scrap heap. It may communicate to him that he is "finished." He may judge himself to be worthless or irreparably injured. With respect to "moral death" or severe threats to the superego, recent studies show that conflicts of values and ethics, because of the severe guilt they induce, are particularly difficult ones in business.[35]

In this discussion, however, rivalry is directed to vanquishing reality problems collectively. The problem is to be overcome. In addition, one competes with his own ego ideal, and that of the leader. He endeavors to make himself more competent, not merely a winner in an economic "life-and-death" struggle. His active striving serves to help him master reality and to become better than his mentors. In this kind of rivalry, he can learn to become stronger even from failure. If he should fail, he can obtain feedback about his competence with which he can alter his direction and strengthen his position. This is in contrast to the contemporary practice of putting people who fail on an "executive shelf" and regarding them thereafter as the defeated ones. The organization is thereby both realistic and supportive; it is not an economic ogre which grinds men up in the interest of making a dollar. Competition with mutually established goals toward solving reality problems rarely destroys men. Men are destroyed when the business becomes a modern-day gladiatorial arena where colleagues, struggling with each other for power, daily stand to lose their innermost sense of competence and self-respect. With accompanying support from superiors and organizational resources, competition directed to real problems alleviates the pressures of the superego and diminishes defensiveness and interpersonal hostility. It thereby diminishes both psychological symptoms and organizational failure.

If the discussion is about rivalry with affection, where does "affection" enter into consideration? Two sources of affection accompany this kind of rivalry. The first lies in the intensification of the cooperative relationship between subordinates and superior. This occurs partly out of common interest in their mutual task and their complementary relationship with respect to it. It also occurs out of the empathy of the superior for the subordinate. Empathy is the ability to put oneself in another's position, to understand what he feels or why he must act in a given way in a particular situation. The research evidence indicates that the superior who can empathize with the subordinate is also more considerate of his needs with respect to accomplishing the task.[36] Those superiors who demonstrate greater consideration engage in more reciprocal two-way communication with subordinates. Such communication is in itself a mark of affection.

The second source of affection lies in winning the approval of the ego ideal. In the course of its development, the ego ideal ultimately incorporates norms, ethics, and social ideals which become part of the person's aspirations.[37] It begins to develop when the child discovers that he is not as omnipotent as in his fantasy he thought he was. Reacting to his disappointment at discovering how small and powerless he is, the child idealizes his parents who are obviously so much bigger and more powerful than he. It seems to him that they know everything and can do anything. He then identifies with them, creating within himself an image representing them, their values, aspirations, and competence. The parents' standards are higher than their achievements, and the child's picture of the parents transcends their actual behavior. In trying to fit that image, he strives to become as competent as he thinks they are. Subsequently, he also identifies with the ideals of heroes, saints, and even the Deity.[38] By doing so, he attempts to recover his earlier feelings of omnipotence. Simultaneously, if the image represents the parents, it is also a substitute for them. When he succeeds, the image approves and grants the love which the parents would have given for the same achievement. The two processes of idealizing himself and idealizing the power gradually become integrated into one goal.[39] When a person meets some of the expectations of his ego ideal, he experiences the applause of the ego ideal with relief, satisfaction, and increased self-respect.[40] The consciousness of deserving this love is felt as pride.

Obtaining the affection of the ego ideal is a more significant factor in occupational satisfaction and achievement than is commonly recognized. Much contemporary management literature on motivation is built on the concept of self-actualization, derived from the work of biologist Kurt Goldstein and others who elaborated similar concepts. Goldstein held that organisms have an inherent growth force.[41] Put simply, they try to become what they are biologically capable of becoming. Maslow, in turn, placed the need for self-actualization at the top of his list of psychological needs. For him, "it refers to a man's desire for self-fulfillment, namely to the tendency for him to become actualized in what he is potentially. This tendency might be phrased as the desire to become more and more what one is, to become everything that one is capable of becoming." [42]

This direct transition from biological theory to psychological theory has omitted one major facet of human personality which differentiates man from other organisms: his psychological capacity for holding a self-image, and the operation of the ego ideal. Self-actualization and self-fulfillment, as used contemporarily, are ego capacities; they leave the super-ego untouched.

Men do strive to become what they are capable of. These pages reflect concurrence with the conception that mastery depends significantly on ego development. Unlike animals, however, men are not content with that achievement. Self-actualization or self-fulfillment are not therefore the highest needs. Even those needs exist in the service of another force: the ego ideal. Men seek to meet the expectations of the ego ideal even when they have "fulfilled" or "actualized" themselves.

To illustrate, Ernest Hemingway and James Forrestal achieved self-actualization and self-fulfillment. Hemingway lived a rich, exciting, varied life in which he became a recognized master at his craft. Forrestal was equally prominent and influential in financial and political life. Yet both men committed suicide. Neither, according to their biographers, could live up to their ego ideals.[43] Neither could love himself for himself.

People strive toward their ego ideals even at the cost of self-actualization or self-fulfillment. Many a man who has the potential for becoming a company president prefers to operate a farm. One often sees people whose talents for other activities are evident between the lines of prosaic accomplishments. They prefer it that way; their present activity meets the needs of their superego. Other achievements, however possible and at whatever heights, would not.

Managerial efforts to motivate people based on self-fulfillment will therefore be only partially successful. Sometimes they will fail dismally. Unless they provide opportunity for people to act in the service of their ego ideals, then the people to whom such efforts are directed will be disillusioned in the organization regardless of their self-actualization.

The key phrase here is "to act." People cannot meet the expectations of their ego ideal by being rewarded. They can meet some ego expectations that way, but not all of the demands of the ego ideal. Their activity toward the latter goal is their major reward. Concepts of participative management are valuable precisely because they enable people to act toward their ego ideals. They permit people to like the images of themselves which they see.

No amount of self-actualization will metamorphize a man into a superman. He will never match the talents of legendary heroes or of the man he imagined his father to be. Only as he acts as he believes they would act does he fit himself to their pattern. As Freud put it, "There is always a feeling of triumph when something in the ego coincides with the ego ideal." [44]

The Need for Consolidation

No one operates as a series of disparate parts or personality traits. One of the major difficulties of most contemporary personality theories, and the managerial applications derived from them, is that they view man as bits and pieces of psychological traits added together: aggressive or passive, masculine or feminine, introvert or extrovert. At best, their picture of man is a profile; the predictions about his behavior derived from such thinking are but statements of the statistical likelihood that more people will tend to behave in one gross way than another.

Just as man is physiologically integrated, so is he psychologically integrated. He must be to function. The quality of his integration will be reflected in the quality of his functioning. It is not a matter of being integrated or not integrated, but rather of levels of integration. [45] A highly intelligent, effective leader has integrated his life experiences into a pattern which is more effective for adaptation and survival than that of a man of similar age and equal intelligence who is demoralized and on the welfare rolls.

Effective adaptation requires the consolidation of a man's lifelong experiences into a composite which is internally consistent, structured of complementary identifications, harmonious values and gratifying avenues for mastery. According to Erik H. Erikson, a psychoanalyst who has given considerable attention to the problems of identity, it also requires finding "a niche in some section of his society, a niche which is firmly defined and yet seems to be uniquely made for him. In finding it, the young adult gains an assured sense of inner continuity and social sameness which will bridge what he *was* as a child and what he is *about to become,* and will reconcile his *conception of himself* and his *community's recognition* of him." [46]

Erikson describes seven stages of development, three of which take place during adulthood. As adults mature, they are likely to seek greater intimacy or closer relationships with others in the form of friendship, combat, leadership, love and inspiration. If they cannot move psychologically closer to others, they become preoccupied with themselves and, as a result, are somewhat stunted in their psychological growth.

Those adults who are able to develop greater intimacy lay the groundwork for the next stage of development: generativity, the interest in establishing and guiding the next generation. People who do not reach this level of development often begin to indulge themselves as if they were their own only child, Erikson says. Finally, only when a person has evolved through these stages is it possible for him to achieve the integrative stage or the stage of integrity. "Only he who in some way has taken care of things and people and has adapted himself to the triumphs and disappointments of being, by necessity, the originator of others and a generator of things and ideas — only he may gradually grow the fruit of the seven stages." [47] When a person achieves such integrity, he accepts himself, accepts his life as his own responsibility, has a sense of comradeship with people of diverse origins and customs, and is ready to defend the dignity of his own life against physical and environmental threats.

Interest in establishing and guiding the next generation is important to the organization which wants each person to contribute to the development of new talent, and to the individual, who must himself do so to achieve the personal strength of consolidation.

Erikson adds that the identity formation of the young man is fostered when those whose activities are significant to him give him a function and a status, and treat him as one whose growth and transformation is important. As his feeling of identity increases, he has a sense of well-being, of direction and assuredness that he will be recognized by those whose recognition counts.

External circumstances, some of which have been described under ministration and maturation needs, are one set of factors in facilitating consolidation. The development of ego skills is another. The ego ideal is yet a third.

When a person can judge his own accomplishments and recognize how well he is living up to his ideal, he provides himself with a reservoir of self-gratification. He meets his own standards with contentment. As a result, he acts as an integrated entity. His actions are in harmony with his aspirations and he feels approved of by his ego ideal for what he has done. He is, then, self-approving. He likes himself; he is an important source of affection for himself. This is not the self-inflation of the egocentric person, which is a compensation for feelings of incompetence and inadequacy, but rather honest self-regard for who one is and what one does. By providing such gratification, the ego ideal supports the ego in dealing with the inevitable disappointments and frustrations of living.[48]

There is another important consequence of the development of the ego ideal. When the child internalizes the "parental function" represented by the ego ideal, psychologically, as the psychoanalyst Roy Schafer indicates, he becomes father to himself. By doing so, he acquires the basic equipment for later becoming father to his children. He has values, aspirations and goals to transmit to them. He also establishes motivation "for learning and perfecting a certain moral, protective and comforting know-how. This know-how is part of being grown-up." [49]

The affection of and gratification from the ego ideal in the adult becomes an important psychological instrument by which the adult as a leader "rears" others. He, too, can then create conditions for ambitious strivings and rivalry with affection. Identification with the leader ultimately leads to personal and organizational strength.

Part Four / Coalition

However complex and frustrating the executive's task may be, it is not something that he need do alone. Every organization has built-in resources to support the executive function. Among these is the personnel function — to date largely miscast and inadequately utilized. This section reconceptualizes the personnel function as a support role for the executive task which the book has so far elaborated. In addition, it illuminates some of the mistakes the executive is likely to make and is likely to experience in carrying out his task. By recognizing and enumerating these errors and conflicts, they are like shoals made evident on a map; though unseen they can be navigated more safely for having been located. The task thus becomes opportunity and the shoals the demarcation of a route rather than a threat to survival.

13 / Not by One Alone

Centering as it has on the leadership-teaching role, the discussion thus far may have given the reader an impression that the executive is to be a superman. Neither as a teacher nor an executive can he be all things to all men. At best, he can be one major influence. As that force, his contribution will not be a global, academic-like one. Rather, his own leadership style will be his basis for teaching. Furthermore, if his subordinates are to be sufficiently broadened to evolve their own styles of leadership, they must have a variety of leadership models with whom to identify. In addition to their contact with him, they will have continuing relationships with those who carry out the major leadership functions.

Leadership Functions

In any organizational situation, three leadership functions are served, as illustrated by the work of Abraham Zaleznik and his colleagues.[1] They speak of the complementary interrelationships of these functions as the executive role constellation. The functions were referred to earlier as the homeostatic, the mediative, and the proactive.

The homeostatic function relates to the maintenance of internal equilibrium in the organization. It is often an informal function, frequently carried on by people who are not officially designated for that role. People who seek to maintain intra-organizational equilibrium are often those who are not in the competitive mainstream of the organization, and who are widely trusted by others. They are intra-organizational shock absorbers, reducing conflicts, repairing hurt feelings, and restoring ruptured relationships. Such a role is like that of a favorite uncle in a family to whom children turn because he exercises neither control nor authority over them, but is encouraging and supportive. They can talk frankly to him about matters they would discuss with no one else. Zaleznik designates this as an "avuncular-permissive" role.

The mediative function applies to the environmental pressure on the organization. Where the chairman of the board is the chief executive officer, the president may be just such a person — executing policy. In another organization that role may be performed by the executive vice-president. It is the "inside man" task as contrasted with the "outside man" activity. The mediative leader sees to it that the organization meets the requirements imposed on it, modulates the stress produced by external demands of the marketplace or constituency. His is a more aggressive role than that of the homeostatic leader, but simultaneously supportive and protective while being demanding. It might be called a "maternal-nurturant" role.

The third function, the proactive, is the "paternal-assertive" role. The proactive leader seeks out the outside environment and is innovative with respect to it. He leads the organization forward to master its environment. His forward leadership creates reality-based tensions within the organization as it strives to meet the challenges to its survival which come from the marketplace or service arena.

These functions may be carefully delineated among three different executives by intention or they may evolve spontaneously in keeping with the complementary skills of the respective leaders. They may vary, some executives carrying on one or another function under different circumstances. Most executives at one time or another will have to undertake each of the three functions, although for most men, one will tend to predominate. The more clearly the roles are defined for each executive, the more selectively will subordinates be able to turn to one for the specific skills he has to offer. From each man a subordinate may learn a specific skill: how to attack reality problems, how to facilitate the work process, how to support others.

The executive-teacher-leader, regardless of his particular style, can rely on the others to complement his activity. He should formally plan to do so. The mediative and proactive leaders will more frequently have to look to someone else for help in implementing their teaching activities. In most organizations that will be the personnel department. Ideally the executive responsible for the personnel department effects the homeostatic function.

Before turning to the personnel department for such help, the executive-teacher should be aware of the problems, difficulties, and shortcomings of that activity or he will find himself disillusioned and frustrated. He may also be making demands that the department is ill-prepared to meet. In some instances, major rehabilitation of the personnel department may be a condition for implementing the concepts advanced in this book.

Personnel Is Not for People

Personnel departments struggle with six major problems: (1) the personnel function is an "added on" activity; (2) often those responsible for personnel activities are assigned rather than chosen; (3) many are poorly trained; (4) they have difficulty defining the role and function of their department; (5) they deal with policies and procedures rather than with people; (6) they have no systematic theory of human behavior.

In most organizations the personnel function is one of four or five major departments. Most departments are concerned with producing and selling the goods or services — manufacturing, finance, sales, and so on. Sometimes there is argument whether an activity such as accounting is a line or staff function, whether it is productive or ancillary. Personnel, however, is always regarded as a staff function; frequently, it is grudgingly borne by the organization.

Most of the personnel function arose from the development of rules and regulations governing wages and hours, and the need for someone to handle collective bargaining.[2] More than half of 249 companies surveyed by the National Industrial Conference Board had no corporate personnel unit before World War II. It is thus an activity "added on" to the functions of manufacturing the product or providing the service, and selling them. It is often viewed by the chief executive and other line executives as a necessary evil, an overhead burden. This is partly because management often cannot see how such a function contributes directly to earning power or productivity. Some organizations view the personnel activity as one they would abolish if they could; others say they are not large enough for such a formal activity.

Since personnel has been viewed as an "added on" function, it is often treated as an organizational stepchild. Only rarely is it regarded as a professional function, similar to engineering or accounting, even by personnel men. There is a tendency in industry to install men in personnel positions when they have been unsuccessful at more competitive or managerial effort. There is also a tendency to disdain executives in personnel work as being preoccupied with "liking people" at the expense of the economic necessities of running the business. How can a tangential issue such as "liking people" be important when the direct task of the organization must be accomplished whether people like it or not?

The textbooks on personnel work describe and enumerate many techniques, methods, and activities.[3] They talk vaguely about the human element in business. In some cases they may even describe the personnel man as a "coordinator." Some go so far as to assert that he is responsible for the "human relations" of the business. For these functions they offer him the tools of a technician: personnel tests, interview schedules, standard forms, formulas, and procedures. If any field of management is characterized by superficial understanding, cliche, and gimmick, it is the personnel field.

The personnel department is divided in varied ways in different companies. The chief officer's title may read "vice-president of personnel and industrial relations" or "vice-president of industrial relations" or simply "personnel director." The job usually encompasses an expansive range of almost unrelated activities. The title of the executive in charge usually reflects the dominant activity of the office holder, and the subordinate nature of his other activities. As a result of being an "added on" function, of having many practitioners assigned and poorly trained, the personnel profession has difficulty in adequately defining its role and function. Typical definitions include an ambiguous generalization or two, followed by the enumeration of specific techniques. Little wonder that the boss' most frequent complaint about personnel men is that they are not sufficiently assertive.[4]

Ask a personnel administrator why he is in the personnel field and he will answer because he likes to work with people. Undertakers give the same reply to the same question. Personnel men rarely work with people; those who actually supervise, work with others. Ask a personnel man what he does, and his reply will indicate that he works mostly with paper — rules and regulations, programs, and projects. Other units view personnel as the "paperwork" department.[5]

Consider the complaint of a department head in a manufacturing plant: "Nothing irks me more than receiving reams of memos discussing regulations and procedures on a hundred different subjects; forms to be filled out on people in my department; questionnaires to be answered. The personnel department is constantly bombarding us with this stuff. If they are so important, why doesn't the personnel manager drop over and talk with me once in a while about them? He would learn a lot more if he would sit down and ask some of these questions, especially if he would take the time to select the forms and questions that actually apply to the members of this department. Furthermore, there are some personnel policies important enough to warrant direct discussion with some of us responsible for large departments."

There are two important considerations here. First, whenever the personnel executive deprives himself excessively of face-to-face relationships with the people in the organization, he denies himself access to their feelings. Personal contacts are essential to understand the feelings and attitudes, the fears and threats which precipitate behavior. That understanding should be his prime responsibility. Indeed, the more the organization has succumbed to systems supported by paper relationships, the greater the need for the personnel department to be attuned to people. The second consideration often overlooked by the personnel manager is that when he is isolated from people, he cannot utilize himself as a professionally trained and sensitive person. His own personality, ideally, should be a key diagnostic instrument for understanding the daily strains of the organization.

In many companies, when the personnel department does become involved with people, its involvement is part of a "buying off" effort to keep employees happy. One company recently reported with pride in a national personnel publication this example of effective personnel relations: five staff members of its personnel division devoted months of time and effort to buying, wrapping, and keeping records on Christmas gifts for employees' children. Countless personnel officers try to cope with less than optimum morale by conceiving ideas of this type — and implementing them. Such efforts are no more than poorly disguised paternalism, attempts to buy affection and loyalty. Palliative efforts never solve problems; they temporarily relieve pain. In the absence of more effective problem-solving, the demand for palliation never ceases.

Frank O. Hoffman, a Los Angeles consultant on personnel practices, complains that personnel men have come to accept the inconsequential as the significant, and they are too often attempting to do someone else's job.[6] He contends that many personnel men build up the inconsequential aspects of their job because they have not been allowed to participate as active members of management. He calls their efforts at compensation for their inadequate role "tail of the dog activities." The personnel executive is doomed to be an "after the fact" irritant if he continues to concentrate on trying to control the decisions of supervision, sell programs and force adherence to procedures.

Despite the discussion of practical psychology and human relations in

both the textbooks and the personnel literature, the personnel executive
has no systematic way of understanding people. He may have acquired
considerable experience in his job. He may have had a smattering of
courses, and in some cases, even a professional degree. Regardless of the
combination of training and experience, he has no explicit theory of motivation by which to understand human behavior. At best, his knowledge is
a pastiche of concepts. The limitations of his knowledge are made explicit
by the wide range of useless psychological tests he buys by the thousands
of copies. These limitations lead to an emphasis on a pragmatic and short-
term, manipulative view of managing people (personnel *managers,* personnel *administrators*), rather than the dynamic, continuous process view
of the interaction of man with the organization in which he works.

Painful evidence of this state of affairs is found in a study of personnel
men in sixteen federal government agencies.[7] Of the 1955 respondents to
the survey, 21 percent had completed high school or less. Most had entered
the field without having a definite occupational choice, and most received
their training on the job. The five most important abilities and skills which
the respondents believed to be essential for work in personnel were: "ability
to write; broad general abilities; ability to conceive of ideas; ability to
plan; and ability to analyze problems." Most felt that the training they
needed most was in personnel administration and general management
theory. People, anyone?

The result of these forces is that the typical use of the personnel division
results in what one observer calls "a kind of schizophrenia" in members of
that department.[8] Being in the unwelcomed position of a fifth wheel, finding a lack of clarity of function, and having no solid professional base from
which to operate, the personnel man's situation is often tenuous and frequently marked by tension. Other effects of this perception are obvious.
As a class, personnel men are the lowest paid executives. Executives often
rise from manufacturing, sales or finance to become company presidents;
personnel executives rarely do.

Another product is that such an organizational role is not functioning
well for any of the parties involved. While personnel is on the organizational
chart, few businesses have succeeded in integrating it well. Comments by
sociologists and professors of business administration point out the ambiguous position of the personnel department: in the organization but not of it.
At best, the authority and responsibility of this department is indirect.

The existence of an ill-defined unit is an irritation to the rest of the organization.[9]

How does the organization liberate itself from this morass? There are no ready-made answers to this problem. Universities mass-produce people with bits and pieces of knowledge, but that is not the answer. Personnel people talk and complain about their plight, but this does nothing to solve the problem. Much of what has been written in the literature has been poorly, if at all, integrated by management so that it is not much help either.

Organizations have tried various kinds of first-aid. They have reduced the functions performed by the personnel department. They have tried to transfer some of the personnel functions to the operating or line divisions. They have divided the duties so that personnel operations and employee development are handled by different people. They have increased and decreased paperwork. They have sent their personnel executives to training programs and group dynamics laboratories. None of these maneuvers seems to have provided an adequate solution.

To be fair, many seriously trained, dedicated personnel executives and professors of personnel practice have been working for years on this problem. Some are highly sophisticated about social science theory. They have made many useful contributions and have gradually elevated the personnel role.

In a 1966 survey by the National Industrial Conference Board, about three-fourths of the respondents said their most important role is to "advise and counsel top management in initiating changes." [10] When describing their most time-consuming duties, they responded, "Services to the line and other staff groups." In the majority of firms surveyed, the top personnel man is a vice-president who reports to the president or chairman. The personnel staff has grown faster than the company's overall work force. It now focuses more on management development, manpower planning, organization planning, employee benefits, and personnel research rather than on labor relations.

The Internal Consultant

There are a number of responses to these complaints about and by personnel men and the personnel function. Tom Lupton, of London's Institute of

Personnel Management, contends that personnel management should modify its present role and practice as a minor administrative aid to management concerned with the way management activities are conducted. Instead, he proposes, the personnel officer should concentrate on analysis of social organizations and structures, and the application of the findings of the behavioral sciences to industrial relations.[11] Frederick Herzberg suggests that the new-style personnel department should concentrate on the human side of man and the psychological growth of personnel.[12] In his view, it would have three main tasks: education of employees and managers in man's dual nature, job enlargement, and remedial work. By "dual nature" Herzberg refers to two motives for working: for profit and for avoidance of pain; and to enjoy the excitement and meaning of achievement. By remedial work he means dealing with technological obsolescence, poor performance, and administrative failures.

Walter H. Powell argues that the role of the personnel department is to "*assist* [italics added] management in improving the ability of its managers to manage, and maximize the utilization of its personnel . . . It is the personnel department which must provide the top management of any company with the coordinative skills needed to attain a high level of internal cooperation." [13] If the personnel department is to do this job, says Powell, it must develop a form of "marketing research which will indicate the prime requirements of the corporate organization." These requirements can then be coupled with the capabilities of people in the context of an environment congenial to simultaneous need satisfaction and profitability. Powell sees the personnel man as a catalytic agent.

These three points of view can be combined and included under a well-defined management role: the personnel executive as an internal organizational consultant in the behavioral sciences. Specifically, he might be viewed as a general practitioner in psychological, sociological, and anthropological processes in organization.

The role of the consultant is an honored one. He makes suggestions from distilled experiences. He is a source of knowledge and support. He does not wield an axe or dispense favors. His is truly an avuncular role in the best sense of that word. In this new role, members of the personnel department will concentrate on diagnosis and preventive maintenance, as does the family doctor. They will discover and define problems of people at work and they will help the organization avoid or eliminate potential difficulties and problems. To do so, they will necessarily require a comprehensive theory of motivation. They will also need a knowledge of the more generally useful techniques applicable in business and industry for facilitating the work of people. For dealing with problems beyond their own skills and competences, they will need to familiarize themselves with sources of specialized help and services.

Some may feel that this conception is not new, that personnel departments are already functioning in this way. Some are. Perhaps the major difference between many contemporary practices and what is suggested here is the difference between a first-aid man and a physician. To suggest such a role is to call for a drastic reconceptualization and upgrading of the personnel function. To the question, "Should the personnel function be professionalized?" the answer is a resounding affirmative. The personnel executive should be an applied behavioral scientist.

The diagnostic aspect of the personnel job involves methods of discovering and defining problems. Traditionally, and often naively, the personnel executive has used entrance interviews and other screening devices to learn the vocational skills and limitations of applicants, and which applicants might fit where in the organization. A more comprehensive effort is the assessment program devised by the American Telephone and Telegraph Company and some other companies.[14] None yet seriously takes into account the concept of the psychological contract and its implications; all such efforts will have to do so as selection becomes more sophisticated. To understand and apply the more refined conceptions, the personnel executive must become more expert and more diagnostically minded. No longer will it be appropriate for a personnel executive to ask, "Are psychological tests any good?" or "What about the Minnesota Multiphasic?"

The personnel executive has also used exit interviews to determine the specific problems people had experienced on the job. He has installed suggestion systems for learning about and correcting unfavorable situations. He has evolved statistics of efficiency such as absenteeism, sickness, tardiness, and turnover figures. While, perhaps, not termed "diagnostic devices" and not even viewed as having to do with diagnosis, their function was and is diagnostic.[15] Yet they are obsolete. To ask people why they have decided to leave after they have made their decision means that they have had no opportunity to express their dissatisfactions in the course of their work. The question arises too late for remedy. To have suggestion systems independent of the task and the work group itself is a mechanistic gimmick. Statistics of efficiency have been used most frequently as indices for culprit-hunting. "Some *one* must be at fault; find him," has been the traditional underlying thesis of such efforts. Morale studies, attitude surveys, opinion polls, and "family-type" or intra-organizational group dynamics laboratories have often been used in the same way.

The diagnostic question must be, "What is going on here among us?" The physician must examine the whole person and the interrelationship of his several systems. The organizational diagnostician must learn to examine the whole organization. He may use some of the traditional tools, but he will have to understand them as only parts of an examination and diagnostic process. Modes of conceiving of the organization as a unit for diagnostic purposes are now being evolved.[16] Methods for bringing problems to the surface other than the traditional questionnaires are already possible. When elicited, conceptualized, and reported as part of the work process, there is a direct interaction between diagnosis and correction. Conceptualization is an important step since most attitude studies simply relate what people have said with minimal understanding and interpretation of what the answers mean. Many statements and complaints are displacements from what actually troubles people. They cannot talk about their troubles if they are limited to multiple choice replies to questions which may have limited relevance to their feelings. Furthermore, it is extremely difficult for many people to verbalize about what they feel. Sometimes the feelings which cause discontent are poorly understood by the complainants themselves. Without a knowledge of unconscious motivation, an organizational diagnostician is like a physician who tries to understand the meaning of the pulse rate without grasping the concept of the circulation of the blood.

Oversimplified and stylized answers are not the fundamental tools of the professional personnel executive. He has a responsibility to assist management in avoiding these pitfalls. Again, he also must be aware of tendencies to develop a personnel program which glibly provides stock answers to department heads and supervisors who face personnel problems in their daily work. Much resentment is generated by personnel administrators who appear to be over-confident and aggressive in requiring their "professional" answers to be accepted and utilized by other executives. The latter balk when they feel there is no genuine understanding of their problem in the proposed solution. To the degree the personnel administrator forsakes his understanding of psychological processes in solving problems, he abdicates his particular responsibility to the management of the organization. A personnel officer must be a managerial guardian against the common organizational hazards of over-simplifying the task of understanding people and their contribution to organizational success.

Diagnosis as an effort to understand psychological process need not become a culprit-finding activity. Neither need it imply corrective activity by the diagnostician himself as a "therapist." This is why any reference to "therapy" is omitted from this discussion. Correction is effected by the persons involved; the diagnostician thereby becomes their ally instead of a spy searching for damaging information. Regardless of its size and level, if the work group itself cannot be self-correcting on the basis of the data it produces or receives, then an outside consultant is needed. This avoids the internal problems that will result if the personnel executive himself tries to undertake correction. For transference reasons, as described in Chapter 3, just as a physician will not treat a member of his family, or a lawyer represent himself, so the internal consultant should limit his own function in his and the organization's interests.

The leader-teacher will need such a diagnostician as a colleague — one who can hear, pinpoint issues, and evolve modes of feedback conducive to self-correction. He should require such competence of his personnel executive. That there are not yet many people trained at this professional level should not deter him.

Personnel functions also include preventive maintenance — the avoidance or elimination of potential difficulties and problems. The personnel executive will be concerned with the degree to which the organization meets ministration, maturation, and mastery needs. He will be knowledgeable about programs and experiences, evolved out of scientific conceptions and managerial practice, which serve these varied needs. He himself need not be a technician in program operation; he will have technical specialists in his department — in personnel research, in management development, in selection, in training, in personal counseling, and in performance appraisal. However, he should be ready to utilize the vast data and productive techniques now being developed.[17] He should be capable of critical thinking about such efforts and have a broad enough perspective of the organization as a social system to adapt and develop programs which can be viable in his organization.

It will be up to the personnel executive not only to formulate programs to meet needs, but also to keep a careful check on how they function. He concerns himself with the process of the man-organization relationship.

His key points of focus are with the starting, supervising, structuring, and support activities of the organization. Structuring means two activities: the composition of complementary roles in work groups of optimum size for the task; and the formation of an organizational structure which meets the requirements of the kind of production or service process of the organization and the kind of people who perform it. He will be interested in what optimal distance people in a given kind of work need from each other and their superiors, and the kind of information about their effectiveness which can be provided directly from the activity of people. He will recognize that intensity of supervision and control will vary with the demands of the job and the experiences of the person in it.

He will be wary of routines. To search for, discover, and then routinize those procedures that appear to meet the demands of a situation is perhaps the goal of most individuals in an organization. Routines and systems are essential for efficiency and productiveness. They provide predictability and security. To the extent that they short-circuit the process of thinking and evaluating, they become stultifying and depressing, obstacles to the achievement of objectives. The danger is that routinized procedures frequently become separated from the needs they originally served. The original purpose fades into oblivion but the form and activity continue — often meaningless to most people.

The support functions of the personnel department include those practices which implement the concept of job security, helping the various levels of supervision with their specialized problems with people, and counseling. The last should include personnel and job counseling, retirement counseling, special help in moving — with particular emphasis on joint planning with husband and wife about the implications and problems of the move. The personnel department should maintain a referral relationship to community agencies to help employees with family, financial, and legal problems. Any activity which mobilizes the resources of the organization behind the person when he needs that help is supportive.

Even this sketchy outline of the major aspects of general practice in human relations by the personnel executive has certain limitations. First, the personnel executive cannot be trained to be equally expert in all of the activities which have been elaborated here. For example, specialized training is required to do morale studies, conduct opinion polls, design sociometric measures, organize work groups, and counsel people. If he is not expert in all areas, he will at least know what these activities are and how such services can be obtained. Surely the personnel executive could and should seek professional consultation without loss of face or embarrassment.

Sometimes it is difficult for the personnel executive to take an objective point of view with respect to the activities of his own organization. Often a personnel officer will find it wiser to call in an outside consultant even when he, by training or experience, is capable of dealing with the situation. An unbiased, unemotional opinion or a special job done by an outsider will, on occasion, be more satisfactory.

Even if he were fully trained to do everything listed under diagnostic and preventive maintenance functions, he cannot possibly undertake all these things himself because of time pressures, if nothing else. In a large business organization with a comprehensive staff and specialists in each area, most things could be done. This kind of a situation is analogous to that in a large teaching hospital with various specialists readily at hand. A general practitioner does not very often have such resources available to him.

Thus the personnel administrator, while defining his scope, must also define his limitations and develop ways of obtaining help in contending with those problems with which he cannot deal himself. In addition to the traditional commercial consultation services, there are many other resources. The trained social workers of family service agencies and child placement agencies can often be useful as consultants in dealing with personal problems and psychological problems in supervision. The departments of psychology, sociology, and business administration in most colleges or universities appreciate opportunities through which their students can learn some of the practical problems of business and industry while developing their scientific acumen in tackling them. Where studies of internal organizational problems are required, often a single individual from a college or university staff can teach members of the business organization how to study a problem and extract valid conclusions.

Thus the executives of the organization will grow and further develop their skills and talents. As the pool of retired executives grows, there will be available the collective experience of many men who are eager to contribute their knowledge, especially to smaller businesses which cannot afford expensive consultations.

Implicit in the concept of the "general practitioner" are two considerations. The first is that one must practice or lose his skills. The second is that one must keep abreast of current trends and developments in his particular field. In the medical field this means refresher courses, attendance at lectures and work toward advanced credits in professional organizations or professional societies. While there are not yet explicit requirements in the personnel field for professional advancement, the conscientious personnel men will not be content with anything less than his best efforts to meet his responsibilities. His senior executive should encourage this aspiration.

There is one difference between the concept of the physician as a general practitioner and that of the personnel officer. The general practitioner treats disease in individuals; when he has to deal with large groups of people he then becomes a public health physician. The public health physician does not treat. He may recognize a problem; he may urge that it be solved in the most constructive way possible. Most often he will concern himself with prevention, or with the diagnosis and presentation of problems to people whose responsibility it is to solve them. As a public health physician, his task is to mobilize community efforts for preventing illness. Many people who are in responsible community positions must join with him to eradicate particular threats to health, whether a stagnant swamp or sub-standard housing. "Treatment" in this sense is action by others who have responsibility.

Often the personnel administrator will discover that what is needed requires action by people other than himself. For example, consider the manufacturing industry suddenly plagued with widespread absenteeism and turnover. The personnel administrator may have the responsibility of analyzing the problem and determining its underlying causes. However, the task of remedying the problem may become that of the entire management staff — implementing widespread measures suggested by the understanding of the problems. In this sense, the personnel administrator is much like the public health physician.

The Executive-Personnel Relationship

The definition of the personnel function that we have formulated calls for a higher order of skills and professional activity than has been customary. Such a man meets this job description, sent to me by the executive vice-president of an electronics firm:

> We have grown very fast in the last fourteen years. We very much need a personnel manager who will spend time thinking with us about

some of our problems from the standpoint of his professional understanding of people — why we behave as we do; what we need in order to be productive; and how industry can enhance self-esteem, dignity and creativity even as it pursues organizational goals. This is a way of describing some of our objectives with which we need help in accomplishing.

We don't want a technician. The manager will have technical specialists in his department. We want a person to bring to us certain attitudes and skills and communicate them in such a way that he will assist our department heads and supervisors in their efforts to understand and handle the problems they face every day that involve human behavior and human relations.

Even if this knowledgeable administrator were fortunate enough to hire the talented personnel executive he describes, could he make effective use of him? This kind of function is (1) comprehensive; (2) interactional; (3) professional. It is a continuous task involving all parts of the organization, and a special kind of relationship with the leader and his immediate colleagues. If the executive does his own diagnosis and treatment of human relations problems, he does not need a personnel professional; he needs a clerk. If he is to make use of such a person he must take into account the special problems which are likely to arise.

Following a study of the relationships between executives and consultants, Seymour Tilles concluded from a Harvard Business School study that many executives fail to achieve satisfaction from consultants for two major reasons.[18] They either think they are "buying the right answer" or that the authority will provide both the diagnosis and the certain cure.

The executive who believes that he will be buying the right answers from a personnel professional will be doomed to failure. Such a personnel professional will provide him with "packaged programs" but no help. Help in the present sense means the opportunity to explore ideas, concepts, programs, problems, and practices — and to make choices which fit the needs of the organization.

The issue of getting answers is confounded by the doctor-patient analogy suggested here for the personnel executive's role. Tilles questions the analogy. In contrast to the patient, the executive does not approach the consultant with the feeling that something is wrong with him. Usually he wants the consultant to do something with someone else. Further, Tilles argues, one of the key issues for the consultant is "How many people is the client?" For the physician there is only one patient; however, an organizational consultant must know with how many groups, divisions, and personnel he is involved. The medical analogy makes no provision for defining the patient in terms of groups. The patient leaves the diagnosis to the physician; the executive cannot. Furthermore, the physician treats the patient, but the consultant must depend on the organization to implement self-help efforts, only sometimes under his guidance. Tilles suggests three questions which the executive must ask if the consulting relationship is to be a process directed toward the achievement of specific organizational results:

1. Toward what end results will the relationship be directed?
2. What is help, as a process, going to consist of?
3. What role will the responsible executive take in the process?

While Tilles' points are well taken and his paper is highly useful for executives, the underlying analogy is nevertheless useful for conceptualizing the role of the personnel executive. Its usefulness will depend on how the executive answers the three questions.

The executive should not approach his internal consultant with the question, "What's wrong?" Rather, he and his personnel professional will continuously be asking of themselves and their colleagues, "What's going on here?" They will be attuned to psychological process just as an automobile mechanic is attuned to the sound of a motor. One of the major human relations skills executives must attain is this kind of "being tuned in." Instead of looking for others to whom something is to be done, the chief executive and his team will be examining their own relationships and their individual and collective impact on their subordinates. They will be raising questions of themselves, not indicting. The client will be the organization as a whole. The organization will undertake self-help efforts unless and until it is necessary to call an outsider in.

The major problem confronting the leader-teacher who would use an internal consultant is his own feeling of dependency. A consulting relationship is often interpreted by the person seeking help to mean that the consultant is somehow superior to him. Few people approach consultation with a physician without apprehension. Furthermore, he who has difficulty allowing himself to be examined and in following medical advice will grasp the parallel problems in accepting the consultant's advice. No one likes to have his inadequacies exposed to another or to feel that he is dependent on another, particularly a subordinate. These feelings will appear in relationship to the personnel executive as a consultant. If such feelings are not recognized and broached for discussion, they can result in the defeat of an effective personnel function. In fact, the presence of such feelings among other executives is probably the single most important reason why the personnel function has not advanced more rapidly. Yet, if they are recognized and dealt with, they need not be a barrier.

The chief executive must therefore not only demand a higher level of performance from the personnel executive, but he must simultaneously make it possible for such performance to occur. As in the other work relationships discussed previously, the two are engaged in a task in which they need each other, and the organization needs their combined talents.

14 / The Failures

Despite his best efforts, the executive as a leader-teacher will have failures. When a man is disappointed with another's response to his efforts, he tends to blame the other person or himself, sometimes alternating between both. The contemporary management scene is characterized by repetitive complaints about the inadequacies of subordinates and potential executive successors. In case discussions in management seminars, executives frequently hold themselves responsible for subordinates' personality problems that cannot be solved by managerial efforts.

The validity of such complaints would seem to be verified by the widespread use of management consultants for every conceivable purpose and the consequent recurrent reorganization of businesses. These phenomena reflect the chronic pain of management, enormous dissipation of human energy and the palliative nature of the attempted cures. Karl Menninger coined the term "polysurgical addiction" to describe people who repeatedly demanded operations to cure their multiple, repetitive complaints.[1] It would not stretch the analogy to speak of "polyconsultative addiction" to describe this frequent mode of solving managerial problems.

This phrase is not meant to reflect adversely on consultants any more than Dr. Menninger's phrase was a criticism of surgeons. Both practitioners serve important purposes. Rather, it refers to a characteristic managerial way of perceiving problems as events caused by someone or something foreign to oneself. Thus perceived, it follows that they are to be resolved by excision or reconstruction, also by someone else. The irony of such a situation is that the executive, like the patient who wants someone else to remove the presumably offensive part, often has within himself the power to cope with managerial problems without either himself or his organization undergoing "therapy." This is especially true with respect to those problems which are of his own, if inadvertent, making.

From cases reported by executives, six common managerial errors in the supervision of subordinates can be discerned. These are: encouragement of power-seeking; failure to exercise controls; stimulation of rivalry; failure to anticipate the inevitable; applying pressure on men of limited ability; and misplacement. The first three are related to the inadequate recognition and management of aggression. The remaining errors stem from failure to consider fully future implications of present decisions.

Inadequate Management of Aggression

No single kind of subordinate pleases his superiors more than the man who is able to assume responsibility during a crisis, plunge into his task with zest, and accomplish it successfully. Such men become the "jets" of industry, the "comers," the "shining lights." They are usually talented, energetic managers who have considerable ability and even more promise. Sometimes they rescue part of the organization from failure or produce outstanding results in resolving difficult problems almost single-handedly.

Naturally, higher management rewards such men for their capacity to organize and mount a vigorous attack on the problem and achieve results. Management encourages them in their wide-ranging pursuit of personal power. At a certain point, management abruptly changes the signals. From then on, further advancement hinges not on what they can do individually but on their ability to lead, not drive, others.

Thus, highly important, talented men become problems at this juncture. As "hard drivers" they characteristically dominate their staffs. They concentrate decision-making in their own hands while exerting heavy pressure on subordinates. They are authoritarian.[2] Their individual achievements result in promotion. For a considerable time, the aura of their record obscures the fact that they are now destroying some part of the organization or failing to build it. They are unable to coach and develop subordinates. These are the men of whom it is frequently said that they could be outstandingly successful if only they could work with people. Since they cannot, they ultimately have to leave their companies or are doomed to the continued frustration of their ambitions. Whether they cannot work well with others because of the kind of people they are or because of organizational pressures to produce is sometimes obscure. *Both factors* usually are involved.

The senior executive has several alternatives in those cases where it is not already too late. If the leader is primarily concerned with building an organization and with making it possible for men to assume larger organizational responsibility, then, contrary to popular conceptions, he must provide for close supervision of them. Such supervision must be directed toward helping them support their subordinates and reward them, rather than toward individual productivity. True, some may not be able to work in harness and therefore may have to leave; however, they will do so without having developed expectations that they can succeed in the organization by vigor alone, and before management develops unrealistic expectations about their future careers.

If a situation demands heroic rescue or rebuilding efforts by a single person, both he and his superiors should recognize the unique value of his talents in the particular crisis and the likelihood that he may have to find a similar task elsewhere when this one is completed. A heroic rebuilding task requires from three to five years. After that, individual efforts, which by then have resulted in an organizational structure, must yield to group action. Rarely is it possible for people who have had unrestrained freedom in an organization to accept increasing circumscription of their behavior. Usually, at the end of the initial building period, a new group of managers must be introduced whose talents lie less in their own vigorous attack and more in coordinating and supporting the problem-solving abilities of groups. This phenomenon is a familiar one in many different contexts: offensive and defensive platoons in football, guerrilla and Ranger units in the military, reform movements in politics. It is not yet widely recognized in business.

Senior executives often seem to condone behavior which grossly exceeds the bounds of common courtesy. The result is devastating to those who are subject to such behavior and detrimental to the organization. Sometimes erratic and discourteous behavior is characteristic of creative people for the reasons discussed in Chapter 11. The kind of behavior which is shattering to others is more hostile than creative, although an inventive person may also be antagonistic. People who are so hostile as to be destructive spew their anger about them — at colleagues, subordinates, and superiors. They are unnecessarily critical. They argue too long and too much. They are crude and rude to others and seem to flay at their working environment. Again, it is sometimes difficult to determine how much of this behavior results from conflicts in the organization. Usually it is apparent that such people get away with angry behavior for a long time, that the undesirable behavior increases in intensity, that others are hurt by it, and that they themselves often feel contrite after their outbursts.

The failure of the senior executive to exercise adequate control is particularly evident in those cases in which self-centeredness is the most conspicuous aspect of the person. The major form this self-centeredness takes is the exploitation of and attack on others as part of the subject's efforts to maintain and increase his own status. These men differ from those who are authoritarian and directive in that they are more manipulative. Self-centered men are more obviously concerned with their own aggrandizement. Often they seem not to care what they do to others in the process, while the authoritarian executives more frequently are sympathetic to others in a paternalistic way.

The astonishing aspect of both the angry and the self-centered executives is the manner in which they are able to intimidate others with impunity. Some of these problems are permitted to go on for years, especially when the man has some particular skill or talent which the organization needs. Even when the responsible executive knows that such behavior is destructive to the organization, the subordinates, and the man himself, he often permits it to continue. He excuses it as "temperament," "the problem you have with creative people," or "he was so nice to his superiors."

Men spew their ire or exhibit their self-centeredness for varying reasons. Such behavior may be a way of demonstrating power or of getting attention. For some people, any attention, whether criticism from superiors or love from oneself, is better than none. Anger or self-centeredness can be an expression of increased insecurity and anxiety, particularly if the job burdens are felt to be onerous and failure threatens. As long as the senior executive condones or tolerates such behavior, the problem is swept beneath the managerial rug.

What seems to happen in such cases is that the superior is startled by the aggressive outbursts or the chronic hostility of the subordinate. The superior may fear the subordinate's anger and be cowed by it; he may then retreat from confrontation or control for fear of precipitating even more anger. The hostility of the subordinate may arouse the superior's wrath to the point where he feels guilty for his anger toward the subordinate. If the superior feels inordinately guilty about his own fury, and doubts his ability to control his feelings once they are unleashed, he may be paralyzed into inactivity as a way of coping with them.

In either case, the subordinate is free to vent his spleen on others. Those who are victims resent both him and the superiors who permit his behavior. Working relationships with colleagues become impaired. The superior feels angry with himself for not stopping the aggressive behavior. The provocative subordinate, whose behavior is actually a cry for help, continues to thrash about to his own detriment and that of the organization. Thus, when the responsible executive does not exercise adequate constraint, he contributes to the malfunctioning of those subordinates who are unable to maintain their own controls.

The first step in the control process is to define the problem. As long as others endure such behavior, the offending executives have no reason to stop it. For them, there is no problem. They can easily feel that they must be justified for their anger or manipulation if everyone allows it, particularly if their own superiors tolerate it despite the complaints and turnover of lower level personnel. Once the superior has defined which facets of the subordinate's behavior are unacceptable, and confronts the subordinate with a statement of that problem as he interprets it, then the two must look at their own relationship. There may be features of the superior's behavior which provoke and sustain the anger of the subordinate. There may be role conflicts among superiors which tear at the subordinate psychologically.[3] Work stresses may take their toll. The subordinate may be unconsciously asking for more support from his superior. Whatever the case, the two of them must examine the situation for possible causal influences. The superior must be alert to possible fears and anxieties which the subordinate cannot express, such as the fear of failure or a sense of inadequacy in the supervision of others.

Regardless of whether there are mitigating circumstances, the superior must draw the line at whatever behavior is destructive in that setting. He must be careful to distinguish between destructiveness and healthy conflict of ideas, which can be both creative and constructive. He cannot permit destructive behavior to continue. If environmental circumstances which precipitate anger cannot be altered, if there seem to be no problems of such proportion as to induce fury, then it is reasonable to assume that the problem is primarily within the individual. He must take the responsibility for correcting it. He may have to seek professional help.[4] The fact that the problem may be an intrapersonal one does not mean that the organization has to suffer such behavior until he solves his problem. If he still cannot control his outbursts after the limits have been drawn, then he should be removed from his job.

However, there is a danger here. The senior executive may fail to recognize the degree of pressure he exerts upon subordinates, which may precipitate or exacerbate such behavior; he may assume that the undesirable behavior can be stamped out by forbidding it. Discussion of problems means just that — self-critical examination by both parties of their working relationship. It does not mean that the superior's responsibility ends when he tells the subordinate he must stop his hostile behavior; with that statement the conversation just begins.

When the superior insists that the subordinate control his behavior, if the behavior is not beyond self-control, this requirement supports the subordinate's own controls. In addition, the superior strengthens the structure of the organization by insisting that the subordinate utilize those organizational avenues, policies, and procedures which presumably are the agreed-upon ways by which problems are dealt with in the company.

When a superior condones such behavior or procrastinates in doing something because the subordinate is "too valuable to lose," probably he is taking an expensive, myopic view of the problem. When confronted with the issue, the senior executive frequently admits that the subordinate is more trouble than he is worth, and his own failure to act arises from his feelings of anger and guilt.

Another recurrent problem results from a rivalry situation. Sometimes the senior executive recognizes the rivalry aspects of the problem; more often he does not. He might, for example, concentrate his attention on the hostility between the two subordinates. Without recognizing why they have become abrasive to each other, the senior executive is likely to try to resolve such problems by exhortation, compulsion, or wishful thinking, none of which is effective.

More subtle aspects of rivalry, particularly his own, tend to escape the notice of the senior executive. For instance, a production-minded president might see the need for a strong sales effort and employ a competent sales executive, only to resent his success. He might then reject or sabotage the sales executive without being aware of or undertanding his actions.

It is not unusual for a man to be promoted to a position in which he becomes a rival of a senior person. At times he is even instructed to "light a fire" under the senior person or is promised the senior man's job; for example, the chairman of the board might choose an executive vice-president to prod the president. In such instances the subordinate may "freeze" in his job, failing to show the previously successful behavior which culminated in his promotion. Sometimes exacerbated feelings of rivalry lead him to try to "take over" from his superior. His seniors cannot understand why.

The destructive effects of rivalry thus stimulated are rarely recognized by the senior executives. Usually they are not aware of the deep-seated psychological roots of rivalry and the guilt feelings which immediate personal competition can arouse in people. Often they consciously encourage rivalry on the assumption that all competition is good. They cannot understand why a forceful competitor might suddenly stop competing, let alone see the psychological trap in which the subordinate has been placed.

Some young executives who are promoted rapidly over the heads of older men have guilt feelings about preempting the opportunities of the older men. Such feelings are rarely recognized by superiors. As a result, they do little to prevent or ameliorate frictions which inhibit the effectiveness of the parties concerned. The issue of rivalry is almost never confronted in discussions about promotion, either by the prospective opponents or by their superiors, as a preparation for dealing with their new jobs.

By definition, rivalry is the essence of competitive enterprise. However, in an enterprise where the desirable outcome is the result produced by the organization, all effort should be focused on the collective attainment of that result. When a superior plays subordinates off against each other, over-stimulates rivalry or acts competitively with his subordinates, he forces them to divert energies from competition with other organizations into interpersonal antagonism. Misdirected rivalry drains collective energy which could be applied to resolving organizational problems. In addition, the subordinates become defensive, destroy cooperative possibilities by attacking each other, or maneuver for the favor of the boss. The more intra-organizational rivalry is stimulated, the more acute the problem of the company becomes.[5]

The discussion and joint solution of mutual problems makes more effective use of the energy which is otherwise dissipated in destructive rivalry. In dealing with this problem the superior must at his own motivation critically examine his own feelings, mindful of these possibilities:

1. He may consciously or unconsciously encourage rivalry because he likes to see a good fight, rationalizing his pleasure by believing that the better ideas or the better men will survive. Men in executive positions have sufficiently intense feelings of competition that they are motivated by problems to be solved, if they have enough freedom to attack them. The range of ideas in any situation is sufficiently expansive to produce differences and critical examination, again if the climate of the organization permits such freedom. Playing men off against each other is merely psychological goad-

ing. Those who are not moved by the problems themselves will not be stimulated by goading either. Instead, they will become even more rigidly paralyzed. One can only wonder about the motivation of an executive who must goad his subordinates into fighting each other, as one would wonder about a parent who did the same with his children.

2. He may be angry at one of the rivals and use the other as a weapon to displace his own hostility. This is a subtle phenomenon which occurs frequently. The senior executive can ask himself to what extent he avoids one subordinate, speaks harshly of him behind his back and disdains his communications. If he finds himself acting in these ways without clearly being aware of it, such behavior is one clue to what may be influencing the conflict between the two subordinates. He would benefit by talking directly to the man with whom he is angry rather than attacking him through an intermediary.

3. He may fear the rivalry of subordinates for his own position, and either keep them off balance or permit them to destroy themselves by encouraging their rivalry of each other. Few men can grow older without envying and fearing the younger men who will take their places, no matter how much they like and respect the younger men. Ascending through executive ranks is similar to playing the children's game, "King of the Mountain." A man often feels as if he is always pushing the man ahead of him off the top — even if it is only a small hill. Inevitably, it is difficult for him to relinquish his position without feeling he is being ejected, too. If he feels that way and is unaware of it, he will perforce defend his position by subtle means. If he can accept such feelings as legitimate, he is in a better position to control their expression.

4. The two rivals may represent the executive's own inner conflicts about his identification with different parts of the business. Often executives rise through the ranks on the basis of a particular capacity, skill, or experience. Upon reaching a high level, they find new business requirements antiquate their old skills or compel them to evolve multiple skills. To illustrate, many a production man has risen to chief executive only to discover that business is now in a marketing era; he must either shift his own focus from production to marketing or become more knowledgeable about marketing.

To broaden one's perception can also mean that a man has to change his self-image. For example, a production man who views marketing as manipulation, may have considerable conflict with his own conscience about becoming a manipulator. Although he may recognize the need for marketing, he may still not want to be a salesman. His internal conflict between the wish to continue being what he always was and the wish to have the organization compete successfully by competitive marketing may then reflect itself in his inability to make decisions.

This kind of a conflict within the senior executive will also reflect itself in antagonism between the men who have to carry on the two responsibilities about which he is in conflict. In hardly discernible ways, he will support one and then the other; make an ally of one and then the other. The two subordinates soon find themselves on opposite sides of a fence whose origin is then attributed to "poor communications" or "salesmen are always like that." Only after the third successive sales vice-president has been fired might it occur to the president that something more than "personality clash" is afoot. The clash within himself reverberates loudly in the behavior of those who report to him.

In the promotion or transfer of any executive, careful attention should be given to the rivalry aspects of the situation. These should be talked about frankly as problems to be dealt with in the new job. For those who must accept a new superior or colleague, it can be helpful to reassure them honestly of their own value. The superior should recognize openly with them the inevitable presence of rivalry feelings, and indicate that, even though such feelings exist, the task is still to be done. He should indicate further that the new boss has his full support in managing that group toward the required goals of the organization.

Inadequate Consideration of the Future

Many experiences in life are painful to people. Some, like aging and its accompanying physical infirmities and incapacities, are the lot of everyone. Others are specific to a man's work life: failure to obtain an expected promotion; the prospect of retirement. Such painful experiences can be conceived of as *psychological injuries*. These injuries are inevitable, yet few companies recognize that they are inexorable and have organized methods for anticipating or relieving them. The result is that those who are hurt in this manner have considerable hostility, which is repressed or suppressed.

Sometimes the thought of retirement hurts. Those men to whom prospective retirement is a psychological injury often stubbornly refuse to train subordinates. They become obstructionists, displacing their repressed or suppressed hostility on both subordinates and the organization. Physical changes such as hearing loss and heart attack also leave residues of resentment as men attempt to deny their incapacity.

A major source of psychological injury is failure to be promoted to a job a man expects, rejecting a man's judgment or giving some of his responsibilities to someone else. In these instances, a man views these events as loss: something has been taken away from him.

Also among the wounded ones are the lonesome people — those who wish they could be gregarious but simply cannot. They, therefore, are hypersensitive to rejection by others. Having previously been often wounded, they are ready candidates for psychological wounds and over-respond to new wounds.

Superiors are more aware of psychological injury than any other form of impairment and try more actively to relieve it. They typically have great difficulty dealing with such problems, especially because the ones who are more subject to these injuries tend to be the older men of long service. Often the senior executive does not know what to do or how to do it, but many do a commendable job of providing support. In the many cases superiors have saved the jobs of such "problem people" by hard work and heroic rescue efforts.

However, such extraordinary measures — and the pain and frustration which usually attend them — can often be made unnecessary by advance preparation in anticipation of possible injury. People not only have a right to know what is likely to happen to them as far ahead as such events can be anticipated, but they also can then prepare themselves for the eventuality or choose between alternatives. If they are not informed and experience a sudden blow from higher management, they have every reason to feel manipulated and exploited.

The organization contributes to executive malfunction when it does not (1) systematically prepare people throughout their work careers for the realities which inevitably will come their way; (2) provide shock absorbers in the form of counseling services to help people cope with psychological injury.

Every important change should be discussed with each man involved before it occurs. A major part of such discussion should be the opportunity for him to express his feelings, without embarrassment or fear, about the change. When a man can tell his superior how he feels about the latter's decision or an organizational decision, the acceptance of his feelings conveys to him that he is accepted and respected as an individual. This supports his feelings of self-esteem and makes it possible for him to deal with the change and his feelings more reasonably. No amount of sugar-coated praise will substitute for being heard.

When a person has help in absorbing the shock of injury and support in recovering from it, he is in the advantageous position of being able to mobilize his resources to adapt to what has happened to him. A senior executive who would quickly offer a supporting hand to a man with a sprained ankle and get him medical attention often has difficulty in perceiving psychological injuries in the same light.

Impulsive men act erratically and without adequate thought. Among them are men who can do their jobs well "when they want to." They are frequently absent, often embroiled in multiple family difficulties, and sometimes irresponsible with respect to completing their work or doing it thoroughly. In this category are the men who, though not alcoholic, drink too much in the presence of their superiors and others whose worst behavior occurs when they are with highest-level superiors. The self-defeating aspects of such behavior are obvious.

Such men present another kind of problem for their superiors. If, in some respects, they are competent, even gifted, the superiors are reluctant to face the problems of their behavior realistically. Too often their "mistakes" or "slips" are attributed to youthfulness with the expectation that they will mature. Poor impulse control and low frustration tolerance usually reflect considerable anxiety and insecurity. More often than not, such behavior indicates a need for professional counsel. Repeated admonitions usually serve little purpose. If the senior executive is reluctant to confront such a problem, he can only continue to chafe at episodic failure the effect of which is to hold a promising man down.

Inflexibility as a personal characteristic is often reflected in an inability to plan or accept change. It may also be the product of environmental events. Some people resist change not because they are personally inflexible, but because the organization has prepared them poorly and they are angry. One company is so rigid that the best man available for any given post will not be promoted if he does not believe in God! Rigid people find their self-protection in well-ordered lives. Often they have high standards for themselves. Those who become more rigid under stress, in effect, build a protective shell for themselves. In the first instance, task responsibilities should be *delimited* in such a way that the person can confine himself to standardized, detailed work with definite policy guidance. It should be made clear to him what his responsibilities do not include. In the second instance, the senior executive should review what demands have made the person more anxious and defensive. Change always requires support from superiors if it is to take place with a minimum amount of stress. Much of the time senior executives take it for granted that people can and will change; few can do so without stress. The most effective kind of support lies in joint problem-solving, so that the person can be master of himself and his fate instead of being arbitrarily buffeted about by anonymous forces over which he has no control.

For various reasons, some men are simply unable to assume responsibility for others or to act on management problems. Although their behavior might be described as dependent, that rubric does not do justice to the complexity of their problems. A frequent corollary of their inability to perform as expected is the fact that these men have previously been suppressed in an extremely authoritarian structure for years. Some are able to function reasonably well so long as they have the close support of their superiors. Some cannot make decisions themselves.

Undoing dependent behavior is no easy task, particularly if the organization continues to demand conformity. Where conformity is the first rule of survival, no amount of exhortation will produce initiative. Where mistakes are vigorously hunted out and prejudice a man's career thereafter, few men will risk making a mistake. In addition to supporting the individual step by small step toward assuming greater responsibility, the senior executive must examine the costs of his doing so. This situation is one in which there is often great conflict among senior executives — between the wish that subordinates demonstrate initiative and the wish to be in complete control.

The repetitive and futile way of trying to deal with men of limited ability is by frontal assault. Characteristically, the senior executive attempts to persuade a rigid person to become flexible, to exhort a dependent person to become independent or to cajole an impulsive person into better self-control. Although often the executive knows that people are inflexible or unable to accept responsibility or assume initiative, he tends to act as if he could compel or stimulate them to do so. It is difficult for him to understand that grown men can be frightened and dependent, and that he should act accordingly. Sometimes, in a misguided effort to stimulate the subordinate, he offers the possibility of greater responsibility and more active participation in decision-making. Such gestures are even more threatening to men who are already immobilized. Sometimes he actually promotes such a person in the vain hope that the subordinate will change when he has more responsibility or when he returns from a management development course.

Senior executives usually do not understand that such pressure on a person who is already devoting great effort to controlling or protecting himself (which is what the aberrant behavior means), only increases the intensity of the undesirable behavior. If a man is characteristically rigid, dependent, or impulsive, he is likely to become more so under increasing stress, which is what the pressure of the boss becomes.

Much too often men are placed in the wrong job; half of the time the job is wrong for them because it has outgrown them. The failure of the senior executive with these two problems is largely failure by omission.

Despite the plethora of psychological consultants, assessment and rating scales, and wide-ranging literature on promotion, there is little *careful* assessment of a man's capacities and limitations. Many personnel men think they are doing an adequate selection job by using tests which they do not understand for jobs which are poorly defined. Usually important personality characteristics are dealt with glibly by reference to norms or profiles. The psychological climate of the organization and the personality of the superior with whom a man will have to work rarely enter into consideration. Little wonder that many men are trapped in tasks which they cannot do well, a situation usually only recognized long after the fact.

With respect to men who are outgrown by their jobs, there seems to be almost no anticipation by senior management that such an eventuality could come about. As a result, in most companies there is no continuing discussion of the problem to help a man become aware of what he should do to maintain or sustain his job. Neither is there support for him in facing his feelings about becoming less competent to do the job, nor having to relinquish it. Instead, whatever the reason a man does not grow, often he is left to flounder in his job because superiors recognize it is not his fault he is failing but theirs for having placed him in that position. Thus the failure is compounded.

Men who are unable to function adequately when confronted by larger responsibilities often have done well in jobs of lesser responsibility. They seem to have promise of being able to assume a more responsible job. Some men, however, are placed in managerial positions despite the fact that their limitations are known, particularly their inability to supervise others. Others move up through the ranks because of their technical knowledge, only to flounder as executives. Still others cannot consistently meet the demands of their present jobs. Often they can do some aspects of their jobs well, but not others.

In most cases when men cannot keep pace with the continuing growth of the organization and the particular jobs they have, the executive simply does not have the knowledge or the skill for the expanding responsibility. His growing job exceeds his training and experiences, or his capacity for organizing and judging. This problem is even more poignant when the incumbent has long service in the position or when he has made significant contributions to organizing and developing an activity, sometimes even the company itself. In these situations the superior bears considerable pain because he feels compelled to take action against a man who has contributed to the organization. His anger toward the man who "forces" him into such a situation arouses his guilt feelings and his superego punishes him severely.

How much of the failure to keep up with the growth of the company is passive aggression — failure to do what a man is capable of doing as a way of defeating the company — is unknown. Often rigidity and plateaus in performance are products of passive aggression. One way of being covertly aggressive is by not changing, not doing what is expected of one, letting the boss down in one way or another. Passive aggression is a widespread phenomenon.

The single most helpful practice for dealing with misplacement is for a company to have a continuing and consistent relationship with a psychological consultant. The concept of a relationship with a professional person is the important one here.[6] Psychological testing and evaluation is no better than the person who does it. His judgments and predictions can be no better than his knowledge of the man, the position, and the company. If he is to serve all three then he must develop a "feel" for the company, knowledge of specific jobs and the men who supervise them, and some understanding of the candidate. Standardized batteries given by psychologists who never see either the company or examine the probable position of the candidate have limited value. Apart from the ethical question involved, mail-order testing has even less. Occasional referral to a local psychologist is not enough to keep such a person in touch with the climate of the organization.

Growth is the essence of living. Everyone likes to feel that he is becoming wiser as he grows older. Most men seek opportunities for continued growth. Some, however, cannot or do not. This problem is likely to occur with increasing frequency as executive roles become more complex. To avoid such failures, companies will have to evolve methods for anticipating and dealing with them before they become a painful and destructive fact. In a continuing professional relationship, the psychologist can be in daily contact with executives, know when they are under particular stress, and provide support and counsel as necessary. In growing companies one of his continuing tasks should be to be alert to those who are faltering.

Most management problems seem to call for increased investment, more experts, and long periods of planning and execution before results can be expected. These do not. Though few managerial problems are more troublesome than those which have to do with people, the solutions to these problems are often relatively simple, given a modicum of attention and sensitivity. The manager needs only to examine more carefully his own actions. Some, like those which arouse feelings of guilt, will remain difficult no matter how simple the solutions seem. Even these, however, will be somewhat easier to handle if the underlying issue is more visible. Perhaps the greatest self-healing managerial talent, as the psalmist would put it, is to make wise the simple.

15 / Epilogue

Despite the longings of many, there is no returning to the comparative quiescence of a rural society. Social institutions will become larger, not smaller.[1] Organizations are already more important for millions of men and women than the cities and states in which those same people reside. The complexities of people's relationships within and to organizations are the central socio-psychological problems of an industrial era.[2] Only as man masters his institutions will he mold his society.

The task for the business leader, posed in these pages, is therefore immense. Some may be appalled at its complexity. All will feel inadequate to meet its demands. But then, few men who have ever founded a business or assumed an impressive responsibility have not felt inadequate at the prospect of its hazards and ramifications. What defeats men is not the insurmountability of their aspirations but the dwindling of their confidence in the radiant luster of their dreams.

The reader will therefore respond to his feelings of being overwhelmed by denial and resistance. Among executives these mechanisms take two characteristic forms. The initial response is rejection of a conception as perhaps appropriate for scientists and intellectuals but not for business. The second is the complaint that, "I'm too busy for all that."

Behind the denial and resistance, only thinly disguised by the rationalizations, are several legitimate concerns. Indeed, there are problems which will become threatening for the man who experiments with some of the ideas expressed here. These must be anticipated and examined or he will retreat to tried methods, however futile, at the first indication of turbulence or strife.

The basic problem with which the executive has to contend is himself. The primary source of the dilemmas which leaders face are their own inner conflicts.[3] To lead successfully, in the sense considered in this book, presupposes having much of one's own psychological house in order. In contemporary innovative organizations, the most successful executive is high in achievement motivation, low in power motivation, and keenly aware of himself, his employees, and the market.[4] The major difference between the most and least successful executives lies precisely in the latters' lack

of awareness. The hallmark of this difference is that the successful executive is critical of his own performance; the unsuccessful, of the performance
of others.

A second problem concerns the issue of hostility, both the hostility of
subordinates and that of the executive. Growth and change always involve
dissatisfaction with the status quo. Much of the time that dissatisfaction is
focused on the leader. It cannot be otherwise. When the leader offers an
ideal to his followers, a direction in which they devoutly wish to go, he
provides an avenue for them to gratify their aspirations. Simultaneously,
however, being a superego goal yet unreached, the ideal induces guilt on
the part of the followers for not yet having accomplished it. This discontent with themselves is then displaced on the father-figure, the leader
whose challenge is both gratifying and guilt-inducing. The subordinates will
fight him even as they esteem him.

The natural tendency of the leader is to respond to hostility with retaliation. When he does not retaliate, and concomitantly does not permit
his subordinates to be completely dependent on him, they have little choice
but to invest their aggressive impulses in the tasks which have been defined
for them. It is difficult for the leader to tolerate hostility; however, unless
he can, he will try to suppress it. Suppression of turbulent feelings inhibits
the possibility of spontaneous change because people who must overcontrol themselves cannot be flexible. Being the target of anger is sometimes
easier to accept if the leader understands that it is only one part of the
feelings about him. If he is a good identification figure, he is also esteemed,
if not loved. One of the major psychological functions of the leader is to
be an object of affection. The fact that his subordinates have feelings of
esteem and affection for him serves to temper their hostility and to channel
it into constructive activities in keeping with the ideal he holds forth.[5]

The leader's own hostility will also trouble him. Most people fear their
aggressive impulses, both because of their fantasies of how destructive
they could be and because of the threat of retaliation by others more powerful than they. Aggressive feelings are always unruly. They become even
more so when exacerbated in conflict and competition. This is one reason
why there is so much conflict between the responsibility to exercise power
and the wish to be liked.[6] Another facet of the same issue is the sense of
loneliness which is the fate of the leader who must make decisions for
which he is then vulnerable to criticism. Even more than others, the leader
fears failure because success is crucial to him and so many people depend

upon him. Despite the drive toward success, that, too, is something to be feared. Each successful step opens new vistas of opportunity — and possible failure.

The executive will confront other anxieties. One is the fear of not being needed. The better he does his job, the more successfully his organization can operate itself, the more he will feel himself to be superfluous. If anything is more forlorn than a cause without a leader, it is a leader without a cause. In such circumstances, a man's superego brands him as being useless.

Beneath the prospective feelings of uselessness is a more subtle fear. Men pursue power because, among other rewards, it provides an illusion of immortality. Not to wield power directly is to threaten that illusion. Furthermore, if a man engages his power with that of others, some will oppose him and thereby threaten the illusion further. He will therefore be under inexorable pressure to assert his leadership role in ways which demonstrate his potency and defeat his rivals. The executive will always be navigating the psychological shoals of his internal struggles.

With these, as with so many other struggles, his ego ideal is an important bulwark. Former ambassador George Kennan put it well: "Professional dedication lifts us repeatedly, like some gigantic spiritual ski-lift, across the abysses of true loneliness and helplessness, moves us up a hill we would never otherwise be able to scale, and gives our lives a meaning they could otherwise never attain." [7]

Struggles and problems notwithstanding, in these pages the reader may have seen another meaning of leadership. Implicit in this discussion is the concept that the relationship between a superior and his subordinates is a dialogue. The superior speaks to his subordinates with his every action. Every policy, every project, every failure or achievement is a phrase in that dialogue. When he speaks or fails to speak, how he acts or fails to act, he reveals what he thinks of himself and how he regards his subordinates. Those who respond to his leadership, though often verbally silent, nevertheless reply in kind whether they produce or fail to do so, whether they develop symptoms of emotional distress, whether they stay or go.

The executive who assumes the full responsibility for his role in the dialogue seeks to fulfill the obligation of the power which is entrusted to him. Being imperfect, and despite his best efforts, he will err. He will thereby sometimes become an agent of stress. But being a leader, and continuing the dialogue, he will have the opportunity again and again to be an agent of strength.

It is the unique privilege of the leader to strengthen men. Nowhere else in contemporary industrial society does that privilege come to grips with opportunity so directly as in the organizations in which men work. To exercise the privilege demands sensitivity to subtlety and forthrightness of action, that creative fusion of aggression and affection which summons forth the highest human talents. The man whose leadership is the product of such fusion in the service of an ideal is aptly called the exceptional executive.

Privilege and opportunity are, however, merely invitations to act. It is no easy task to fully utilize them. He who would use his power to strengthen others must therefore be prepared for frustration and disappointment for he will taste these more than success. When he sees the results of his personal investment in others, he will know the copious richness of leadership.

Prominent names and imposing edifices are testimony to the fact that some men build organizations as monuments to themselves. The most enduring monuments, however, are those images perpetuated in the minds of men. Each of us, however humble his place in the scheme of things, can engage in his dialogue in such a way that the imagery of his being endures in the being of others.

Notes

Notes

Part One

Chapter 1 Imbroglio

1. Warren G. Bennis, "Beyond Bureaucracy," *Trans-action,* 2:5 (July–August 1965), 31–35; D. Ronald Daniel, "Team at the Top," *Harvard Business Review,* 43:2 (March–April 1965), 74–82; Clark Kerr, "The Multiversity," *Harper's,* 227:1362 (November 1963), 37–42; Joseph Kraft, "Johnson's Talent Hunt," *Harper's,* 230:1378 (March 1965), 40–46; Martin Mayer, "The Man Who Put the Rhinestones on Miami," *Harper's,* 230:1378 (March 1965), 61–68; Bernard J. Muller-Thym, "Practices in General Management: New Direction for Organizational Management," Paper no. 60-WA-59, American Society of Mechanical Engineers (1960), and "The Real Meaning of Automation," *Management Review,* 52:6 (June 1963), 40–48; Philip E. Slater and Warren G. Bennis, "Democracy is Inevitable," *Harvard Business Review,* 42:2 (March–April 1964), 51–59; Paul B. Wishart, "Wanted: 200,000 Top Business Managers," *Management Review,* 54:3 (March 1965), 4–14.

2. Chester I. Barnard, *Organization and Management* (Cambridge, Mass.: Harvard University Press, 1956), p. 112.

3. Harry Levinson, *Emotional Health: In the World of Work* (New York: Harper & Row, 1964).

4. "Labor Relations: A Thorn in Corporate Mergers," and "Courts Rule on Thorny Question of Sub-Contracting," *Industrial Relations News* (April 11, 1964), 2, and (October 2, 1965), 1.

5. Harry Levinson *et al., Men, Management, and Mental Health* (Cambridge, Mass.: Harvard University Press, 1962).

6. Mortimer R. Feinberg and Benjamin Balinsky, "Bias: How it Clouds Management's Thinking," *BFS Reports* (September 1965), p. 1.

7. Barnard, *Organization and Management,* p. 27.

Chapter 2 The Pillars of Survival

1. Sigmund Freud, "The Ego and the Id," *The Standard Edition of the Complete Psychological Works of Sigmund Freud,* vol. 19 (London: Hogarth Press, 1961); Charles Brenner, *An Elementary Textbook of Psychoanalysis* (New York: International Universities Press, 1955); Fritz Redlich and June Bingham, *The Inside Story* (New York: Alfred A. Knopf, 1953); William C. Menninger and Munro Leaf, *You and Psychiatry* (New York: Charles Scrib-

ner's Sons, 1948); Calvin Hall, *A Primer of Freudian Psychology* (New York: World Book Co., 1954).

2. Eleanor Wintour, "Bringing Up Children: The American Way vs. the British Way," *Harper's,* 229:1371 (August 1964), 58–63; Henry Fairlie, "American Kids?" *New York Times Magazine* (November 14, 1965), 116 ff.; Sheffield White, "The Underdeveloped British Businessman," *Atlantic,* 217:3 (January 1966), 75–78; Howard R. Wolf, "British Fathers and Sons: 1773–1913: From Filial Submissiveness to Creativity," *Psychoanalytic Review,* 52:2 (Summer 1965), 53–70.

3. "The Halfhearted Economy," *Time* (December 25, 1964), 60–61.

4. Norman Bradburn, "Interpersonal Relations Within Formal Organizations in Turkey," *Journal of Social Issues,* 19:1 (January 1963), 61–67.

5. Luigi Barzini, *The Italians* (New York: Atheneum, 1964); John Fischer, "The Japanese Intellectuals: Cliques, Soft Edges, and the Dread of Power," *Harper's,* 229:1372 (September 1964), 14–15 ff.

6. Daniel P. Moynihan, "When the Irish Ran New York," *Reporter* (June 8, 1961), 32–34.

7. Some classical examples of such studies are: Daniel Katz, Nathan Maccoby, and Nancy C. Morse, *Productivity, Supervision and Morale in an Office Situation* (Ann Arbor: University of Michigan, Survey Research Center, Institute for Social Research, 1950); Daniel Katz et al., *Productivity, Supervision, and Morale Among Railroad Workers* (Ann Arbor: University of Michigan, Survey Research Center, Institute for Social Research, 1951); E. A. Fleischman, E. F. Harris, and Harold Burtt, *Leadership and Supervision in Industry* (Columbus: Ohio State University Press, 1955). Summaries of such studies may be found in the following, among others: Rensis Likert, *New Patterns of Management* (New York: John Wiley & Sons, 1961); Morris S. Viteles, *Motivation and Morale in Industry* (New York: W. W. Norton, 1953); Victor H. Vroom, *Work and Motivation* (New York: John Wiley & Sons, 1964).

8. Irving Knickerbocker, "Leadership: A Conception and Some Implications," *Journal of Social Issues,* 4:3 (Summer 1948), 23–40.

9. Nancy C. Morse and Robert S. Weiss, "The Function and Meaning of Work and the Job," *American Sociological Review,* 20:2 (April 1955), 192.

10. Viteles, *Motivation and Morale,* and Vroom, *Work and Motivation.*

11. Frederick Herzberg, Bernard Mausner, and Barbara Snyderman, *The Motivation to Work* (New York: John Wiley & Sons, 1959).

12. Edward E. Lawler and Lyman W. Porter, "Perceptions Regarding Management Compensation," *Industrial Relations,* 3:1 (October 1963), 41–49.

13. Eli Ginzberg, *The Unemployed* (New York: Harper & Bros., 1943).

14. J. Stacy Adams, "Wage Inequities, Productivity and Work Quality," *Industrial Relations,* 3:1 (October 1963), 9–16.

15. "Splitting Cost Cuts," *Business Week* (December 22, 1962), 20.

16. Hannah Arendt, *The Human Condition* (Chicago: University of Chicago Press, 1958); Daniel Bell, *Work and Its Discontents* (Boston: Beacon Press,

1956); W. N. Evans, "The Cultural Significance of the Changed Attitude Toward Work in Great Britain," *Bulletin of the Menninger Clinic,* 13:1 (January 1949), 1–8; Eugene H. Friedman and Robert J. Havighurst, *The Meaning of Work and Retirement* (Chicago: University of Chicago Press, 1954); Sol W. Ginsburg, *A Psychiatrist's View on Social Issues* (New York: Columbia University Press, 1963); A. R. Heron, *Why Men Work* (Stanford, Calif.: Stanford University Press, 1948); Everett C. Hughes, *Men and Their Work* (Glencoe, Ill.: Free Press, 1958); Aaron Levenstein, *Why People Work* (New York: Crowell-Collier, 1962); Karl Menninger, *Love Against Hate* (New York: Harcourt, Brace, 1942); Walter S. Neff, "Psychoanalytic Conceptions of the Meaning of Work," *Psychiatry,* 28:4 (November 1965), 324–333.

17. Victor Obenhaus, "The Churches and the Change," *Christian Century,* 79:50 (December 12, 1962), 1523–1525.

18. Kenneth Boulding, *The Organizational Revolution* (New York: Harper & Row, 1963).

19. Douglas McGregor, *The Human Side of Enterprise* (New York: McGraw-Hill, 1960); Likert, *New Patterns of Management;* Floyd Mann and Richard Hoffman, *Automation and the Worker* (New York: Henry Holt, 1960).

20. "Self-Employed Have Place at Top of Top Pay Group," *Wall Street Journal* (July 15, 1963).

21. Elliott Jaques, "Social Systems as a Defense Against Persecutory and Depressive Anxiety," in Melanie Klein, ed., *New Directions in Psychoanalysis* (New York: Basic Books, 1955).

22. Melanie Klein, "A Contribution to the Psychogenesis of Manic-Depressive States," in Klein, ed., *Contributions to Psychoanalysis, 1921–1945* (London: Hogarth Press, 1948).

23. Sigmund Freud, "The Dynamics of the Transference," *Works of Sigmund Freud,* vol. 12 (London: Hogarth Press, 1958); Otto Fenichel, *The Psychoanalytic Theory of the Neuroses* (New York: W. W. Norton, 1945); Ives Hendricks, *Facts and Theories of Psychoanalysis,* 3d ed. (New York: Alfred A. Knopf, 1958); Anna Freud, *The Ego and the Mechanisms of Defense* (New York: International Universities Press, 1946).

24. Philip Selznick, *Leadership in Administration* (Evanston, Ill.: Row, Peterson, 1957).

25. Ernst Simmel, "Psychoanalytic Treatment in a Sanitorium," *International Journal of Psychoanalysis,* 10 (January 1929), 78.

26. Norman Reider, "Transference to Institutions," *Bulletin of the Menninger Clinic,* 17:2 (March 1953), 60.

27. H. A. Wilmer, "Transference to a Medical Center," *California Medicine,* 96:3 (March 1962), 173.

28. Aldous Huxley, *The Devils of Loudun* (New York: Harper & Bros., 1952), pp. 20–21.

29. Theodore Purcell, *The Worker Speaks His Mind on Company and Union* (Cambridge, Mass.: Harvard University Press, 1953). See also, Geraldine

Pedersen-Krag, quoted in "Job 'Family' Seen as Basis of Strife," *New York Times* (January 15, 1955).

30. Fred G. Lesieur, *The Scanlon Plan* (New York: John Wiley & Sons, 1958).

31. Herzberg, Mausner, and Snyderman, *The Motivation to Work.*

32. Levinson *et al., Men, Management, and Mental Health.*

33. Karl Menninger, *Theory of Psychoanalytic Technique* (New York: Basic Books, 1958).

34. Joseph Adelson, "The Teacher as a Model," *American Scholar,* 30:3 (Summer 1961), 383–406.

35. Peter F. Drucker, *The Practice of Management* (New York: Harper & Bros., 1954).

36. William F. Whyte, *Money and Motivation* (New York: Harper & Bros., 1955); David Mechanic, "The Power to Resist Change Among Low-Ranking Personnel," *Personnel Administration,* 26:4 (July–August 1963), 5–11.

37. Leonard I. Pearlin, "Alienation from Work: A Study of Nursing Personnel," *American Sociological Review,* 27:3 (June 1962), 314–326.

Chapter 3   Leading by Following

1. Seymour M. Lipset and Reinhard Bendix, *Social Mobility in Industrial Society* (Berkeley: University of California Press, 1959), p. 14.

2. Ferenc Merli, "Group Leadership and Institutionalization," *Human Relations,* 2:1 (January 1949), 23–39.

3. Eli Ginzberg, "Man and His Work," *California Management Review,* 5:2 (Winter 1962), 22.

4. A. H. Raskin, "Rumbles from the Rank and File," *Reporter* (January 28, 1965), 27–29; Raskin, "Labor's Crisis of Public Confidence," and "The Big Strike," *Saturday Review* (March 30, 1963), 21–25; (November 16, 1963), 20–22.

5. Luigi Barzini, "The Next Pope," *Harper's,* 213:1277 (October 1956), 27–34.

6. C. Wright Mills, *Power, Politics, and People* (New York: Oxford University Press, 1963).

7. Daniel S. Greenberg, "Who Runs America? — An Examination of a Theory that Says the Answer is a 'Military Industrial Complex,'" *Science* (November 16, 1962), 797–798; Luther J. Carter, "Anti-Missile Missile: Next Entry in the Arms Race?" *Science* (November 25, 1966), 985–987.

8. Boulding, *The Organizational Revolution* (New York: Harper & Row, 1963).

9. John J. Ryan, "American Catholics," *Wall Street Journal* (July 29, 1963).

10. Thomas O'Hanlan, "What's A Trade Association Worth?" *Dun's Review,* 85:3 (March 1965), 32–33.

11. Eric Hoffer, "A Time of Juveniles," *Harper's,* 230:1381 (June 1965), 17–24.

12. Alvin W. Gouldner, "Cosmopolitans and Locals: Toward an Analysis of Latent Social Roles, I," *Administrative Science Quarterly,* 2:3 (December 1957), 281–306.

13. "The Blue Collar Revolution," *Forbes* (January 15, 1967), 13–15; "Our Surprising Economy," *Wall Street Journal* (January 31, 1967); "Working Wives: Rise of Married Women in Labor Force has Wide Economic Effects," *Wall Street Journal* (October 30, 1963). See also "Rising Pay Lifts More Blue Collar Men into a New Affluent Class," *Wall Street Journal* (April 5, 1965).

14. "Machines Won't Take Over After All," *Business Week* (October 8, 1966), 93–96.

15. Harry Bernstein, "The Aerospace Worker," *Nation* (December 15, 1962), 419–421.

16. "Labor Force Projections," *Industrial Relations News* (September 24, 1966), 4.

17. Herman P. Miller, "Is the Income Gap Closed?" *New York Times Magazine* (November 11, 1962), 50–58.

18. U.S. Department of Labor, *Handbook on Women Workers* (Washington, D.C.: U.S. Government Printing Office, 1963).

19. "Working Wives."

20. Ginzberg, "Man and His Work," p. 22.

21. "Name of Prescription Should be on Label, AMA Council Asserts," *Wall Street Journal* (July 29, 1963); "As Long as You are Up, Get Their Attention," *Time* (April 23, 1965), 17. See also William Greer, "Quality vs. Quantity in American Medical Education," *Science* (August 26, 1966), 956–961.

22. Ginzberg, "Man and His Work," p. 22.

23. Rensis Likert, *New Patterns of Management* (New York: John Wiley & Sons, 1961).

24. See Urie Bronfenbrenner, "The American Child: A Speculative Analysis," *Journal of Social Issues,* 17:1 (1961), 6–18.

25. Floyd Mann and Richard Hoffman, *Automation and the Worker* (New York: Henry Holt, 1960).

26. E. A. Fleischman, E. F. Harris, and Harold Burtt, *Leadership and Supervision in Industry* (Columbus: Ohio State University Press, 1955). See also Edwin A. Fleischman and James A. Salter, "Relation Between the Leader's Behavior and his Empathy Toward Subordinates," *Journal of Industrial Psychology,* 1:3 (September 1963), 79–84; Harold Oaklander and Edwin A. Fleischman, "Patterns of Leadership Related to Organizational Stress in Hospital Settings," *Administrative Science Quarterly,* 8:4 (March 1964), 520–532.

27. Fred E. Fiedler, *Leader Attitudes and Group Effectiveness* (Urbana: University of Illinois Press, 1958).

28. Daniel Bell, "The Invisible Unemployed," in Sigmund Nosow and Wil-

liam H. Form, eds., *Man, Work, and Society* (New York: Basic Books, 1962).

29. Dick Bruner, "Why White Collar Workers Can't Be Organized," *ibid.*

30. D. W. Dobler, "Implications of Parkinson's Law for Business Management," *Personnel Journal,* 42:1 (January 1963), 10–18.

31. C. Northcote Parkinson, *In-Laws and Outlaws* (Boston: Houghton Mifflin, 1962), p. 200.

32. Albert Porter, "Books and the Bramble Bush," *Advanced Management,* 1:12 (December 1962), 20–21.

Chapter 4   The Executive's Denials

1. Helen M. Davidson, Frank Reissman, and Edna Meyers, "Personality Characteristics Attributed to the Worker," *Journal of Social Psychology,* 57:1 (June 1962), 155–160.

2. Mason Haire, Edwin E. Ghiselli, and Lyman W. Porter, *Managerial Thinking: An International Study* (New York: John Wiley & Sons, 1966), p. 24. See also Raymond E. Miles, "Human Relations or Human Resources?" *Harvard Business Review,* 43:4 (July–August 1965), 154.

3. "IR Key: Innovation, not Improved Administration," *Industrial Relations News* (September 28, 1963), 2.

4. "The IR Degree: A Step Toward Professionalism?" *ibid.,* IRN Special Report (July 1963).

5. Philip Selznick, *Leadership in Administration* (Evanston, Ill.: Row, Peterson, 1957), p. 5.

6. Bernard Barber, "Resistance by Scientists to Scientific Discovery," *Science* (September 1, 1961), pp. 601–602.

7. Charles M. Solley and Gardner Murphy, *Development of the Perceptual World* (New York: Basic Books, 1960).

8. William C. Schutz, "The Interpersonal Underworld," *Harvard Business Review,* 36:4 (July–August 1958), 123–135.

9. E. A. Fleischman, E. F. Harris, and Harold Burtt, *Leadership and Supervision in Industry,* pp. 93–100.

10. Harry Levinson, "A Psychologist Looks at Executive Development," *Harvard Business Review,* 40:5 (September–October 1962), 69–75.

11. Lester Coch and John R. P. French, Jr., "Overcoming Resistance to Change," *Human Relations,* 1:4 (August 1948), 512–532.

12. Fred G. Lesieur, *The Scanlon Plan* (New York: John Wiley & Sons, 1958); "More Companies Give Blue-Collar Employees Greater Responsibility," *Wall Street Journal* (March 14, 1966).

13. Chris Argyris, *Personality and Organization* (New York: Harper & Bros., 1958).

14. Peter F. Drucker, "Our Emerging Industrial Society," *Social Progress,* 53:6 (April 1963), 28–40.

15. August B. Hollingshead and Frederick C. Redlich, *Social Class and*

Mental Illness (New York: John Wiley & Sons, 1958); and Arthur Kornhauser, *Mental Health of the Industrial Worker* (New York: John Wiley & Sons, 1965).

16. See William F. Whyte, *Money and Motivation* (New York: Harper & Bros., 1955); and "Willful Damage Presents a Bigger Problem Than Many Firms Will Admit," *Wall Street Journal* (December 13, 1966).

17. David Riesman, *The Lonely Crowd* (New Haven: Yale University Press, 1950); Erich Fromm, "Personality and the Marketplace," in Sigmund Nosow and William H. Form, eds., *Man, Work and Society* (New York: Basic Books, 1962).

18. "Campus Stealing Rises Rapidly — A 'Thing to Do,' " *National Observer* (November 7, 1966).

19. C. S. Lewis, *The Screwtape Letters* (New York: Macmillan, 1962), p. x.

Chapter 5   The Pressures of Technology

1. Robert W. Austin, "Responsibility for Social Change — Business or Government?" *Harvard Business Review,* 43:4 (July–August 1965), 52.

2. David G. Wood, "How Businessmen Can Fight 'Big Government' — and Win," *Harper's,* 227:1362 (November 1963), 77–81; Thomas J. Watson, Jr., "Four Million People Who Want to Work," *Brown Alumni Monthly,* 64:4 (January 1964), 12–16; Ralph C. Gross, "War on Poverty," *Industrial Relations News* (November 13, 1965), 1–2.

3. Charles E. Silberman, "The Real News About Automation," *Fortune,* 31:2 (January 1965), 124–129 ff.; "Automation Alarm is Proving False," *Wall Street Journal* (December 23, 1965).

4. "If the Machine Wants Our Jobs, Let's Buy It," *Life* (August 14, 1964), 4.

5. See Michael Harrington, *The Other America* (New York: Macmillan, 1962); "Decline in Charity Cases," *Wall Street Journal* (December 27, 1963); "In an Affluent Society, a Shortage of Cadavers," *National Observer* (February 20, 1967).

6. See, for example, Dwight McDonald, "Our Invisible Poor," *The New Yorker* (January 19, 1963), 82–132.

7. Ben Wattenberg, Jr. and Richard M. Scammon, *This U.S.A.* (New York: Doubleday, 1965).

8. "Some 8 Million in U.S. Receive Public Aid, A 33% Rise Since 1955," *Wall Street Journal* (February 9, 1964).

9. Herman P. Miller, "Is the Income Gap Closed," *New York Times Magazine* (November 11, 1962), 50–58.

10. "How Our Income is Divided," U.S. Department of Commerce, Bureau of the Census, Graphic Pamphlets, GP60-2.

11. Bayard Rustin, "Black Power and Coalition Politics," *Commentary,* 42:3 (September 1966), 35–40; "White-Negro Gap Still Widens," *Montreal Gazette* (December 15, 1966).

12. See Michael Harrington, "The Economics of Racism," *Commonweal* (July 7, 1961); "Automation Worry," *Wall Street Journal* (July 1, 1964); "Notable and Quotable," *ibid.* (December 1, 1965); *Meeting the Manpower Challenge of the Sixties with 40-Plus Workers* (Washington, D.C.: U.S. Department of Labor, BES No. E-189, November 1960); "More Workers Hold Two Jobs as Others Go Unemployed," *Wall Street Journal* (February 14, 1964); Seymour Wolfbein, "View from Washington," *American Child* (Automation: Outlook for Youth), 44:4 (November 1962), 1–3; A. H. Raskin, "Labor's Crisis of Public Confidence," *Saturday Review* (March 30, 1963), 21–25; "Socialists Hear Views on Poverty," *New York Times* (April 18, 1965); *The Challenge of Jobless Youth* (Washington, D.C.: President's Commission on Youth Employment, 1963); "Campus Economists Probe Unemployment Factors," *Industrial Relations News* (December 28, 1963), 2–3; I. John Billera, "Human Problems: A Challenge to Automation," *ibid.* (December 8, 1962), 2; Charles E. Silberman, "The Comeback of the Blue Collar Worker," *Fortune,* 81:2 (February 1965), 153–156 ff.; "More Firms Transfer Idled Laborers to Jobs In Distant Localities," *Wall Street Journal* (September 10, 1965).

13. Fredric Solomon, Walter L. Walker, Garret J. O'Connor, and Jacob R. Fishman, "Civil Rights Activity and Reduction in Crime Among Negroes," *Archives of General Psychiatry,* 12:3 (March 1965), 227–236.

14. John W. McConnell, "Welfare in an Age of Automation," *ILR Research,* 7:3 (Winter 1962), 14.

15. *Mental Health Problems of Automation,* WHO Technical Report, series no. 183 (Geneva: World Health Organization, 1959), pp. 6, 9.

16. See, for example, William A. Faunce, "Automation and the Automobile Worker," in Nosow and Form, eds., *Man, Work, and Society;* "All the News That's Fit to Automate," *Time* (July 6, 1963), 2.

17. David A. Goldstein and C. Raymond Hulsart, "Automation: A Clinical Study," *Journal of Occupational Medicine,* 6:4 (April 1964), 169–173.

18. "Push the Button, Strain the Heart," *University Daily Kansan* (May 12, 1964).

19. "Tape Can Run the Machine Better," *Business Week* (March 30, 1963), 100–105; M. V. Mathews, "The Digital Computer as a Musical Instrument," *Science* (November 1, 1963), pp. 553–557; "Computers Turn to Conversation," *New York Times* (June 29, 1964).

20. James D. Hodgson, "Automation: A Study in Promise, Problems and Polemics," *Management of Personnel Quarterly,* 2:3 (Autumn, 1963), 2–9; William A. Faunce, "Automation and the Division of Labor," *Social Problems,* 13:2 (Fall 1965), 149–160; Jack Siegman and Bernard Karsh, "Some Organization Correlates of White Collar Automation," *Sociological Inquiry,* 32:1 (Winter 1962), 108–116.

21. Howard Baumgartel and Gerald Goldstein, "Some Human Consequences of Technical Change," *Personnel Administration,* 24:2 (July–August 1961), 32–40.

22. Quoted by William Gomberg, "The Controversy Ahead," *American Child* (Automation: Outlook for Youth), 44:4 (November 1962), 1–3.

23. Albert Kushner, "People and Computers," *Personnel*, 40:1 (January–February 1963), 27–34.

24. Siegman and Karsh, "Some Organization Correlates of White Collar Automation"; Ida R. Hoos, "When the Computer Takes Over the Office," and Robert Merton, "Machine, Worker, and Engineer," in Nosow and Form, eds., *Man, Work, and Society;* Albert A. Blum, "Job Skills for Automated Industry," *Management of Personnel Quarterly*, 4:4 (Winter 1966), 24–31.

25. Baumgartel and Goldstein, "Some Human Consequences of Technical Change."

26. See Bernard Muller-Thym, "Practices in General Management: New Direction for Organizational Management," Paper No. 60-WA-59, American Society of Mechanical Engineers, 1960.

27. Anthony J. Celebrezze, "Aim for the Top Jobs of '67," *This Week* (June 16, 1963); "Growth in Office Force Since '47 Far Outpaces Blue-Collar Job Loss," *Wall Street Journal* (May 7, 1963); "Every Other Person Will Fill a Key Slot," *Industrial Relations News* (December 14, 1963), 4.

28. "White Collar Cutback: Firms Try to Reverse Trend to Ever-Larger Office, Technical Staffs," and "New Devices, Systems Bring Sharp Showdown in White Collar Hiring," *Wall Street Journal* (January 3, 1963); (May 5, 1964); "Automation's Relation to Jobs," *Industrial Relations News* (December 1, 1962), 3.

29. W. S. Buckingham, "The Effects of Automation on White Collar Workers," *Employee Relations Bulletin,* Report No. 839 (January 2, 1963), 1–5.

30. Thomas R. Brooks, "New Fit to the White Collar," *Dun's Review*, 80:3 (September 1962), 63–65.

31. Albert Kushner, "People and Computers," p. 30.

32. *White Collar Restiveness — A Growing Challenge* (New York: Industrial Relations Counselors, 1963).

33. Howard B. Jacobson, quoted in "Warning of Shift in White Collar Management Orientation," *Industrial Relations News* (June 29, 1963), 1–2.

34. Clark C. Caskey, "White Collar Employees — A Union Dilemma and a Management Challenge," *Management of Personnel Quarterly*, 1:3 (Spring 1962), 9–13.

35. "Why White Collar Workers Can't Be Organized," in Nosow and Form, eds., *Man, Work, and Society.*

36. Albert H. Blum, *The Prospects for Office Employee Unionization,* reprint series no. 66, 1963–64 (East Lansing: Michigan State University, School of Labor and Industrial Relations); "Factors Favoring White Collar Unionism," "Salaried Unions Stand Strong," "Automation: A Catalyst for White Collar Unionism?" "Three Pincers Pilot White Collar Unionization Offensive," "White Collar Workers Voice Concern," "Life in White Collar

Drive," and "Administrative Management Society Report — White Collar Workers," *Industrial Relations News* (January 12, 1963), 1; (March 16, 1963), 3; (August 31, 1963), 4; (October 26, 1963), 1–2; (May 16, 1964), 1; (March 12, 1965), 2; and (August 14, 1965), 1. See also "Labor Briefs," *Business Week* (April 9, 1966), 148.

37. Paul Jacobs, "David Dubinsky: Why His Throne is Wobbling," *Harper's,* 225:1351 (December 1962), 75–84.

38. Blum, *The Prospects for Office Employee Unionization;* Everett Kassalow, "The Prospects for White-Collar Union Growth," *Industrial Relations,* 5:1 (October 1965), 37–47; Carl D. Snyder, "The UAW and White Collar Unionization," *Management of Personnel Quarterly,* 4:4 (Winter 1966), 11–19; Solomon B. Levine, "The White Collar, Blue Collar Alliance in Japan," *Industrial Relations,* 5:1 (October 1965), 103–115; "Changes in Leadership, Program could Inject New Vigor in Labor," *Wall Street Journal* (February 19, 1965); Herbert Harris, "Why Labor Lost the Intellectuals," *Harper's,* 228: 1369 (June 1964), 79–86; Bernard Goldstein and Bernard P. Indik, "Unionism as a Social Choice: The Engineers' Case," *Monthly Labor Review,* 86:4 (April 1963), 365–369; "Many Seek to Acquire New Skills as Demand Softens, Layoffs Mount," *Wall Street Journal* (February 20, 1964).

39. Harold J. Leavitt and Thomas L. Whisler, "Management in the 1980's," *Harvard Business Review,* 36:6 (November–December 1958), 41–48.

40. Charles E. Silberman, "The Real News About Automation," *Fortune,* 31:2 (January 1965), 124–129 ff.; Jack B. Wiener, "Cutback in Middle Management," *Dun's Review,* 84:1 (July 1964), 33–34; "Increased Job Hopping by Junior Executives Vexes Personnel Men," *Wall Street Journal* (January 21, 1965).

41. Peter F. Drucker, "Is Business Letting Young People Down?" *Harvard Business Review,* 43:6 (November–December 1965), 49–55; Lyman W. Porter, "Job Attitudes in Management: I. Perceived Deficiencies in Need Fulfillment as a Function of Job Level," *Journal of Applied Psychology,* 46:6 (December 1962), 383; Hjalmar Rosen, "Managers Predict Their Futures," *Personnel Administration,* 25:3 (May–June 1962), 49–52.

42. Donald Shaul, "What's Really Ahead for Middle Management?" *Personnel,* 41:6 (November–December 1964), 8–16.

43. Robert Merton, "Machine, Worker and Engineer," in Nosow and Form, eds., *Men, Work, and Society.* See also Clarence Randall, "Business, Too, Has its Ivory Towers," *New York Times Magazine* (July 8, 1962), 5 ff.

44. Eugene Raskin, "The Modular Man," *Columbia University Forum,* 5:3 (Summer 1962), 27.

45. Richard H. Rahe *et al.,* "Social Stress and Illness Onset," *Psychosomatic Medicine,* 25:5 (September–October 1963), 494.

46. John D. Adamson and Arthur H. Schwale, Jr., "Object Loss, Giving Up, and the Onset of Psychiatric Illness," *ibid.,* 493.

47. "A Common Thread of Trouble," *Time* (November 20, 1964), 57.

48. "The Middle Management Enigma," *Dun's Review,* 82:1 (July 1963), 29.

Part Two

Chapter 6 The Tasks of Top Management

1. Thomas J. Watson, Jr., *A Business and Its Beliefs* (New York: McGraw-Hill, 1963), p. 4.

2. Peter Drucker, "Our Emerging Industrial Society," *Social Progress,* 53:6 (April 1963), 31.

3. Frederick Pollock, *Automation* (New York: Praeger, 1957).

4. See Aaron Levenstein, *Why People Work* (New York: Crowell-Collier, 1962).

5. Donald McDonald, *An Interview with Hans Bethe* (Santa Barbara, Calif.: Center for the Study of Democratic Institutions, 1962), p. 6; Thomas A. Cowan, "Decision Theory in Law, Science and Technology," *Science* (June 7, 1963), 1067–1068.

6. Donald L. Johnson and Arthur L. Kobler, "The Man-Computer Relationship," *Science* (November 23, 1962), 873.

7. *Ibid.,* 879.

8. See Stanley A. Rudin, "The Personal Price of National Glory," *Transaction,* 2:6 (September–October 1965), 4–9.

9. Phillip M. Boffey, "American Science Policy: OECD Publishes a Massive Critique," *Science* (January 12, 1968), 176–178.

10. "More of Today's Executives Speak the Language of Science," *Personnel,* 42:4 (July–August 1965), 7; Andrew Hacker, "The Making of a Corporation President," *New York Times Magazine* (April 2, 1967), 26–27 ff.

11. Alvin C. Eurich, "Mastery of Ideas: The Key to the Future," *Congressional Record* (June 16, 1965), 13823–13825; Robert Hutchins, *Science, Scientists and Politics* (Santa Barbara, Calif.: Center for the Study of Democratic Institutions, 1963).

12. Seymour M. Lipset and Reinhard Bendix, *Social Mobility in Industrial Society* (Berkeley: University of California Press, 1959), p. 138.

13. Vance Packard, *The Pyramid Climbers* (New York: McGraw-Hill, 1962).

14. Eugene S. Uyeki and Frank B. Cliffe, Jr., "The Federal-Scientist-Administrator," *Science* (March 29, 1963), 1267–1270.

15. Andrew Hacker, "The Elected and the Anointed: Two American Elites," *American Political Science Review,* 55:3 (September 1961), 539–549; "Fathers and Sons," *Wall Street Journal* (December 14, 1966).

16. "Talent Edges Out Wealth at 'Big 3,'" *New York Times* (March 14, 1964).

17. Harold J. Leavitt and Thomas L. Whisler, "Management in the 1980's," *Harvard Business Review,* 36:6 (November–December 1958), 41–48.

18. Pollock *Automation,* p. 83.

19. Lipset and Bendix, *Social Mobility in Industrial Society,* p. 143.

20. Donald N. Michael, *Cybernation: The Silent Conquest* (Santa Barbara, Calif.: Center for the Study of Democratic Institutions, 1962), p. 35.

21. Leonard Sayles, *Individualism and Big Business* (New York: McGraw-Hill, 1963).

22. James S. Hekemian and Curtis H. Jones, "Put People On Your Balance Sheet," *Harvard Business Review,* 45:1 (January–February 1967), 105–113; Jay W. Forrester, "A New Corporate Design," Massachusetts Institute of Technology (September 20, 1965, mimeographed).

23. "The Changing American Executive," *Dun's Review,* 83:1 (January 1964), 38–41 ff.; Theodore M. Alfred, "Checkers or Choice in Manpower Management," *Harvard Business Review,* 45:1 (January–February 1967), 157–169.

Chapter 7   The Business as an Educational Institution

1. A. H. Raskin, "Automation: Key to Lifetime Jobs," *Saturday Review* (November 28, 1964), pp. 14–16 ff.; "Allan Wood, USW Draft Novel Agreement on Security for Workers," *Wall Street Journal* (January 11, 1965).

2. Fred A. Auman, "Retraining: How Much of an Answer to Technological Unemployment?" *Personnel Journal,* 41:10 (November 1962), 505–507; "Why Retraining Results Are So Often Disappointing," and "Displaced Workers Who Stay That Way," *Personnel,* 40:4 (July–August 1963), 5, and 40:2 (March–April 1963), 21; A. R. Weber, *Retraining the Unemployed* (Chicago: University of Chicago, Graduate School of Business, 1963); "Packing up an Armour Plant," and "When Job Retraining Helps," *Business Week* (July 20, 1963), 80, and (November 16, 1963), 50; "Scoreboard for Legislated Training Effort," *Industrial Relations News* (February 5, 1966), 2; "Technology's Impact: Du Pont Eases it by Locating New Plants Near Those it Closes, Pushing Retraining," and "IBM's Watson Fields Queries on Russia, National Anthem and Lunches at Meeting," *Wall Street Journal* (December 18, 1962) and (May 1, 1963).

3. Ben H. Bagdikian, "I'm Out of a Job, I'm All Through," *Saturday Evening Post* (December 18, 1965), 32–36 ff.

4. Allen R. Dodd, Jr., *The Job Hunter* (New York: McGraw-Hill, 1965), p. 193.

5. Tom Collins, "Retirement Results in Void," *Topeka State Journal* (May 4, 1965).

6. Harold G. Wolff, "What Hope Does for Man," *Saturday Review* (January 5, 1957), 42–45.

7. David C. McClelland, "Thinking Ahead," *Harvard Business Review,* 43:6 (November–December 1965), 178; David A. Kolb, "Achievement Motivation Training for Underachieving High-School Boys," *Journal of Personality and Social Psychology,* 2:6 (1965), 783–792; Ida R. Hoos, "Retraining in the United States: Problems and Progress," *International Labour Review,* 92:5 (November 1965), 410–425.

8. S. P. Goodwin, *Experience in Group Hiring, Training, and Adaptation* (Clifton, N.J.: Goerlick's, 1963).

9. "Morality Play," *Forbes* (August 15, 1966), 30–31.

10. "Industrial Program to Curtail High School Dropouts," and "Disadvantaged Youth Have a Friend at Chase Manhattan," *Industrial Relations News* (October 9, 1965), 1–2, and (May 7, 1966), 1.

11. "Can Today's Unemployables Become Tomorrow's Salesmen?" *Merchandising Week* (March 29, 1965); "Peace Corps Stresses On-the-Scene Training Over Classroom Work," *Wall Street Journal* (August 24, 1966).

12. "Learning Pools Advocated," *Industrial Relations News* (July 17, 1965), 3–4; "New Drive to 'Fulfill These Rights,' " *Business Week* (May 28, 1966), 38–40; "Significant Training Legislation Updated," *Industrial Relations News* (September 18, 1965), 2; "A Bill to Amend the Internal Revenue Code of 1954 to Allow a Credit Against Income Tax to Employers for the Expenses of Providing Training Programs for Employees and Prospective Employees," Sen. 2509, 89th Cong., 1st sess. (September 9, 1965); Thomas J. Watson, Jr., "Four Million People Who Want to Work," *Brown Alumni Monthly,* 64:4 (January 1964), 12–16.

13. John P. Crane, "Impact of Automation Today and Tomorrow," *Personnel Administrator,* 7:6 (November–December 1962), 20–22.

14. U.S. Department of Labor, *Training of Workers in American Industry* (Washington, D.C.: Government Printing Office, 1964).

15. *Technological Change & Employment in the Automotive Industry* (Detroit: Automobile Manufacturers Association, 1965).

16. Harold A. Foecke, "Continuing Education for Engineers," *Science* (May 13, 1966), 880–883.

17. "Many Officials Find They Cannot Adjust to Business Changes," *Wall Street Journal* (January 24, 1966).

18. Richard B. McAdoo, "Sabbaticals for Businessmen," *Harper's,* 224:1344 (May 1962), 39–52; Lassor A. Blumenthal, "Should Management Take Sabbaticals?" *Dun's Review,* 83:1 (January 1964), 45–46 ff.

19. John W. Macy, Jr., "The Scientist in the Federal Service," *Science* (April 2, 1965), 51–54; Lawrence Stessin, "They're not Trying to Succeed in Business," *New York Times Magazine* (March 28, 1965), 76 ff.

20. "Bringing the Campus to the Office," *Business Week* (December 25, 1965), 72–73; "A Master's Degree for Everyone," *Training,* 3:3 (March 1966), 15–19; see also C. D. Wilkerson, "A Results-Oriented Development Plan," *Conference Board Record,* 3:3 (March 1966), 40–45.

21. "Manpower Shortages Predicted for Top and Bottom Echelons," *Industrial Relations News* (May 18, 1963), 1–2.

22. "Preparing the Engineer and Scientist for Management," *Industrial Relations News,* Special Report (January 1964).

23. "Editor to Reader," *Personnel Journal,* 45:3 (March 1966), 134.

24. "Notable and Quotable," *Wall Street Journal* (September 9, 1965); Eugene E. Jennings, "The Emergence of New Managerial Style," a paper presented to the Upper Midwest Hospital Conference (May 14, 1964). See also Kenneth Andrews, "There are Some Tricks Only Old Dogs Can Learn," *Columbia Journal of World Business,* 1:4 (Fall 1966), 101–108.

25. Robert A. Gordon and Edwin H. Jones, *Higher Education for Business* (New York: Columbia University Press, 1959).

26. Paul Goodman, "For a Reactionary Experiment in Education," *Harper's,* 225:1350 (November 1962), 61.

27. George J. Odiorne, "Managerial Narcissism — the Great Self-Development Binge," *Management of Personnel Quarterly,* 1:3 (Spring 1962), 21–25.

28. Harry Levinson, "A Psychologist Looks at Executive Development," *Harvard Business Review,* 40:5 (September–October 1962), 69–75.

29. Raymond A. Bauer, "Social Psychology and the Study of Policy Formation," *American Psychologist,* 21:10 (October 1966), 933–942.

30. Nathaniel Cantor, *The Learning Process for Managers* (New York: Harper & Bros., 1958).

31. John W. Gardner, "The Need for Leaders," *Science* (January 21, 1966), 283; "Foundation Programs Attempt to Develop More Future Leaders," *Wall Street Journal* (February 18, 1966).

Chapter 8   The Role and the Learners

1. "The Changing American Executive," *Dun's Review,* 83:1 (January 1964), 38–41 ff.

2. Crawford H. Greenewalt, "Sensing Who Can Command," *Nation's Business,* 53:10 (October 1965), 40 ff.; William D. Patterson, "David Rockefeller, Creative Banker, Champion of Change," *Saturday Review* (January 9, 1965), 39–40 ff.; "Looking Backward," *Time* (February 7, 1964), 52.

3. Noel Buckley, "The Most Wanted Men in Industry," *Dun's Review,* 83:2 (February 1964), 49 ff.; Dale Yoder, "The Two Roads to Success in Industrial Relations," *Personnel Administration,* 27:6 (November–December 1964), 3–6; Thomas R. Donovan, "Opportunism and Executive Behavior," *Management of Personnel Quarterly,* 1:3 (Spring 1962), 6–9; Lawrence A. Appley, "Now!" *Supervisory Management,* 9:2 (February 1964), 13–15; "VP for the Future," *Time* (May 10, 1963), 89; George J. Odiorne, "Managerial Narcissism — the Great Self-Development Binge," *Management of Personnel Quarterly,* 1:3 (Spring 1962), 21–25.

4. Bernard J. Muller-Thym, "Practices in General Management: New Directions for Organizational Management," Paper no. 60-WA-59, American Society of Mechanical Engineers (1960).

5. Ithiel de Sola Pool, "The Head of the Company: Conceptions of Role and Identity," *Behavioral Science,* 9:2 (April 1964), 147–155.

6. Harold J. Leavitt and Thomas L. Whisler, "Management in the 1980's," *Harvard Business Review,* 36:6 (November–December 1958), 41–48.

7. W. Van Dusen and W. Rector, "A Q-Sort Study of the Ideal Administrator," *Journal of Clinical Psychology,* 19:2 (April 1963), 244.

8. Abraham Zaleznik, "Managerial Behavior and Interpersonal Competence," *Behavioral Science,* 9:2 (April 1964), 156–166.

9. Henry Brandon, "Schlesinger at the White House," *Harper's,* 229:1370 (July 1964), 56.

10. John Fischer, "The Editor's Trade," *Harper's,* 231:1382 (July 1965), 20–23.

11. Henry A. Kissinger, "The Illusionist: Why We Misread de Gaulle," *Harper's,* 230:1378 (March 1965), 70.

12. Douglas McGregor, *The Human Side of Enterprise* (New York: Mc-Graw-Hill, 1960).

13. Edith Jacobson, *The Self and the Object World* (New York: International Universities Press, 1964), p. 54.

14. Heinz Eulau, "Bases of Authority in Legislative Bodies: A Comparative Analysis," *Administrative Science Quarterly,* 7:3 (December 1962), 309–321.

15. Peter Drucker, "Our Emerging Industrial Society," *Social Progress,* 53:6 (April 1963), 28–40.

16. Eugene Jennings, "The Emergence of New Managerial Style," a paper presented to the Upper Midwest Hospital Conference (May 14, 1964).

17. H. Marshall McLuhan, "Address at Vision 65," *American Scholar,* 35:2 (Spring 1966), 205.

18. John W. Gardner, *Self-Renewal* (New York: Harper & Row, 1963), p. 10.

19. Edgar H. Schein, "How to Break-In the College Graduate," *Harvard Business Review,* 42:6 (November–December 1964), 68–76.

20. Peter Drucker, "Is Business Letting Young People Down?" *ibid.,* 43:6 (November–December 1965), 49–55.

21. Lawrence Stessin, "They're not Trying to Succeed in Business," *New York Times Magazine* (March 28, 1965), 76 ff.

22. Arthur Letcher, "Understanding Today's Students," *Journal for College Placement,* 26:3 (February–March 1966), 91–92; Duncan Norton-Taylor, "The Private World of the Class of '66," *Fortune,* 73:2 (February 1966), 128–132 ff.; "Xerox Chairman Emphasizes Social Objectives of the Corporation as a Way of Attracting Bright New Leadership," *Industrial Relations News* (April 23, 1966), 1. See also Robert M. Hutchins, "Why They Don't Want Business Careers," *Think,* 32:5 (September–October 1966), 2–5; "Notable and Quotable,"

Wall Street Journal (February 28, 1967); Elinor Langer, "The Berkeley Scene, 1966 (II): Educational Reform," *Science* (May 27, 1966), 1220–1223.

23. "Thinkers and Doers — A Survey," *Management Review,* 51:11 (November 1962), 14.

24. "Lack of Purpose in Business Careers," *Industrial Relations News* (January 1, 1966), 4.

25. Richard Nason, "Harvardmen vs. Big Business," *Dun's Review,* 83:1 (January 1964), 41–42 ff.; "Business School Grads Increasingly Choose Posts at Small Firms," *Wall Street Journal* (April 7, 1967).

26. Roger M. Blough, "Business *Can* Satisfy the Young Intellectual," *Harvard Business Review,* 44:1 (January–February 1966), 49–57.

27. John S. Fielden, "The Right Young People for Business," *Harvard Business Review,* 44:2 (March–April 1966), 76–83.

28. Drucker, "Is Business Letting Young People Down?" *ibid.,* p. 50.

Part Three

Chapter 9   The Executive as a Teacher

1. Joseph Adelson, "The Teacher as a Model," *American Scholar,* 30:3 (Summer 1961), 394–404. Additional literature on the teaching role includes: John Fischer, "The Editor's Trade"; Loren Eiseley, "The Glory and the Agony of Teaching," *Think,* 28:9 (October 1962), 22–25; Karl A. Menninger, "The Doctor as a Leader," *Bulletin of the Menninger Clinic,* 13:1 (January 1949), 9–15; Jacques Barzun, *Teacher in America* (Boston: Little, Brown, 1965); Raphael Demos, "Doctors, Philosophers and Teachers," *Harvard Alumni Bulletin,* 64:2 (October 14, 1961), 65–67; Paul Goodman, "For a Reactionary Experiment in Education"; Edgar H. Schein and Douglas T. Hall, "The Student Image of the Teacher," *Journal of Applied Behavioral Science,* 3:3 (July–August–September 1967), 305–337; "When *You* Will Hit Your Peak," *Nation's Business,* 51:1 (January 1963), 64–66.

2. Sigmund Freud, "Group Psychology and the Analysis of the Ego," *Standard Edition of the Complete Psychological Works of Sigmund Freud,* vol. 18 (London: Hogarth Press, 1955), p. 105.

3. Edith Jacobson, *The Self and the Object World* (New York: International Universities Press, 1964), p. 66.

4. See Jeanne Lampl-de Groot, *The Development of the Mind* (New York: International Universities Press, 1965), p. 266.

5. Ruth Mack Brunswick, "The Preoedipal Phase of Libido Development," *Psychoanalytic Quarterly,* 9:2 (April 1940), 293–319.

6. Joost A. M. Meerloo, "Plagiarism and Identification," *Archives of General Psychiatry,* 11:4 (October 1964), 421–424.

7. Taken by permission from a tribute to Mrs. Roosevelt in *The New Yorker* of November 17, 1962.

8. See, for example, Harry F. Harlow and Margaret Kuenne Harlow, "Social Deprivation in Monkeys," *Scientific American,* 207:5 (November 1962), 136–146; J. P. Scott, *Animal Behavior* (Chicago: University of Chicago Press, 1958); Wladyslaw Sluckin, *Imprinting and Early Rearing* (Chicago: Aldine Publishing Co., 1965); Edward H. Hess, "Imprinting In Birds," *Science* (November 27, 1964), 1128–1138; J. P. Scott, "Critical Periods in Behavioral Development," *Science* (November 30, 1962), 949–958; Robert G. Patton and Lytt I. Gardner, "Influence of Family Environment on Growth: The Syndrome of Maternal Deprivation," *Pediatrics,* 30:6 (December 1962), 957–962; Sally Provence and Rose C. Lipton, *Infants in Institutions* (New York: International Universities Press, 1962); Gardner Murphy, "Communication and Mental Health," *Psychiatry,* 27:2 (May 1964), 100–106; Albert Bandura and Carl J. Kupers, "Transmission of Patterns of Self-Reinforcement Through Modeling," *Journal of Abnormal and Social Psychology,* 69:1 (July 1964), 1–9.

9. Irving Knickerbocker, "Leadership: A Conception and Some Implications," *Journal of Social Issues,* 4:3 (Summer 1948), 23–40.

10. Freud, "Group Psychology and the Analysis of the Ego," p. 108.

11. Suzanne H. Rudolph, "Self-Control and Political Potency: Ghandi's Asceticism," *American Scholar,* 35:1 (Winter 1965–66), 79–97.

12. Freud, "Group Psychology and the Analysis of the Ego," p. 116.

13. Robert Waelder, "Conflict and Violence," *Bulletin of the Menninger Clinic,* 30:5 (September 1966), 272.

14. William M. Easson, "The Ego Ideal in the Treatment of Children and Adolescents," *Archives of General Psychiatry,* 15:3 (September 1966), 288–292.

15. Samuel Strauss, "Career Choices of Scholars," *Personnel and Guidance Journal,* 44:2 (October 1965), 153–159; Shirley Tuska and Benjamin Wright, "The Influence of a Teacher Model on Self-Conception during Teacher Training and Experience," *Proceedings of the 73rd Annual Convention of the American Psychological Association* (1965), 297–298; Philip H. Abelson, "What are Professors For?" *Science* (June 18, 1965), 1546.

16. W. Schindler, "The Role of the Doctor in Group Therapy," *International Journal of Group Psychotherapy,* 16:2 (April 1966), 198–202; Joseph C. Bailey, "Clues for Success in the President's Job," *Harvard Business Review,* 45:3 (May–June 1967), 97–104.

17. Harold G. Hubbard, "Career Choices of Successful Business Executives," *Personnel and Guidance Journal,* 44:2 (October 1965), 147–152.

18. Anna Freud, *The Ego and the Mechanisms of Defense* (New York: International Universities Press, 1946), p. 121.

19. See James Mann, "Psychoanalytic Observations Regarding Conformity in Groups," *International Journal of Group Psychotherapy,* 12:1 (January 1962), 8–10.

20. Edwin A. Fleischman and David R. Peters, "Interpersonal Values, Leadership Attitudes, and Managerial 'Success,'" *Personnel Psychology,* 15:2 (Summer 1962), 127–143.

21. Selwyn W. Becker, "Personality and Effective Communication in the Organization," *Personnel Administration,* 27:4 (July–August 1964), 28–30.

22. David G. Bowers, "Self-Esteem and Supervision," *Personnel Administration,* 27:4 (July–August 1964), 23–26.

23. Jacobson, *The Self and the Object World,* p. 68.

24. Karl Menninger, "Human Needs in Urban Society," *Menninger Quarterly,* 13:3 (Fall 1959), 1–8.

25. Knickerbocker, "Leadership: A Conception and Some Implications."

26. "The Integrated Society," *Time* (December 23, 1966), 22.

27. Warren G. Bennis, *Changing Organizations* (New York: McGraw-Hill, 1966).

Chapter 10   Ministration Needs

1. William C. Schutz, *FIRO: A Three-Dimensional Theory of Interpersonal Behavior* (New York: Henry Holt, 1958).

2. Harry Levinson *et al., Men, Management, and Mental Health* (Cambridge, Mass.: Harvard University Press, 1962).

3. Earl R. Gomersall and M. Scott Myers, "Breakthrough in On-the-Job Training," *Harvard Business Review,* 44:4 (July–August 1966), 62–72.

4. Edgar H. Schein, "How to Break-In the College Graduate," *Harvard Business Review,* 42:6 (November–December 1964), 68–76.

5. Duncan Norton-Taylor, "The Private World of the Class of '66," *Fortune,* 73:2 (February 1966), 128–132 ff.

6. Peter Drucker, "Is Business Letting Young People Down?" *Harvard Business Review,* 43:6 (November–December 1965), 55.

7. Richard Nason, "Harvardmen vs. Big Business," *Dun's Review,* 83:1 (January 1964), 41–42 ff.

8. *White Collar Restiveness: A Growing Challenge* (New York: Industrial Relations Counselors, 1963).

9. David E. Berlew and Douglas T. Hall, "The Socialization of Managers: Effects of Expectations on Performance," *Administrative Science Quarterly,* 11:2 (September 1966), 207–223.

10. Douglas McGregor, *Leadership and Motivation* (Cambridge, Mass.: MIT Press, 1966), p. 51.

11. Norman Reider, "Psychodynamics of Authority with Relation to Some Psychiatric Problems in Offices," *Bulletin of the Menninger Clinic,* 8:2 (March 1944), 55–58.

12. S. R. Parker, "Type of Work, Friendship Patterns, and Leisure," *Human Relations,* 17:3 (August 1964), 215–219.

13. Harold Lasswell and Abraham Kaplan, *Power and Society* (New Haven: Yale University Press, 1963).

14. Selwyn W. Becker, "Personality and Effective Communication in the Organization," *Personnel Administration,* 27:4 (July–August 1964), 28–30.

15. Levinson *et al., Men, Management, and Mental Health,* p. 63.

16. Michael Aiken and Jerold Hage, "Organizational Alienation: A Comparative Analysis," *American Sociological Review,* 31:4 (August 1966), 497–507; Elliott Jaques, "Too Many Management Levels," *California Management Review,* 8:1 (Fall 1965), 13–20; Rensis Likert, *Applying Modern Management Principles to Sales Organizations* (Ann Arbor, Mich.: Foundation for Research on Human Behavior, 1963).

17. John W. Gardner, *Self-Renewal* (New York: Harper & Row, 1963), p. 16.

18. Frederick Herzberg, Bernard Mausner, and Barbara Snyderman, *The Motivation to Work* (New York: John Wiley & Sons, 1959).

19. David G. Bowers and Stanley E. Seashore, "Predicting Organizational Effectiveness with a Four-Factor Theory of Leadership," *Administrative Science Quarterly,* 11:2 (September 1966), 238–263.

20. Rensis Likert, *New Patterns of Management* (New York: McGraw-Hill, 1961).

21. Norman R. F. Maier and L. Richard Hoffman, "Financial Incentives and Group Decision in Motivating Change," *Journal of Social Psychology,* 64:2 (October 1964), 369–378.

22. David G. Bowers, "Self-Esteem and Supervision."

23. Floyd C. Mann, "Toward an Understanding of the Leadership Role in Formal Organization," in Robert Dubin *et al.,* eds., *Leadership and Productivity* (San Francisco: Chandler Publishing Co., 1965).

24. Likert, *New Patterns of Management,* p. 103.

25. Eric L. Trist *et al., Organizational Choice* (London: Tavistock Institute, 1963).

26. Salomon Rettig, "Group Discussion and Predicted Ethical Risk Taking," *Journal of Personality and Social Psychology,* 3:6 (June 1966), 629–633.

27. S. L. A. Marshall, *Men Against Fire* (New York: William Morrow, 1947), p. 136.

28. Eric L. Trist, "Socio-Technical Systems," Address, University of Cambridge, November 18, 1959.

29. Robert Dubin, "Supervision and Productivity: Empirical Findings and Theoretical Considerations," in Dubin *et al., Leadership and Productivity,* p. 30.

30. Leonard R. Sayles, "Managing Organizations: What We Know Now that We didn't Know Before," *Management Review,* 56:1 (January 1967), 50–53.

31. Thornton B. Roby, Elizabeth H. Nicol, and Francis M. Farrell, "Group Problem Solving Under Two Types of Executive Structure," *Journal of Abnormal and Social Psychology,* 67:6 (December 1963), 550–556.

32. Abraham H. Maslow, *Motivation and Personality* (New York: Harper & Bros., 1954).

33. Martin Patchen, "Supervisory Methods and Group Performance Norms," *Administrative Science Quarterly,* 7:3 (December 1962), 275–294.

34. Lyndall F. Urwick, "The Line/Staff Impasse — A Footnote," *Management Review,* 56:1 (January 1967), 50–53.

35. Gardner, *Self-Renewal*, p. 73.

36. F. Reif, "The Competitive World of the Pure Scientist," *Science* (December 15, 1961), 1957–1962.

37. Ralph Cordiner, "The Nature of the Work of the Chief Executive," Address, General Electric Co., Schenectady, N.Y., September 16, 1963.

38. Eugene E. Jennings, "Two Schools of Thought About Executive Development," *Personnel Journal,* 37:10 (March 1959), 370–372.

39. George J. Odiorne, "Managerial Narcissism — The Great Self-Development Binge," *Management of Personnel Quarterly,* 1:3 (Spring 1962), 21–23.

40. Raymond A. Katzell, "Reflections on Educating Executives," *Public Administrative Review,* 19:1 (Winter 1959), 4–6.

41. McGregor, *Leadership and Motivation,* p. 25.

42. M. Gene Newport, "Problems of Middle Management Development," *Personnel Administration,* 28:2 (March–April 1965), 17–20; Warren C. McGovney, "Start at the Top," *Advanced Management,* 1:2 (February 1962), 11–12.

43. Robert J. House, "Managerial Reactions to Two Methods of Management Training," *Personnel Psychology,* 18:3 (Autumn 1965), 311–320.

44. Jerome S. Bruner, "The Will to Learn," *Commentary,* 41:2 (February 1966), 41. See also Bruner's *The Process of Education* (Camrbridge, Mass.: Harvard University Press, 1961).

45. Bruner, "The Will to Learn," p. 46.

46. Nathaniel Cantor, *The Learning Process for Managers* (New York: Harper & Bros., 1958), p. 75.

47. David S. Ewing, "The Knowledge of an Executive," *Harvard Business Review,* 42:2 (March–April 1964), 91–100.

48. Mortimer R. Feinberg, quoted by Harwood F. Merrill in "The Listening Post," *Management News,* 38:2 (February 1965), 1.

49. Walter R. Mahler, "Improving Coaching Skills," *Personnel Administration,* 27:1 (January–February 1964), 28–33.

50. Robert L. Katz, "Human Relations Skills Can Be Sharpened," *Harvard Business Review,* 34:4 (July–August 1956), 61–72.

51. Jurgen Ruesch and Weldon Kees, *Nonverbal Communication* (Berkeley and Los Angeles: University of California Press, 1956); Eric L. Berne, *Games People Play* (New York: Grove Press, 1965).

52. Norman R. F. Maier, Allen R. Solem, and Ayesha A. Maier, *Supervisory and Executive Development* (New York: John Wiley & Sons, 1957).

53. Charles A. Curran, "Counseling Skills Adapted to the Learning of Foreign Languages," *Bulletin of the Menninger Clinic,* 25:2 (March 1961), 78–93.

54. Robert L. Sutherland, "Can an Adult Change?" *Advanced Management,* 17:3 (March 1952), 2–6.

55. Earl M. Bowler and Frances T. Dawson, *Counseling Employees* (Englewood Cliffs, N.J.: Prentice-Hall, 1948); Nathaniel Cantor, *Employee Counseling* (New York: McGraw-Hill, 1945); Benjamin Balinsky and Ruth Berger,

The Executive Interview: A Bridge to People (New York: Harper & Bros., 1959); William J. Dickson and F. J. Roethlisberger, *Counseling in an Organization: A Sequel to the Hawthorne Researches* (Boston: Harvard University Graduate School of Business Administration, 1966); Felix M. Lopez, Jr., *Personnel Interviewing: Theory and Practice* (New York: McGraw-Hill, 1965).

56. Gertrude R. Ticho, "On Self-Analysis," *International Journal of Psychoanalysis,* 48:2 (April 1967), 308–318.

57. Edwin Thomas, Norman Polansky, and Jacob Kounin, "The Expected Behavior of a Potentially Helpful Person," *Human Relations,* 8:2 (May 1955), 165–174.

58. Lawrence L. Ferguson, "Better Management of Managers' Careers," *Harvard Business Review,* 44:2 (March–April 1966), 139–153.

Chapter 11   Maturation Needs

1. John W. Gardner, *Self-Renewal,* p. 35.

2. Abraham H. Maslow, "The Need for Creative People," *Personnel Administration,* 28:3 (May–June 1965), 3–5 ff.

3. Arthur Koestler, *The Act of Creation* (New York: Macmillan, 1964), p. 96.

4. Rene Dubos, "Humanistic Biology," *American Scholar,* 34:2 (Spring 1965), 179–198.

5. Alex F. Osborn, *Applied Imagination: Principles and Procedures of Creative Thinking* (New York: Charles Scribner's Sons, 1953).

6. Gardner, *Self-Renewal,* p. 71.

7. Donald W. MacKinnon, "The Nature and Nurture of Creative Talent," *American Psychologist,* 17:7 (July 1962), 485, 488.

8. "Why the Creative Student is Out of Step in School," *National Observer* (January 13, 1964).

9. Robert Presthus, "University Bosses: The Executive Conquest of Academe," *New Republic* (February 20, 1965), 20–24.

10. Gardner Murphy, *Human Potentialities* (New York: Basic Books, 1958), pp. 129–131.

11. Jacob W. Getzels and Mihaly Csikszentmihalyi, "Portrait of the Artist as an Explorer," *Trans-action,* 3:6 (September–October 1966), 34.

12. Murphy, *Human Potentialities,* p. 141.

13. Rensis Likert, "Conditions for Creativity," *Management Review,* 51:9 (September 1962), 70.

14. Donald C. Pelz and Frank M. Andrews, *Scientists in Organizations* (New York: John Wiley & Sons, 1966).

15. Albert E. Meyers, "Performance Factors Contributing to the Acquisition of a Psychological Advantage in Competition," *Human Relations,* 19:3 (August 1966), 283–295.

16. Raymond E. Miles, "The Affluent Organization," *Harvard Business Review,* 44:3 (May–June 1966), 106–114.

17. See Carolyn Bird, *The Invisible Scar* (New York: McKay, 1966), pp. 315–317.

18. "Fund Supports Technical Innovation," *Industrial Relations News* (February 5, 1966), 3.

19. Seymour Levy and D. Miriam Stene, "Construct Revalidation of a Forced-Choice Rating Form," *Journal of Applied Psychology,* 49:2 (April 1965), 122–125.

20. Crawford H. Greenewalt, "Notable and Quotable," *Wall Street Journal* (November 15, 1965).

21. Daniel M. Colyer, "The Good Foreman — As His Men See Him," *Personnel,* 28:2 (September 1951), 140–147.

22. "How You Look to the Man Under You," *Management Methods,* 14:5 (August 1958), 22–28.

23. Lyman W. Porter and Edwin E. Ghiselli, "The Self Perceptions of Top and Middle Management Personnel," *Personnel Psychology,* 10:4 (Winter 1957), 400, 402.

24. Ralph M. Stogdill and Ellis L. Scott, "How Does Top Management's Conception of Its Own Responsibility and Authority Influence Behavior Down the Line?" *Industrial Relations News* (June 8, 1957), 1–2.

25. Lawrence K. Williams, William F. Whyte, and Charles S. Green, "Do Cultural Differences Affect Workers' Attitudes?" *Industrial Relations,* 5:3 (May 1966), 105–117.

26. Hjalmar Rosen, "Managers Predict Their Futures," *Personnel Administration,* 25:3 (May–June 1962), 49–52.

27. Dero Saunders, "Executive Discontent," *Fortune,* 54:4 (October 1956), 155.

28. Robert W. White, "Ego and Reality in Psychoanalytic Theory," *Psychological Issues,* 3:3 (Monograph 11, 1963), 35.

29. Douglas McGregor, *Leadership and Motivation* (Cambridge, Mass.: MIT Press, 1966), p. 29.

30. John W. Gardner, "Notable and Quotable," *Wall Street Journal* (December 15, 1965).

31. Robert Dubin, "Supervision and Productivity:[Empirical Findings and Theoretical Considerations," in Robert Dubin *et al.,* eds., *Leadership and Productivity* (San Francisco: Chandler Publishing Co., 1965), p. vii.

32. Rensis Likert, *New Patterns of Management* (New York: McGraw-Hill, 1961).

33. Donald C. Pelz and Frank M. Andrews, "Autonomy, Coordination, and Stimulation, in Relation to Scientific Achievement," *Behavioral Science,* 11:2 (March 1966), 97.

34. Jerald G. Bachman, Claggett C. Smith, and Jonathan A. Slesinger, "Control, Performance, and Satisfaction: An Analysis of Structural and

Individual Effects," a paper presented to the American Psychological Association (1965).

35. Robert L. Peabody, "Perceptions of Organizational Authority: A Comparative Analysis," *Administrative Science Quarterly,* 6:4 (March 1962), 463–482.

36. Louis A. Allen, "Leaders Who Fail Their Companies," *Business Horizons,* 8:2 (Summer 1965), 79–86.

37. Moss Hart, *Act One* (New York: Random House, 1959), pp. 107–108.

38. Peter J. Burke, "Authority Relations and Disruptive Behavior in Small Discussion Groups," *Sociometry,* 29:3 (September 1966), 237–250.

39. Edwin E. Ghiselli, "Psychological Properties of Groups and Group Learning," *Psychological Reports,* 19:1 (July–December 1966), 17–18.

40. Abraham Zaleznik, "The Human Dilemmas of Leadership," *Harvard Business Review,* 41:4 (July–August 1963), 49–55.

41. Joel D. Singer, "Human Behavior and International Politics," in Joel D. Singer, ed., *Contributions from the Social-Psychological Sciences* (Chicago: Rand McNally, 1965).

42. Eric L. Trist *et al., Organizational Choice* (London: Tavistock Institute, 1963).

43. John Gardner, *Self-Renewal.*

44. George C. Homans, "Effort, Supervision and Productivity," in Dubin, *et al., Leadership and Productivity.*

45. White, "Ego and Reality in Psychoanalytic Theory," p. 68.

46. T. H. Fitzgerald, "Appraisals: Personality, Performance, and Persons," *California Management Review,* 8:2 (Winter 1965), 81–86.

47. Herbert H. Meyers, Emanuel Kay, and John R. P. French, Jr., "Split Roles in Performance Appraisal," *Harvard Business Review,* 43:1 (January–February 1965), 123–129.

48. Harry Levinson, *Emotional Health: In the World of Work* (New York: Harper & Row, 1964), p. 268.

49. Peter F. Drucker, *The Effective Executive* (New York: Harper & Row, 1967), p. 83.

50. "The Bookworm Turns: More Collegians Now Grade Their Teachers," *Wall Street Journal* (January 3, 1966).

51. I. R. Andrews and Mildred M. Henry, "Management Attitudes Toward Pay," *Industrial Relations,* 3:1 (October 1963), 29–39.

52. Leopold W. Gruenfeld and Peter Weissenberg, "Supervisory Characteristics and Attitudes Toward Performance Appraisals," *Personnel Psychology,* 19:2 (Summer 1966), 143–151.

53. See Homans, "Effort, Supervision and Productivity."

Chapter 12 Mastery Needs

1. Edith Jacobson, *The Self and the Object World* (New York: International Universities Press, 1964).

2. H. Marshall McLuhan and Quentin Fiore, *The Medium is the Message* (New York: Random House, 1967).

3. H. G. van der Waals, with the collaboration of Martin Mayman, "Normal and Pathological Narcissism," unpublished paper, 1964.

4. Leo Cherne, "Mediocrity in the Future?" *Industrial Relations News* (July 17, 1965), 4.

5. John W. Gardner, *Self-Renewal,* p. 59.

6. Douglas McGregor, *The Professional Manager,* ed. Warren G. Bennis (New York: McGraw-Hill, 1967), p. 129.

7. Virgil B. Day, Address, Congress of American Industry, National Association of Manufacturers, New York (December 5, 1963).

8. John D. Williams, "Increased Job Hopping by Junior Executives Vexes Personnel Men," *Wall Street Journal* (January 21, 1965).

9. Richard Nason, "Harvardmen vs. Big Business," *Dun's Review,* 83:1 (January 1964), 41–52 ff.

10. Lyndall F. Urwick, "The Line/Staff Impasse — A Footnote," *Management Review,* 56:1 (January 1967), 50–53. See also R. B. Zajonc and O. M. Wolfe, "Cognitive Consequences of a Person's Position in a Formal Organization," *Human Relations,* 19:2 (May 1966), 139–150.

11. Roy W. Menninger, "What Values Are We Giving Our Children?" Address, Values Conference, Denver, Colorado (October 12, 1963).

12. Harry Levinson *et al., Men, Management, and Mental Health* (Cambridge, Mass.: Harvard University Press, 1962), p. 141.

13. Bernard J. Muller-Thym, "Practices in General Management: New Directions in Organizational Practices," Paper No. WA-59, American Society of Mechanical Engineers, p. 7.

14. Quoted in Henry Brandon, "Schlesinger at the White House," *Harper's,* 229:1370 (July 1964), 56.

15. Edwin G. Boring, "Cognitive Dissonance: Its Use in Science," *Science* (August 14, 1964), 680–684.

16. Harold J. Leavitt, "Unhuman Organizations," *Harvard Business Review,* 40:4 (July–August 1962), 90–98.

17. David C. McClelland, "Business Drive and National Achievement," *Harvard Business Review,* 40:4 (July–August 1962), 99–112.

18. David C. McClelland, "That Urge to Achieve," *Think,* 32:6 (November–December 1966), 19. See also: Ralph D. Norman, "The Interpersonal Values of Parents of Achieving and Non-Achieving Gifted Children," *Journal of Psychology,* 64:1 (September 1966), 49–57.

19. Paul E. McGhee and Richard C. Teevan, "The Childhood Development of Fear of Failure Motivation," paper presented to the American Psychological Association, September 4, 1965.

20. McClelland, "That Urge to Achieve."

21. David C. McClelland, "Toward a Theory of Motive Acquisition," *American Psychologist,* 20:5 (May 1965), 321–333; Robert A. Stringer, "Achieve-

ment Motivation and Management Control," *Personnel Administration,* 29:6 (November–December 1966), 3–5.

22. David G. Bowers and Stanley E. Seashore, "Predicting Organizational Effectiveness with a Four-Factor Theory of Leadership," *Administrative Science Quarterly,* 11:2 (September 1966), 238–263.

23. McClelland, "Toward a Theory of Motive Acquisition."

24. Gardner, *Self-Renewal,* p. 20.

25. Hudson Hoagland, "Notable and Quotable," *Wall Street Journal* (May 5, 1964).

26. Shirley Tuska and Benjamin Wright, "The Influence of a Teacher Model on Self-Conception during Teacher Training and Experience," *Proceedings of the 73rd Annual Convention of the American Psychological Association* (1965), 297–298.

27. Robert L. Swinth, "Certain Effects of Training Goals on Subsequent Task Performance," *Occupational Psychology,* 40:3 (July 1966), 164.

28. David E. Berlew and Douglas T. Hall, "The Socialization of Managers: Effects of Expectations on Performance," *Administrative Science Quarterly,* 11:2 (September 1966), 221.

29. Leo Cherne, "Mediocrity in the Future?" p. 4.

30. Crawford H. Greenewalt, Address, International Industrial Conference, San Francisco (September 13, 1965).

31. Abram T. Collier, *Men, Management, and Values* (New York: Harper & Row, 1962); Louis W. Norris, "Moral Hazards of an Executive," *Harvard Business Review,* 38:5 (September–October 1960), 72–79; Raymond C. Baumhart, "How Ethical Are Businessmen?" *Harvard Business Review,* 39:4 (July–August 1961), 6–7 ff.

32. William D. Guth and Renato Tagiuri, "Personal Values and Corporate Strategy," *Harvard Business Review,* 43:5 (September–October 1965), 123–135.

33. L. S. Ewing, "Fighting and Death from Stress in a Cockroach," *Science* (February 27, 1967). For relevance to human work groups see: Fred E. Fiedler, "The Effect of Inter-Group Competition on Group Member Adjustment," *Personnel Psychology,* 20:1 (Spring 1967), 33–44.

34. Robert Waelder, "Conflict and Violence," *Bulletin of the Menninger Clinic,* 30:5 (September 1966), 270, 274.

35. Edgar H. Schein, "The Problem of Moral Education for the Business Manager," *Industrial Management Review,* 8:1 (Fall 1966), 3–14.

36. Edwin A. Fleischman and James A. Salter, "Relations Between the Leader's Behavior and his Empathy Toward Subordinates," *Journal of Industrial Psychology,* 1:3 (September 1963), 79–84.

37. Jeanne Lampl-de Groot, "Ego Ideal and Super Ego," *Psychoanalytic Study of the Child,* vol. 17 (New York: International Universities Press, 1962).

38. Ernest Jones, *Papers on Psychoanalysis,* 4th ed. (London: Balliere, 1938), p. 53.

39. Heinz Hartmann and Rudolph M. Lowenstein, "Notes on the Superego," *Psychoanalytic Study of the Child,* vol. 18.

40. Roy Schafer, "The Loving and Beloved Superego," *ibid.,* vol. 15.

41. Kurt Goldstein, *The Organism* (New York: American Book Co., 1939), p. 88.

42. Abraham Maslow, *Personality and Motivation* (New York: Harper & Bros., 1954), p. 91.

43. See A. E. Hotchner, *Papa Hemingway* (New York: Random House, 1966); and A. A. Rogow, *James Forrestal, a Study of Personality, Politics, and Policy* (New York: Macmillan, 1964).

44. Sigmund Freud, "Group Psychology and the Analysis of the Ego," *The Standard Edition of the Complete Psychological Works of Sigmund Freud,* vol. 18 (London: Hogarth Press, 1961), p. 131. See also: Joseph Sandler, "On the Concept of Superego," *Psychoanalytic Study of the Child,* vol. 15.

45. Karl Menninger, with Martin Mayman and Paul Pruyser, *The Vital Balance* (New York: Viking Press, 1963).

46. Erik H. Erikson, "Identity and the Life Cycle," *Psychological Issues,* 1:1 (1959), 111.

47. *Ibid.,* p. 98.

48. Lampl-de Groot, "Ego Ideal and Super Ego."

49. Schafer, "The Loving and Beloved Superego," p. 183.

Chapter 13 Not by One Alone

1. Richard C. Hodgson, Daniel J. Levinson, and Abraham Zaleznik, *The Executive Role Constellation* (Boston: Harvard Graduate School of Business Administration, Division of Research, 1965).

2. *Personnel Administration: Changing Scope and Organization* (New York: National Industrial Conference Board, 1967).

3. Some representative texts are Dale S. Beach, *The Management of People at Work* (New York: Macmillan, 1965); Wendell French, *The Personnel Management Process* (Boston: Houghton Mifflin, 1964); Walter D. Scott, Robert C. Clothier, and William R. Spriegel, *Personnel Management* (New York: McGraw-Hill, 1954); George Strauss and Leonard Sayles, *Personnel: The Human Problems of Management* (Englewood Cliffs, N.J.: Prentice-Hall, 1960); Paul Pigors and Charles A. Myers, *Personnel Administration: A Point of View and a Method* (New York: McGraw-Hill, 1947); and Dale Yoder, *Personnel Policies and Principles* (Englewood Cliffs, N.J.: Prentice-Hall, 1959).

4. See *Personnel Administration: Changing Scope and Organization.*

5. Elliott Jaques, *Equitable Payment* (New York: John Wiley & Sons, 1961).

6. Frank O. Hoffman, "Keeping Them Happy Isn't Your Job," *Personnel Administrator,* 12:1 (January–February 1967), 18–22.

7. Albert P. Maslow, "Personnel Execs in Government Service," *Industrial Relations News* (November 26, 1966), 4.

8. David S. Brown, "The Personnel Officer's New Dilemma," *Personnel Administration,* 27:4 (July–August 1964), 4–6.

9. Leonard Sayles, "Inherent Conflicts in the Personnel Function," *Employee Relations Bulletin,* no. 829 (October 17, 1962), 1–5.

10. *Personnel Administration: Changing Scope and Organization,* p. 16.

11. Tom Lupton, *Industrial Behavior and Personnel Management* (London: Institute of Personnel Management, 1964). For a similar point of view see also Dale Yoder, "The Two Roads to Success in Industrial Relations," *Personnel Administration,* 27:6 (November–December 1964), 3–6 ff.

12. Frederick Herzberg, *Work and the Nature of Man* (Cleveland: World Publishing Co., 1966), p. 172.

13. Walter H. Powell, "Are We Managers or Technicians?" *Personnel Administrator,* 11:5 (September–October 1966), 26.

14. Douglas W. Bray and Donald L. Grant, "The Assessment Center in the Measurement of Potential for Business Management," *Psychological Monographs: General and Applied,* 80:17 (1966), 1–27.

15. Willard Merrihue, "General Electric's Employee Relations Index," *Personnel Series,* no. 168 (New York: American Management Association, 1959), 51.

16. Harry Levinson, "Organizational Diagnosis," manuscript in preparation.

17. Lawrence L. Ferguson, "Better Management of Managers' Careers," *Harvard Business Review,* 44:2 (March–April 1966), 139–154.

18. Seymour Tilles, "Understanding the Consultant's Role," *Harvard Business Review,* 39:6 (November–December 1961), 87–99.

Chapter 14   The Failures

1. Karl Menninger, *Man Against Himself* (New York: Harcourt, Brace, 1938).

2. Robert R. Blake and Jane S. Mouton, *The Managerial Grid* (Houston: Gulf Publishing Co., 1964), p. 19; Eugene E. Jennings, *The Executive: Autocrat, Bureaucrat, Democrat* (New York: Harper & Row, 1962), p. 114.

3. Robert F. Kahn *et al., Organizational Stress: Studies in Role Conflict and Ambiguity* (New York: John Wiley & Sons, 1964); David Moment and Abraham Zaleznik, *Role Development and Interpersonal Competence* (Boston: Harvard University Graduate School of Business Administration, Division of Research, 1963); Eugene E. Jennings, *The Executive in Crisis* (East Lansing: Michigan State University, Graduate School of Business Administration, 1965).

4. Harry Levinson, *Emotional Health: In the World of Work* (New York: Harper & Row, 1964).

5. Edgar H. Schein, *Organizational Psychology* (Englewood Cliffs, N.J.: Prentice-Hall, 1965).

6. Harry Levinson, "The Psychologist in Industry," *Harvard Business Review,* 37:5 (September–October 1959), 93–100.

Chapter 15 Epilogue

1. Nathan Glazer, "The Good Society," *Commentary,* 36:3 (September 1963), 226–234.

2. Aaron Levenstein, *Why People Work* (New York: Crowell-Collier, 1962).

3. Abraham Zaleznik, *Human Dilemmas of Leadership* (New York: Harper & Row, 1966).

4. Harry Schrage, "The R & D Entrepreneur: Profile of Success," *Harvard Business Review,* 43:6 (November–December 1965), 56–69.

5. Edward A. Shils and Michael Young, "Meaning of the Coronation," *Sociological Review,* n.s., 1:2 (December 1953), 63–81.

6. Zaleznik, *Human Dilemmas of Leadership,* p. 98.

7. George F. Kennan, "Why Do I Hope," *Washington Post* (December 25, 1966).

Index

Index

HIEBERT LIBRARY

3 6877 00122 1877

HF
5500.2
L375
Levinson, Harry.
    The exceptional executive; a psychological conception.
Cambridge, Mass., Harvard University Press, 1968.

    x, 297 p.   25 cm. $6.95

    Bibliographical references included in "Notes" (p. [259]-286)

HIEBERT LIBRARY
Pacific College - M. B. Seminary
Fresno, Calif. 93702

13275

    1. Executives.   I. Title.

HF5500.2.L375   658.42   68-25615
                                                                MARC

    Library of Congress